A SOLDIER IN THE COCKPIT

Other titles in the Stackpole Military History Series

THE AMERICAN CIVIL WAR
Cavalry Raids of the Civil War
Pickett's Charge
Witness to Gettysburg

WORLD WAR II
Armor Battles of the Waffen-SS, 1943–45
Australian Commandos
The B-24 in China
Backwater War
Beyond the Beachhead
The Brandenburger Commandos
Bringing the Thunder
Coast Watching in World War II
Colossal Cracks
D-Day to Berlin
Exit Rommel
Flying American Combat Aircraft of World War II
Fist from the Sky
Forging the Thunderbolt
The German Defeat in the East, 1944–45
Germany's Panzer Arm in World War II
Grenadiers
Infantry Aces
Iron Arm
Luftwaffe Aces
Messerschmitts over Sicily
Michael Wittmann, Volume One
Michael Wittmann, Volume Two
The Nazi Rocketeers
On the Canal
Packs On!
Panzer Aces
Panzer Aces II
The Panzer Legions
Retreat to the Reich
The Savage Sky
Surviving Bataan and Beyond
The 12th SS, Volume One
The 12th SS, Volume Two
Tigers in the Mud

THE COLD WAR / VIETNAM
Flying American Combat Aircraft: The Cold War
Land with No Sun
Street without Joy

WARS OF THE MIDDLE EAST
Never-Ending Conflict

OTHER
Desert Battles

A SOLDIER IN THE COCKPIT

From Rifles to Typhoons in World War II

Ron Pottinger

STACKPOLE
BOOKS

Published in paperback in 2007 by
STACKPOLE BOOKS
5067 Ritter Road
Mechanicsburg, PA 17055
www.stackpolebooks.com

Cover design by Tracy Patterson

Printed in the United States of America

10 9 8 7 6 5 4 3 2 1

FIRST EDITION

Library of Congress Cataloging-in-Publication Data

Pottinger, Ron, 1919–
  [View from the office]
  A soldier in the cockpit : from rifles to Typhoons in World War II /
Ron Pottinger.
    p. cm. — (Stackpole military history series)
  Previously published as: A view from the office. 2005.
  ISBN-13: 978-0-8117-3368-7
  ISBN-10 0-8117-3368-8
    1. Pottinger, Ron, 1919– 2. World War, 1939–1945—Aerial operations, British. 3. World War, 1939–1945—Prisoners and prisons, German. 4. World War, 1939–1945 —Personal narratives, British. 5. Fighter pilots—Great Britain—Biography. 6. Prisoners of war—Great Britain—Biography. 7. Prisoners of war—Germany—Biography. I. Title.

D786.P64 2007
940.54'4941092—dc22
[B]
                                                                2006101098

Table of Contents

Introduction

This is the story of the small part I played in World War II from 1939 to 1945, as I saw it then and remember it now. It has not been written by someone much decorated or of high rank, with insight into higher strategy or reasoning, but by an ordinary working-class chap pitch-forked out of an ordinary life into an environment—or rather environments—completely foreign to him, but to which he had to adapt; a chap who fell in line as ordered and did what was asked of him without quibble or hesitation.

You could say that I had an "interesting" war, but the fact is, I survived it, for which I am grateful, and I know I was very lucky. As you read on, you will find so many occasions when I could so easily have come to a sticky end, and somehow luck held, and I came through unscathed. So many didn't. Luck also kept me from some of the times of greatest danger. In the army we didn't quite get to join the B.E.F. in France, and Hitler held off the expected invasion of our shores. Before the battalion could be posted to any other theatre of war I had transferred to the R.A.F. and was having a wonderful time training in Florida. The Battle of Britain was long won by the time I reached a squadron, and the R.A.F. fighters had command of the sky. Enemy planes were rarely seen, and when they were, they didn't stay to fight. By then they were probably more concerned with the day and night raids on their home cities than with a few nuisance raids by fighters over occupied territory. Again during the push across the Rhine into Germany, I was comparatively safe in a not-very-comfortable prison camp.

By the end of the war, after six years of service, I had seen enough for any gloss there might once have been to have worn thin. War is a dirty business at best.

On arriving home to a civilian life, which was at least as foreign to me as service life had been six years before, everyone wanted to hear exciting tales of "derring-do," but I felt reluctant to oblige. I'd put it all behind me; the chapter was closed. I only wanted to tell them how unglamorous the whole business really was, and then get on with life. I clammed up to the extent that Joy, my wife, only learned of some of the events described in the following pages when reading an early draft copy. A colleague in the office I was

The author and a Typhoon
1B at Manston, 1943.

working in during 1950 pestered me to write a book on my experiences. To me, at the time this would have seemed almost akin to prostitution.

So how is it that the story has eventually been told after all this time? Well, it's all down to my son, Mark. In his late teens and early twenties, he would ask me about my time during the war, and at the end I would explain, "There was not really much glamour about it, you know!" He'd reply, "I know, Dad, but it's history, isn't it? You old b——s are getting pretty thin on the ground now, and we ought to get as much out of you as we can, while we can."

Eventually, I was persuaded to put the story down on paper for my family—especially Mark and my two grandsons, Matthew and George. Inevitably, when the story was half told, while clearing out one corner of our loft, two old diaries came to light. One covered part of my time in the army, from August 1940 to March 1941; the other covered my time with 3 Squadron R.A.F., from May 1943 to November 1944. We already had a diary of my time in prison camp, written, I am sure, shortly after my release.

Mark was amazed at how accurate my memory had been in many of the events already described. I was appalled at how differently I remembered some events from the way they were described some fifty years ago. Many extracts from the diaries are included verbatim. In other places it was better to write the diary into the general text.

This all filled out the account, and I am persuaded that it is worth publication. For Mark, who has done so much work nudging, bullying, and otherwise pushing me along to completion, and in addition has typed the whole thing up, I hope the result will prove worthy of his effort.

CHAPTER 1

Army Days

The years following the Great War were a difficult time for the western world. Being born in 1919, I remember events from the latter part of the 1920s and 1930s well: the General Strike, the Jarrow hunger march, and the Great Depression that lasted well into the 1930's. There was unemployment that reduced skilled men who had previously held secure jobs to selling buttons and boot laces out of a suitcase door to door.

However, across the Channel in mainland Europe, something far more sinister was brewing. Adolf Hitler was appointed Chancellor of Germany in 1933, and after a programme of open rearmament, he sent troops into the demilitarised Rhineland. In his bid to establish German rule over Europe, his first move was to annex Austria and Czechoslovakia, and it became obvious to the world that he wasn't going to stop there. Despite Chamberlain's declaration of 'Peace in our time', I think we all, while not relishing it, slowly faced the fact that there was almost certainly going to be a showdown, and the odds were it would end in war.

My friends and I realised that being in our late teens, we would be directly in line, but at that age you tend not to believe that the worst can happen to you. Our elders, veterans and survivors of the 14 to 18 holocaust, told us horrific tales of blood and mud in the Flanders trenches, adding to the general air of apprehension. There was a generation of people out there with very vivid memories of the 'war to end all wars', and of the relief and gladness with which they had celebrated the armistice only twenty-one years before.

Because of the Depression, and a strong disarmament lobby, Britain's defences had been run down to a pathetic level, and we were in no position to stop a Germany whose slogan, in contrast to Chamberlain's, had for some years been 'Guns before butter!' However, during the early part of 1939, someone in a position of power must have woken up, for conscription was announced. They called this new fighting force 'The Militia'. I was just the right age, and was in the second batch to attend an interview and a medical examination.

This took place in a Territorial Army drill hall near Clapham Common. The medical was quite cursory, and the interview was, to say the least, a complete farce. I was seen by an elderly army officer who asked me which service I would like to apply for. I thought the Navy sounded interesting. "Sorry," I was told, "no vacancies there!" Well then, how about the Air Force as second choice. "Sorry, no vacancies there!" "I suppose it will have to be the Army then." I'm not sure this went down too well. "What branch?" I was asked. I hadn't much idea about what any of the jobs in the forces comprised, and it certainly wasn't explained to me. However, the Royal Engineers sounded as if they might do something a bit more interesting than the P.B.I. ('Poor Bloody Infantry'), and that's how it was left.

It was not long afterwards that the showdown came over the annexing of Poland, and war was declared on 3rd September 1939. I had just returned from a cycling holiday on the Isle of Wight. I was boarding up a downstairs window at the back of our house in south west London, and all around were sounds of hammering and banging as others did the same. We stopped long enough to listen to Chamberlain's declaration of war on the wireless, and then rather subdued I went back to my hammering.

Almost immediately the air raid sirens sounded—an unearthly sound. There was clatter all around of tools being dropped, and then absolute dead silence. I don't know where everyone went to. We didn't yet have air raid shelters, and hiding under the bed wouldn't have helped much. As everyone now knows, nothing happened. It was a false alarm, or perhaps the authorities wanted to impress on everyone the gravity of the situation we were in.

Soon after, I arrived home one evening to find my call-up papers waiting for me. Not into the Navy, the Air Force, or even the Royal Engineers, but into the infantry. So much for the interview!

I was being drafted into the London Scottish, and my main concern was that I might be expected to wear hats and a kilt, which seemed ridiculous to me.

On 18 October 1939, I reported for duty at the New Horticultural Hall off Vincent Square in Victoria. Despite my protests my mother insisted on coming with me. I felt a proper fool as we approached the hall, and the situation wasn't improved by the two buxom women in aprons and mop caps standing on the corner opposite the entrance, one of whom I heard say to the other, "Poor little buggers, hardly got the nappy marks off their bums yet!"

I was duly parted from mum, and the various contingents were each gathered under an N.C.O. from the unit they were joining. Our brood mother was an immense Sergeant McLeod. He gave the impression of being at least seven feet tall and broad with it. When he marched up to the officer's desk and halted, his knees came up to his chest and his big boots the size of packing cases crashed down one after the other, the sound reverberating throughout the building.

Eventually, we were all sorted out, and about a hundred of us were marched through the streets to Chelsea barracks where the 1st Battalion of

The London Scottish was stationed. Not many of us had ever walked that far, much less marched. Keeping step was something we had yet to learn, and with a suit case clutched in one hand, banging the legs of both those in front and behind, it was a shambles.

At Chelsea barracks we were installed in a large room with beds all round the walls and a large table near the centre. The floor was bare boards, wax polished to a gloss you could see your face in. It almost dared you to walk on it.

Our first shock was the beds, which were constructed from iron, the bottom half sliding back under the top. The base of the bed was made from three-inch-wide interwoven iron strappings, and the mattress consisted of three 'biscuits', straw-filled canvas cases so old the straw had crumbled into dust.

The second shock came during the deepest part of a most uncomfortable, almost sleepless night when we were awoken by the most awful caterwauling below our window: reveille played on the bagpipes! To be roused at the ridiculous (to us) hour of six o'clock by such an alien sound was an affront to the senses. We found that all the calls—cookhouse, lights out, fatigues, last post, and the rest—were all played on the pipes.

That day, we were kitted out—thank goodness—in battle dress and forage caps, not kilts. The London Scottish was a pretty snooty territorial unit, and we found out later that they were not pleased at having sassenach conscripts drafted onto them. We didn't even have cap badges.

We were vaccinated, inoculated, and initiated into foot drill. We were shown a guards barrack room and were told that this was how ours had better look in the future. The place was spotless. Not a speck of dust anywhere. All the bed biscuits were piled one on top of another on each bed and the blankets folded on top, square to within a fraction of an inch. The floor was polished boards with not a smudge or smear anywhere. Their rifles were laid out in a semicircle on the table. Cleaned and glistening with a smear of oil. The bolts laid out in a separate semicircle above them, all again positioned as accurately as if they had all been measured out with a rule. It was certainly going to take some practice to match this.

We also watched the Scots Guards doing foot drill as a block of about twelve men by twelve men marched to and fro across the parade ground, led by a sergeant major who hardly moved from one spot. "Le tur, ri tur, harbow tur". They hardly took three paces in any one direction before the next command. Their response to each command was perfect; the lines always kept perfectly straight in each direction. It was an impressive sight.

Rifles were issued, and we were initiated into the rituals of pull throughs, four by two, and gun oil. The four by two, a small piece of flannel material, was dampened with gun oil, and pulled through the barrel of the gun, thus cleaning and lubricating it. On inspection the barrel had to gleam brightly. A speck of anything, much less rust, was enough to bring the heavens down. The pull through and a small brass tube of oil were kept in a specially drilled out compartment in the butt of the gun—that is, if the pull through was carefully coiled exactly as instructed.

While at Chelsea, we conscripts were interviewed individually by the C.O. and questioned carefully about our ancestry. They were eager to find us Scottish forbears if possible, and this was the first of about three such interviews along these lines. To be honest, they made such a thing about being Scottish that they seemed almost as bad as the Germans and their search for 'Aryans'. In modern times, they would have definitely fallen foul of the race relations act. My hackles were definitely up, and I stated that I was born in London, if not within sound of Bow Bells, and so were all my relations and ancestors that I was aware of, and I was quite happy with it that way.

Then without warning we were moved to Womanswold in Kent, about seven miles on the Dover side of Canterbury. We conscripts were billeted in the old vicarage, which appeared to have been empty for years. The basement was flooded, and the first task for most of our number was to stand in water waist deep baling with our drinking bowls into buckets which were passed to and fro along a chain of men and emptied into the gutter.

I thought I was lucky when a sergeant major took me aside to a pile of logs and a long-handled axe. He wanted the pile split and chopped into short lengths since we had no other fuel for cooking or heating. He demonstrated what was required on one of the logs by hitting it about a foot from one end. This opened up a split about three quarters of the way along its length. These were each split again and then broken into short lengths. I took the axe from the sergeant major and hit the next log with all my strength. The log didn't split and the axe head buried itself deep in the wood. It took about the next ten minutes and all my strength to get the axe out again. This happened with most of the logs. Occasionally, one would split but more often the axe stuck hard in the wood and wouldn't move. I'd never worked so hard in my life, and I almost came to envy the balers. The sergeant major wasn't too pleased about my meagre pile of chopped wood either. There was obviously a knack to this which I was yet to learn.

The Pioneers arrived and performed miracles in the stables and the loft above them. They ran two galvanised pipes into the stables, each fitted with taps at regular intervals. Below the taps they placed a sheet metal trough to take away the waste water. This was to be our ablutions. At soon after six in the morning, we would be lining up to wash and shave. There were no lights in the stables and only cold water. It was freezing and pitch black. It was a miracle no one lost an ear or a nose shaving. During the first trip into Canterbury, some of us bought matches and candles. By this light you could at least see if you were shaving your own face or somebody else's. But of course, when the owner of a candle finished his ablutions, picked up his candle, and walked out, there were howls of protest and a near riot broke out.

I particularly remember an Irishman, a real country character. He used to shave with just the blade of an open 'cut throat' razor, which he kept in an old tobacco tin held together with an elastic band. The blade had no handle and was wrapped in a piece of dirty-looking cloth. The thought of putting such a lethal implement near one's throat in pitch black was bad enough. Watching him wash it when he was finished, wipe it on the piece of cloth, and strop it on the heel of his palm before wrapping it up and putting it away in the tin filled me with awe. I never saw it receive any other sharpening than a quick strop on his hand.

Over the stables was a loft that had been converted into our mess room. Since it was in the roof space, it had sloping walls and wooden beams. Two long tables ran the length, and there was always a rush to get to the inner sides of the tables. On the outer sides, you couldn't sit upright, and if you were unfortunate enough to end up by one of the beams, it was even worse.

Food was cooked in the kitchen of the house and had cooled somewhat by the time it had crossed the yard and up to where we were sitting. There wasn't enough room to serve the meals in the loft, so a table was set up at the top of the stairs. Each meal had to be served as you filed up the stairs and past the table. This resulted in some most peculiar combinations of food. One breakfast I shall never forget consisted of stodgy porridge with a pilchard in tomato sauce plopped in the centre of it.

Armistice Day, 11 November, arrived, and we were marched to Broome Hall, the battalion headquarters, where we formed up in a square with the rest of the battalion. There was an Armistice Day service with two minutes of silence, and then a file of half a dozen pipers wended their way through the wooded slopes above the house playing the last post. In that setting and atmosphere, the sight was most impressive and brought a lump to even my throat.

A few days later, those of us who hadn't been able to dig out a Scottish skeleton from some dark cupboard were to be reposted, half to the 8th Battalion Royal Fusiliers and half to the 9th. Rumour said the London Scottish had petitioned the King, who was Colonel of the Regiment, to get rid of us. I was posted to the 9th and was sent to their headquarters at Chapelwood Manor near Nutley in Sussex.

Chapelwood Manor was approached through an arched gatehouse with rooms above it used by the fusiliers as a guardroom. At the end of a drive that was about half a mile long and ran through parkland and eventually sadly neglected gardens stood a large Tudor-style house. The stables, coach houses, and servants quarters were in a separate complex to the side.

The Battalion headquarters was quartered here, and temporarily they found space for us where they could. A chap called Ibbotson and myself were billeted with a headquarters section called 'Drums'. Our billet was situated over the stables in what used to be the servants quarters. Drums were responsible for the bugle calls and there was a great pre-occupation with time. On many an occasion a bleary-eyed, half-dressed bugler was pushed out of the door by his mates to blow reveille five minutes late. The late blowing of 'defaulters', with an irate sergeant major tapping his foot and the bugler could find himself lining up on 'jankers' with the rest of those who hadn't quite matched up to the army's expectations of them.

You could understand why the section was billeted away in the stables. They were always practising on the drums and fifes. They used to have great fun letting us try to play the fifes. I don't think Ibby or I ever extracted a sound from one. I didn't do much better with a bugle. You had to be careful with this anyway. You didn't want the troops lining up at the cookhouse for food half an hour early. The Battalion also had a full brass band billeted elsewhere. Very impressive it was, too: they didn't really mix with our lot, considering themselves real musicians.

Here we were initiated into the mysteries of military tactics. We would have exercises in the park and surrounding countryside. Tramping through mud and stream. On command flinging ourselves flat into wet knee high bracken, arriving back without a clue what had been going on, wet, weary, and hating all in authority, with barely enough time to clean it all up for the next parade, only to get all muddy again the next day.

The author as a Fusilier
in the 9th Royal Fusiliers,
November/December 1939.

H.Q. Company, 9th Battalion Royal Fusiliers at Chapelwood Manor, Nutley.

These jaunts were only ever livened up for us when one of the local dogs came along for the ride. He was a brown and white Scottie and was good at catching rabbits among the bracken. Having caught a rabbit he would bring it over to one of our number looking all pleased with himself. We would rarely come back with less than a couple, which would be roasted over the open fires we had in our billets and enjoyed by all.

While we were at Chapelwood Manor, one of the fusiliers was given leave to get married and one of his ex territorial friends lent him his peace-time uniform. Peaked cap, belted tunic with brass buttons and all. Many of these peacetime, part time soldiers had brought their own uniforms with them to get a good fit. Nevertheless, on his return, still in a rosy daze from his honeymoon, he was put on a charge by the quarter master sergeant for borrowing another man's equipment. The Q.M.S. was not very popular, and he revelled in it. He was tall and rather portly with black hair and a black waxed moustache. He was every man's idea of what a professional soldier should look like, and was known to all and sundry as 'Black Joe'.

Our newlywed, the story went, came from a farming family in Lincolnshire. He had recently inherited eleven thousand pounds, a vast sum in those days. For his sins he was incarcerated in the guard house over the gate. From here he climbed out of the window, dropped to the ground, and vanished, presumably back to Lincolnshire and the arms of his loving wife. He was eventually found, brought back, court marshalled, and sent off to the dreaded 'glasshouse'. He did his term and came back to the battalion, certainly the fittest, and smartest soldier I ever saw, and within days had vanished

again. He kept this up for the whole two years nearly that I knew him. Sometimes they didn't even get him to the glasshouse, he would vanish en route.
At one time our guardhouse was a bell tent situated at the entrance to a large
private school. Having been found and escorted back by a couple of 'red
caps' he got under the side of the guard tent and yet again vanished into the
night. You heard terrible stories of the treatment meted out to offenders at
the glasshouse, but it didn't seem to deter this chap in the slightest.

After a couple of weeks or so at Chapelwood Manor, we conscripts were
moved out to the rifle companies. Ibbotson and I went to 'C' Company at
Coopers Green, Buxted, about two miles north of Uckfield.

'C' Company was billeted in another vicarage. These old Victorian vic-
arages were usually large, gloomy houses, but this one was in better condition
than the one at Womanswold. No baling out of basements was needed here.

At the back of the house, there was a large, raised lawn which looked as
if it might have once been a tennis court. This was to be our parade ground.
On the opposite corner of the road was the entrance to Buxted Manor, a fine
country house standing in a large, walled park. We used the park for exercises and manoeuvres, and the mud was just as difficult to remove from boots
and battle dress as that at Chapelwood Manor.

The winter of 1939–40 was particularly severe, and we had quite a heavy
layer of snow over the ground for several weeks. This made the training even
more arduous. You can imagine that after crawling through the snow for several hours, we were soaked and frozen to the marrow. The evenings were
spent wearing greatcoats over underwear, while our battle dress steamed
gently around the stove.

One night, I was on guard duty outside the front entrance of the house
during a blizzard. Our company sergeant major came out of the house and
said in a very friendly manner, "Lousy night for that job, isn't it?"

"It certainly is," I agreed.

"WELL STAND TO ATTENTION WHEN YOU ADDRESS AN N.C.O.!"
he roared and stamped off into the night.

Drill out on our lawn in about a foot of fresh snow was pretty hilarious,
too.

Then one night after the snow had thawed, we were roused at around
midnight and taken out on parade without arms and into Buxted Park at a
jog trot. Word went back along the line that Buxted Manor was on fire, and
as we came out of the tree-lined drive, we could see the glow in the sky.

Although we used the park for our exercises, the house was occupied
and fully furnished with servants still living there. We were divided into
groups and sent to save whatever we could. The upper floors were well alight,
and impossible now to get to, but a lot of furniture was brought out and

stacked on the lawns, including a grand piano which came out through French windows onto a terrace and down a dozen or so stone steps with a marvellous jangling noise. The most concern was for paintings that had been crated up and moved down from London for safety. Not only were these valuable, but they were also irreplaceable. Some of the crates were very large, around ten feet by twenty-one and a half feet deep, but many hands managed to move them out onto the lawns. A chain was formed to empty the kitchen stores. They must have had sufficient food to keep an army for a year.

No attempt was made to put the fire out. It was beyond anything we could have done, and the whole place was gutted by flames. My most vivid memory of the night was seeing a double-iron bedstead with brass knobs on its posts crashing down through two floors amidst a great flurry of burning timbers and great showers of sparks. Next morning, we were allowed to lie in, official—the only time I remember that happening in the army.

I don't recall hearing what caused the fire, but a couple of weeks after, the owner, Mr Ionides, bought the whole company dinner and drinks in a restaurant on the outskirts of Uckfield.

By then we had moved from Buxted into Uckfield and were billeted in a small school near the top of the hill, opposite the cinema.

We ate in an old territorial army drill hall at the bottom of the hill, and when the weather was really foul, we used to do training exercises in the same hall. They had us stripping down and reassembling a Bren gun against a stopwatch 'ad infinitum' and doing arms drill till we could hardly hold the rotten thing.

In front of the drill hall was an open space used as a bus terminus, and they put up showers for us at the front of the hall. The only trouble was that the doors to the showers faced the buses so that whenever a door was opened, people on the buses had a fine view of a row of naked soldiers with only soap suds to hide their embarrassment.

The weather hadn't finished with us either. One morning, as we marched down the hill to breakfast, we found that the whole surface of the road was covered in a sheet of ice. Nothing could be heard but the slithering of hob nail boots, curses, and the clatter of plates and drinking bowls as they rolled down the hill. There were plenty of bruises but it was amazing that there were no broken limbs. They hadn't got round yet to issuing proper mess tins, and we were using galvanised iron plates and bowls like small pudding basins.

For an exercise we were taken to heath land near Crowborough and told to dig a defensive trench system. We started in pairs, each digging a slit trench about four feet by two by three feet deep, in a pattern laid out by our N.C.O. These were then to be joined, and eventually, a six-foot-deep trench would be dug behind, making up the trench system.

After several days the Brigadier came and inspected our progress. He was appalled. Most of the slit trenches had been joined up, but hardly any of the deeper communication trenches behind had reached anywhere near their full depth. I think we were expected to 'dig in' in hours rather than days. Anyway, he decreed that we were to man the trenches for three days and nights—whether for edification or punishment, I'm not sure.

This was in the early part of 1940, and it was still very cold and wet, and the nights were very long. Food and drink were brought to us at very irregular intervals and were mostly cold by the time it reached us. To add to our misery, he sent the London Irish to attack our lines, which they did with relish. This meant that there could be no relaxing. It was heads low, and a good lookout kept.

One night, our Lance Corporal Norris was about to enjoy a mess tin of warm tea when a clod of earth hit it, sending tea into his face and the tin into the mud. At the end of the third night, a truck came to collect us. In one of the trucks, there was a large billy full of cocoa, and we were delighted to find that it was laced with rum. I was convinced it saved my life. A sorrier, wetter, more bedraggled, drawn, grey-looking bunch of scarecrows it would be hard to imagine.

The 16th April 1940 was my twenty-first birthday. This was supposed to be a special occasion, and the army certainly made sure I wouldn't forget it.

For a start it was my turn on the roster for cookhouse fatigues. I was down at the cookhouse by the side of the drill hall from crack of dawn. delivering early morning tea (universally known as 'Gunfire') and breakfast, whilst eating my own on the move. After breakfast a couple of us were set to cleaning out the cookers. These were boilers like the old fashioned coppers used by housewives for boiling up laundry in those days. They consisted of a heavy cast-iron structure with a firebox at the bottom. Above this was fitted a boiler that was about two feet in diameter by about two in depth and was cylindrical with a hemispherical bottom. The fires burnt wood and coal, and the heat was difficult to regulate, so the porridge inevitably got burnt onto most of the bottom part of the boiler. This had to be scraped off as best we could, and the interior cleaned with a cloth and ashes in cold water—a most unpleasant job.

This took most of the morning and was followed by the continuous stream of billies and other utensils for washing up. Potato peeling was almost a relief, and six of us sat around a sack and a billy of water scraping furiously. Another took away the billies full of potatoes and brought back fresh ones filled with water. The 'janker wallahs' joined us for this chore.

By the time we were finished, it was about dark. We thought we had finished for the day when an N.C.O. came over from the company office and told us that 'B' Company was out of coal. Four of us were detailed to go with shovels in a 30-hundredweight truck to a depot where we shovelled coal into the truck. We then moved on to 'B' Company at Maresfield, where we shovelled it all back out again.

Then we went back back to Uckfield, where we hoped we would be allowed to collapse on our beds, only to find that the whole company had been given their first T.A.B. injections, and we were told to seek out the M.O. in order to receive ours. Finally, we were allowed to return to our billet at the top of the hill. After a clean up I knocked on the side door of the cinema opposite, where our favourite usherette let me in, and I sank thankfully into the nearest seat. I reckoned I was safe from further imposition at last. I didn't suffer seriously from the effects of the injections, but some did. Two or three got sick in the cinema that night and had to be helped back to their beds.

Some time afterwards, Fred Newman from 'B' Company and I were selected to go on a sniper's course. This was held on the edge of the Ashdown Forest somewhere near Crowborough. I'm not sure what the basis was for the selection to go on the course. It certainly had nothing to do with shooting ability. Up until then, I had only fired about ten rounds on the shingle at Pevensey, without any spectacular results.

I found the course very enjoyable, being mainly concerned with things I already had some experience with, such as map and compass work and field sketching. Much of a sniper's work was reckoned to be the sending back of information, and most of the time was spent on this aspect of the job: moving over ground without being seen, setting up an observation post, mapping, and sketching.

We did go on the range with the Ross rifle with telescopic sight. Most of the time was spent zeroing the sight and not more than twenty rounds fired at one and two hundred yard ranges. We were suitably impressed by the accuracy, for at these ranges it was easy to get all the shots within about a four-inch-diameter circle.

Fred came first on the course, and I came second out of about a dozen, and we returned to our companies, where we promptly forgot all about it.

During our time at Uckfield, we did a couple of three-day exercises. The Battalion would leave, marching somewhere between fifteen to twenty miles the first day. Another Battalion in the brigade, usually the London Irish, would have left their home base on a different route so that at the end of the first day, the two battalions faced one another somewhere around a couple of miles apart.

Neither side knew exactly where the other was, so the first night was spent sending out scouting parties. A successful scouting party, one who found the enemy without detection, often turned into a raiding party, and turfs and other missiles were hurled at bivouac tents, probably empty, their owners most likely at the same game at our camp. On at least one occasion, a camp kitchen was wrecked.

The following day would see a mock battle. I don't know if the scouting parties were all that successful, for I don't remember ever seeing the enemy. The day was spent crouching in one hollow after another, climbing hedges, falling in ditches, racing up and down hillsides, all without the faintest idea what was happening. No one ever told us. Nor were we ever told who had won the battle. Presumably, someone learnt something from it. But I surely didn't.

Then, on the second morning of the last of these exercises, we were rounded up somewhere behind Shoreham and taken back to Uckfield in trucks. Back at our billets, we were given half an hour to pack our kit and get back on parade. We were then issued with the universal haversack ration: one fish paste sandwich and a slab of biliously yellow cake. We knew something was up when we were also issued with a five-round clip of live ammunition, the first I'd seen away from the ranges. Then we got back on the trucks and drove across into Kent. 'C' Company ended up at Fordwich about four miles north of Canterbury.

By now rumour had passed up and down the Battalion, and we knew about the 'Blitzkrieg' in France and the withdrawal of the B.E.F. through Dunkirk. We gathered that we and five rounds of ammunition apiece were to man the beaches and repulse the might of the Nazi invaders.

However, we were busy filling our palliases with straw when an officer drove up in a khaki-coloured Austin and asked for me. He informed me that I was to be transferred from 'C' Company into the Battalion's intelligence section as a sniper. I collected my kit together again and climbed into the Austin and was driven to Headquarters Company, which was settling in at Hall Place at Harbledown.

Arriving at Hall Place, I found Fred Newman, who had already been collected from 'B' Company. We quickly set about finding ourselves a place to settle and as much as we could about the set up. We found the Intelligence Section office and from amongst the heaped equipment found two Ross rifles with telescopic sights.

Hall Place was a big old house standing in a park at Harbledown about three miles west of Canterbury on the London Road. Most of the flooring was rotten and unsafe. The C.O. had an office in the house, and there was also an orderly room and the intelligence office. The rest of the building was out of bounds for safety reasons. All headquarters personnel were in bell tents on the lawns in front of the house.

The rank and file were housed twelve to a tent and slept with feet towards the centre pole, heads around the outside. The only trouble was that the lawns were on a steep hill, and the two at centre top ended up draped round the centre pole, the remainder in a heap half in and half out under the edge of the lower brailings. Sleep was, to say the least, difficult.

During the day the brailings were rolled up and tied with tapes. Kit and bedding, impeccably folded of course, was left in twelve neat heaps around the circumference of the tent, which was most impressive looking along the rows. However, one day while we were all out on an exercise, the camp was hit by a storm and cloudburst. The water washed down the hill in a torrent, taking much of our gear with it. That which remained was sodden. When we arrived back, we were all set to digging drainage channels—much too late— and the rain stopped before we finished them and didn't start again for the rest of our stay at Hall Place.

By now, what became known as the Battle of Britain was well under way. Formations of maybe thirty or so bombers were crossing Kent daily, with their fighter escorts tiny black specks high above them. Then would come the Hurricanes and Spitfires, diving on the tail ends of the bomber formations. We could hear the *rat-tat-tat* of the guns. Then the fighters would pull up beneath the formation for another squirt before turning away. Up above, dog fights would develop between the fighters, and we followed the progress of these by the vapour trails left in the sky. We carried on with whatever we were doing unless the fight was right overhead. Then the alarm would be sounded, and we would all pile into a ditch—dry, thank goodness—which ran down behind the brick wall boundary of the estate. I wouldn't say that I felt safe in the ditch; in fact, I'm certain that if a bomb landed on the road that ran on the other side of the wall, it would have brought the whole thing down on top of us.

Part of the job of snipers and the intelligence sections generally was to set up observation posts and pass information back to the decision makers. So it was decided that we would set up and man an observation post to plot the movements of aeroplanes, numbers, types, directions, approximate height, and other specifications, as well as the location of any planes shot down, bombs dropped, or parachutes seen. An obvious location for the O.P. was on top of a water tower situated high on the hill northwest of Canterbury about two miles along the road to Whitstable, opposite St Edmunds School. It was about a mile walk across country from Hall Place.

The tower was a concrete structure, the lower support column being about twenty-five feet in diameter by eighty feet in height. The tank was probably an additional ten feet in diameter and twenty feet in height. The way to the top was decidedly scary at first sight. This led up vertical ladders up the inside wall, then across an open stairway, leading up at forty-five degrees to a platform in the centre, then up another vertical ladder through a hole in the tank, and out through a trap door onto the top, where a low concrete wall ran round the edge. The view was certainly spectacular.

We did duty in pairs perched up on this eyrie for two hours at a time. From here we had a good view of the fight above, although we felt somewhat exposed when things came too near. We did, however, console ourselves with the fact that we were probably safer than under that wall at Hall Place.

Then one day, Sergeant Pierce decided to pay us a visit. The first we knew of this was when we heard him call from below. Leaning over the wall we could see him shouting but couldn't hear a word. I decided to go down and find out what it was all about. After a chat about how we were set up, he decided that he wanted to go up to the top of the tower and see for himself. By now we were fairly used to those ladders, but they were still pretty intimidating at first sight. After a little hesitation, he set off first, with me following behind. He had gone up about fifty feet when he suddenly wrapped his arms around the ladder and froze. Nothing I could say would make him move, and the longer we stayed there, the more tired we both became. Eventually, I yelled to my mate, who was still up on top of the tank. He came down to see what all the fuss was about, and with one of us above and one below, we managed to coax him down rung by rung, with me guiding his feet from one step to the next.

On the other hand, when Manny Rossen visited us, he ran round the small ledge that was on the outside of the wall on top of the tank. This was a wager which I would have had no hesitation in backing away from.

During the first few weeks following Dunkirk, when an invasion by air or sea seemed a fairly likely occurrence, all leave was cancelled. Then this was relaxed, and we were allowed an evening pass, but still had to carry our full equipment with us in case the Nazis started dropping from the sky.

On one such evening, I went on my own to the cinema in Canterbury. Getting to a seat, past other people, clutching a rifle in one hand, pack on back with gas cape and tin hat to boot was difficult enough, but sitting down was almost impossible. Eventually, I saw the show round, and made my way out. Passing through a door and down a corridor I noticed a couple of women going the opposite way, giving me funny looks. I thought it was my get up. It wasn't. I was wandering into the ladies toilet.

We were only at Hall Place a short time, probably not more than four weeks. Then during August 1940, Headquarters Company moved to Milner Court in Sturry about four miles north of Canterbury.

Milner Court was a fairly large public school. We were quartered in one of the dormitories in a new part of the school, clean, dry, and warm—which was absolute heaven after bell tents. It even had a good swimming pool out back.

Our O.P. was set up on the church roof, which was fine until the first Sunday when the bells were rung for morning service. The two of us were sitting on the tower when the bells, about four feet below us, started their peal. Not only was the noise deafening, I also thought the tower was coming down with the vibration. Soon after this time, church bells were reserved for warning of invasion only, but before that happened, they had found us another O.P. The church was ancient, dating back to about the eighth century, and I doubt our hob nail boots were doing its roof much good.

The new O.P. was in the school building above our dormitory. There was access to the roof space and from there into a small cupola which might have been intended for a bell but was actually empty. A slat was taken out at eye level on all sides and this gave a good view all round.

It was from this O.P. that I saw a Dornier shot down by Spitfires, said to have been a Polish squadron. About four attackers were buzzing around the bomber like angry bees, firing into it almost continuously. It passed our O.P. only a few hundred yards away and barely above roof height. It crashed on open ground less than a quarter of a mile from the school near the village of Broadoak. When freed from duty, I went up to see the plane. The wreck was hardly recognisable as an aeroplane, and there were no survivors. Looking into the plane, I could see a seat with several holes in it where shots had gone through from the back. It had pieces of torn cloth and flesh still clinging to the jagged edges of the holes. A guard had been mounted to discourage souvenir hunters, and one of them led me to a nearby bush. Pulling a branch aside, he revealed a leg. Clothing and boot gone, it had been torn off at the thigh, was broken at the ankle, and was missing the big toe. The flesh was a bright red and the skin a dark bluey grey. God knows what had happened to the rest of the body.

On the edge of Sturry, just over the level crossing where the road forks to Whitstable and Sarre, there used to be a garage. Piled up alongside was a heap of crashed aeroplanes from both sides, the wings removed and stacked alongside the fuselages, probably twenty feet high.

Another Dornier came down in a cornfield near Westbere. It was pretty well intact, and the crew were taken prisoner by 'D' Company, which was billeted nearby. A pretty arrogant bunch they were said to be, too. They were convinced they would not be prisoners long, and they told us to beware their friends when they arrive.

A local farmer took a suspiciously keen interest in the crash. He stood around taking photographs, and when the prisoners were collected and taken away, he followed the van on a motor bike. Unfortunately for him, his activities had been noticed, and he was soon arrested and his film confiscated.

'D' Company's guard had grand fun messing around in the crashed plane, sitting in the pilot's seat and playing like children. Unbeknown to them, one of the machine guns had been left on 'fire', and when the wrong button was pressed, bullets sprayed out across Westbere Marshes. It's lucky they didn't kill one of their mates.

Accidents happened more often than they should have once live ammo was issued. An incident involving 'D' Company occurred when an anti-tank rifle—with a half-inch bore and a kick like a mule—was being cleaned in a billet. The magazine had been taken off, but a round was inadvertently left 'up the spout'. The trigger was pulled, and the shot went right through two partition walls, an outer wall, and vanished out over the Kent countryside. Luckily, nothing much else intervened, and no one was hurt.

Another duty found for us was to search the East Kent area for possible landing points, both sea and air, and possible routes for an invading force to follow. This we did in pairs on bicycles, and maps were constructed from our reports.

Around the coast, defences had been built. Sometimes they were made of concrete, but more often metal scaffolding poles were arranged as a continuous fence with the ends pointing seawards at about high-water level and with barbed wire loosely draped over the lot. Inland any field on which a plane or glider could be landed had twenty-foot poles set up in them at staggered intervals. Road routes were covered by pill boxes and block houses.

We had to look for holes through these defences, and it was suggested that it might be possible to find a way up to Canterbury by following the Stour Valley and Westbere Marshes. Two of us were sent to seek out the warden, and he explained that there was indeed a way through the marshes on foot.

We asked to be shown these routes, with the intention of plotting them on our map. Our guide took us to a store and fitted us out with thigh-length boots, and we found that most of the so-called paths through the marshes were under water, sometimes as deep as two feet. We didn't think the Blitzkrieg would come that way.

Local people regularly reported seeing suspicious lights over the marshes at night and noises in the woods sounding like generators. We had to investigate all of these, and many sleepless nights were spent creeping through woods, listening for anything untoward. Reports of strange happenings in Trenleypark Wood persisted for most of our stay, but we never did find anything suspicious. The reported lights, if found, always turned out to be quite innocuous.

After repeated reports of lights out on the marshes, 'Pip' Appleby, our Intelligence Officer, gave us a chit to commandeer a rowboat from the Fordwich Arms on the river at Fordwich. As instructed, we rowed up to Chislet

Dornier and captured crew that was forced to land in a cornfield in Westbere, summer 1940.

Colliery, where we could leave it moored for future use. The theory was that when the lights were reported we would take the boat and maybe pinpoint where the lights were. En route down the river, we were nearly swept over a small waterfall, and my companion, a fellow called Eric Sanders, caught a crab, and we lost a rowlock overboard. Down toward the colliery, there were thick weeds, and with only one oar, we had great difficulty getting through them. When we reached the colliery landing stage, half a dozen grimy kids were playing there. They watched silently as we secured the boat, and their eyes followed us as we walked away up the slope. I bet that as soon as we were out of sight they were in the boat like a shot. One of the colliery workers whom we talked to said that any boat found by the local kids would inevitably end up sunk. So perhaps it didn't matter too much how many rowlocks we had. To my knowledge, the boat was never used as intended and was never retrieved, and I've no idea what eventually happened to the oars and solitary rowlock that cluttered up our office for weeks.

One old lady persistently reported seeing lights from the bedroom of her cottage in the main street of Sturry. Sgt Rogers and two of us fusiliers kept a watch from her room until suddenly one night she said, "There, there it is!"

And sure enough, we could see a faint light on which we quickly took a bearing. This was plotted on a map and appeared to be somewhere along the north side of the marshes. The two of us were sent off to follow the bearing as closely as possible over fields, gardens, and back alleys until we were out near Hersden. We could find nothing out of the ordinary, except a railway signal on the line near Westbere village. We telephoned Sgt Rogers, and he said we were to climb the signal and cover it with a cap at ten o'clock. We tossed for the job; I lost and climbed the thing, feeling very vulnerable up there, hoping no enthusiastic Home Guard would come along with a loaded rifle. We phoned Sgt Rogers again, and that was definitely the light.

While at Sturry, I was sent to attend a one-day unarmed combat course. The course was quite interesting, and I managed to survive without serious injury, though someone did stand on my hand while wearing hob-nailed boots, which was quite painful for a few days. When I got back to Milner Court, I found the section digging slit trenches on a slope at the back of the house.

Sergeant Rogers demanded to be shown what we had learnt, and rushed at me with hands outstretched to grab me round the neck. I grasped his wrists, stepped across in front of him, and bent down, and he sailed over my head and landed, luckily, on a heap of soil that had been dug out of the trench. Sgt Rogers must have weighed about fourteen stone—portly would be a kind description—and was a good deal older than the rest of us. Although he wasn't hurt, he was quite shaken. No further demonstration was required.

While we were at Sturry, I suppose to keep everyone occupied, we started having 'spit and polish' inspections and parades. Everyone had to learn the art. A new pair of army boots came with a rather greasy 'orange peel' finish. First, this was ironed out with an old spoon heated in the fire. Then black boot polish was worked in with a cloth, and finally, a little spit and a lot of rotary action would produce a surface like glass. Brass buckles, tabs, buttons, and badges were first smoothed with 'wet or dry' paper and then worked on with metal polish until they glistened like precious metal. Webbing equipment had to be blancoed and left to dry where it wouldn't be marked before slipping it on to go on parade.

Guard duty was one such parade where this was taken to extreme lengths. An extra man was detailed for guard duty, and when the guard was inspected, the man with the best turn out would be selected as the 'stick man'. This was a sought-after job because you remained in the nice warm guard room unless there were any messages to be run. It was much better than standing out in the weather for two hours at a stretch, snapping to attention and saluting any officer who passed or, at night, challenging anyone who approached.

Selecting the stick man could sometimes be difficult. All of the guard wanted the job and had spent the previous day cleaning and polishing to the limit. A putty not quite tied as neatly as perfection or a buckle slightly out of position was enough to lose you the job. On at least one occasion, the last two were down to removing equipment, then their battle dress blouses, and when one was found to a have a trouser button loose, the other man got the job.

Mounting the guard was sometimes undertaken in real ceremonial style with the band playing, and all the movements were initiated by drum taps, not spoken command. It was difficult to memorise the sequence of movements, and Lord help anyone who got it wrong.

We also had church parades with the band playing and marching round the village after the service. On one occasion we had a service in Canterbury Cathedral. The band not only played marches for us into the cathedral grounds and away but also inside for the service. The Archbishop conducted the service. The march to the cathedral from Sturry was approaching three miles, and the band played only at the beginning and end each way. I didn't envy them carrying those instruments that distance, but blowing into a euphonium at the same time would have been too much for even the army to expect.

Lt 'Pip' Appleby and Sgt Rogers had been transferred into the intelligence section only a short time after I had, and neither seemed to know that Fred and I were snipers, so we found ourselves treated as any other two on the section. One day, out of the blue, I was asked to draw a map of an area. I enlarged the relevant section of a one-inch-to-a-mile ordinance survey map to six-inches-to-a-mile, putting in the extra detail wanted. I was always quite good at drawing, and when they realised this, I was frequently given this sort of job to do. Sometimes, it would be an enlargement as I've just described for the planning of an exercise or route march. Sometimes, it would be an even larger drawing to show locations of positions, pill boxes, and trenches. On a couple of occasions, this was done in chalk on a blackboard for a C.O.'s briefing. I enjoyed this work, and it also got me out of less interesting activities. Sometimes, it was necessary to go out on a bicycle to fill in detail, and for the further reaches, I was even allowed to use the section's motor bike. Once, I was driven to East Hoathly to draw the site of a road accident which had happened before we left the Uckfield area.

The motor bike was normally for the use of Sgt Rogers, but Pip decreed that we all should learn to ride it. Of the section, only 'Nobby' Norris and myself laid claim to ever having ridden a motorbike before. I don't know about Nobby, but I had a friend who owned a 250cc Velocette which I had ridden a few times, but not on any public highway. Neither of us had ever possessed a driving licence. This, apparently, was all the experience they were looking for, and we were detailed to teach the rest of the section all we knew.

We took the first two or three pupils out to a field at the back of Milner Court with the motor bike, a 500cc side-valve B.S.A. The field was an ideal place for it, except that at the far end there was a ditch and along one side ran a paling fence.

Nobby sat the first man on the bike, describing the various controls and explaining how to use them. He then got him to start the bike, pull in the clutch, foot into gear, and let out the clutch as you open the throttle. At least that was how it should be done. Well the throttle was twisted so that the engine screamed, the clutch was let go with a bang, and Fusilier Sanders and bike vanished down the field, leaving the rest of us staring through a cloud of smoke and dust at a large skid mark in the grass.

Nobby and I raced after him. By now Sanders was screaming, "How do I stop it! How do I stop it!", and fast reaching the end of the field. He tried to turn but didn't make it before vanishing over the lip of the ditch with a crash. All that could be seen was the back wheel sticking up out of the ditch.

Luckily, the ditch was dry, and we dragged poor Sanders out more or less unscathed. The bike was less fortunate and had to be sent back to the transport section to have the forks straightened. It had hardly been returned to us before someone else drove it into the paling fence with further damage. I'm sure the transport section must have been fed up with the sight of that bike before we were through.

I had a lot of fun on the bike though, and was often sent on errands. On one of my mapping trips I had to cross the River Stour using the Grove Ferry. There is a fine bridge there now, but in those days it really was a ferry.

This consisted of a wooden platform with a rail either side and you crossed by hauling on a cable which rose dripping from the river bed at one end of the platform and dropped back into the water at the other. With several people, it was easy, but alone with the bike, I had to haul the ferry across from the far side, drive the bike on, set it on its stand, and then haul the whole lot back across the river. This was much more fun than a bridge but no good if we were in a hurry.

Another good game they found for us was the coding and de-coding of messages. We used syllabic code, picking pairs of letters from a chart each representing a syllable and in this way your message could be built up. One of us had to spend the night in our office awaiting the arrival of a practice message. It would have originated from a ship in the channel and would be sent via coastguards, ourselves, brigade, division, and onto army headquarters in London, each using their own particular code. The results were never revealed, and I often wondered if the original and the final messages received were anything alike.

In early September 1940, the state of the moon and tides were favourable for the awaited invasion so that for about a week, very few of us got any sleep. Our section was divided into pairs. One pair to each of the four rifle companies and one in the battalion command post.

Stan Humphreys and I were sent to 'B' Company command post, which was situated on a hill on the Canterbury side of Stodmarsh. There was little for us to do unless the balloon went up, and we were advised to get what sleep we could. There was so much noise in the command post that we rolled up in a blanket with our gas capes over us and slept under a nearby water tower. During one night it rained, and our blankets got wet, but this was a small price to pay for being out of that stuffy, noisy command post.

For some time I had been missing my forage cap. There was always a lot of petty pilfering going on in the army. So I couldn't believe my luck when I spotted a cap lying in the long grass beneath the water tower. It looking a bit worn and weather beaten, but it was a forage cap all the same. I had been dreading the next kit inspection, so I gladly thanked providence and slapped it on my head. After about a day, I had a nasty, raw sore behind my ear which spread rapidly all over my face. I attended sick parade and was rushed to an army sick bay near Canterbury, where they said I had impetigo.

I was whipped straight into bed. I couldn't see why; I was perfectly fit apart from a few sores. I suppose it stopped me spreading it around.

These days, they would have some wonder drug, but at that time, a perfectly lovely nurse sat on the side of my bed twice a day and picked all the scabs off of my sores with tweezers and then painted them with antiseptic of some kind. It was half an hour of pure agony each time, and lovely or not, I began to dread the sight of my tormentor. Nor for a week had the sores got any better. Then they decided to move some of us up to a temporary hospital in Maidstone.

About eight of us were taken in an ambulance, and for the journey they had bandaged our sores, again I suppose to stop any contact and spreading. The ambulance was losing water and boiled for the second time on the run down to Harrietsham. We stopped near a café that laid back from the road, and the motherly old lady running it assumed we were wounded from the recent Dunkirk evacuation,. She insisted on plying us with tea and cakes while the driver filled the radiator. Rotten lot that we were, no one enlightened her.

I spent about a further week at Maidstone. Thank goodness there was no more picking of scabs, but I looked a pretty sight I must say with gentian violet dabs all over my head. At least it quickly cleared up and I returned to Sturry.

After a while it became apparent that the arrival of Nazi hordes charging up the beaches was not that imminent, and things relaxed a little. Some leave was allowed, and we no longer had to take rifles and equipment wherever we went.

I got a short leave and was easily able to get home. It was the first time I had been in London since Dunkirk and the start of the 'Blitz'. I hadn't realised the extent to which the London underground railway stations were used as shelters from the air raids. It came as quite a shock when on going down to catch a train I found the whole platform covered in sleeping bodies, right up to within two or three feet from the edge of the platform. Every few minutes a train would arrive pushing a great waft of stale air ahead of it, or sucking it along behind. It was always noisy and draughty, but I suppose at least they felt safe.

At home there were air raids every night, and I went with my parents to the Anderson shelter at the bottom of our garden when the siren sounded. Our dog, Danny, had the most amazing hearing and would worry at the back door several minutes before we could detect the slightest sound of a warning. As soon as the door was opened he would race down the garden and into the shelter, where he remained trembling until the 'all clear' sounded and we trooped back indoors.

One raid came close when a stick of bombs fell along the back of our house. The noise of the explosions was terrific and through it all came the awful sound of a woman screaming. This went on for probably ten or twenty seconds then stopped. There was nothing to be heard except for the clatter of falling debris, followed by a strange hissing sound as all the dust and lighter pieces floated down. The bomb had scored a direct hit on an air raid shelter about sixty yards from ours. Three people were killed and a fourth injured.

We were perfectly alright in our shelter, except for ringing ears! Our house did suffer damage though. The back door was blown through the house and ended up near to the front door. A long case clock in the hall was matchwood, and our piano had digs and scrapes and a split end. Some windows were blown out and we lost some tiles from the roof, but at least we were unhurt.

Exercises once again commenced, though usually of shorter duration. For these exercises the intelligence section was split up into pairs again, one pair being attached to each of the rifle companies and one pair in the battalion command post as before. This usually meant riding in the back of a truck next to a signals chap with his radio, telephone, and other gear. Receiving messages from our colleagues in the field, logging them and passing them on to one of the C.O.'s aides. This was the plum job which we all liked. Those attached to the companies went forward with them. There was not always a radio or telephone handy so each pair had a bicycle. For observing the enemy, a brass-bound telescope in a leather case was provided. This on top of all our other equipment meant that, when the infantry took to the hills and advanced cross country we had little hope of keeping up. Usually a good deal of fun could be had if you could keep your sense of humour.

27 September 1940

Another scheme in the district of Chartham. Was with Advance Headquarters, which at this time was situated at a cross roads. Three enemy Bren gun carriers could be seen coming along the road only about a hundred yards away.

Everyone scattered like rabbits looking for the anti-tank rifles, and finally someone got a Bren trained on the carriers. An argument developed over who were the victors, but since we had two lieutenants and a captain and they only had a sergeant, needless to say we won! Pip Appleby called out to them.

"Alright you're all dead, we have a Bren trained on you!"

Poor Sgt Reed tried to remind him that they had had several Brens trained on us for quite ten minutes before ours was in action, but by then an umpire, Major Deeks had arrived and shouted.

"Damme man, don't argue!"

So what could he do! Later, Pat Coyne, Don Hylkema and I were sent forward to establish an observation post. We moved round to the far side of a wood, but found our view obstructed by another

wood a few hundred yards further on. Pat said he would go forward and recce. Don and I sat down and munched our fish paste
sandwiches. Pat didn't return and through my telescopic sight I
could see what looked like an L.M.G. position. We couldn't be sure
if they were enemy or not since Pat had our telescope. We settled
down in cover and later picked out several who we could see were
enemy. I sent Don back with a message and while he was away 'D'
company advanced through into the attack. When they reached
the far wood, enemy attackers and an umpire stood around in
groups talking, I thought the objective had been gained, and sent
another message to say so. However, when I joined them, the
umpire said 'D' company would have been wiped out by the
L.M.G. I chipped in and said I was a sniper and had picked off at
least twenty men around the L.M.G. and the umpire, Major
Roberts, said, 'Don't talk rot, anyway the attack failed!' I pointed
out that I had only shown myself thinking the attack successful and
I was told I was a casualty. Later Don came looking for me having
passed on his false message, and was 'taken prisoner!' We sat in the
woods finishing our dinner 'till a truck came to take us back to
Sturry.

On the second of November I said farewell to Milner Court, and went
with an advance party to sort out new billets at Highland Court on the Dover
side of the village of Bridge. Highland Court is a mansion standing in a large
park, and looked like Buckingham Palace to me, with stone pillars and
wrought iron gates across a terrace in front of the house. The large entrance
hall was finished in dark green marble and had oil paintings still hanging. I
remember there were pillars and large marble fireplaces. At the back of the
hall a white marble staircase curved up to an upper landing and we were
allocated a room off to one side. This still had a fitted carpet, and the whole
house had concealed central heating.
    Part of the house was still occupied and a farm on the site was still being
run from the house. It was a tremendous billet and I wondered if it wasn't
too good to last. Still the exercises continued and another entry in the diary
reads as follows.

6 December 1940
    Early morning 'C' Company had to attack 'B' Company in their
billets. 'B' Company hadn't been forewarned and Pip Appleby,
Stan and I had to go and raise the alarm. On our arrival everyone
was either in bed, or washing and shaving and we caused quite a
commotion. Soon after, 'C' Company's Corporal Robson walked in

dressed as a farm labourer carrying a Tommy gun under his rain coat. He had just walked right past a guard, and what by now was supposed to be alert defences. He was disarmed in the company office and he told us to be careful since the gun was loaded. On taking the magazine off, sure enough it was full of live ammo. Later C.S.M. Crump was brought in also dressed as a farm hand. No one had searched him, and he suddenly whipped a revolver out of his pocket and 'shot' Pip. However, a 'B' Company member said he had shot Crump half an hour ago so Pip was resurrected. After that 'B' company boys shot all disguised prisoners out of hand. Robson and Crump had one more try to escape and Robson went for me with a chair. My imaginary bullets didn't make him stop. However, Pip came in and pronounced him dead, and apart from one short sharp scuffle outside the office door we had no further fun. Further along the line we heard that 'C' Company Commander Captain Warren drove straight past the guards on a tractor, dressed in an old shooting jacket looking just like every mans idea of a country squire. The guards then, having been blasted for that, refused to let the Batt. C.O.'s car past until they'd had everyone out and checked them over.

While the defenders were playing games with the amateur actors, 'C' Company attacked from the rear yelling blood curdling war cries as they came. Everyone got over excited and things became a little heated. In the hand to hand 'fighting' rifle butts came into play, and knowing 'C' Company of old I wasn't surprised. I reckoned 'C' Company won that war!

Manny Rossen had joined our section by now, and one evening suggested that we get ourselves down to the village hall in Bridge where the signals section were running a dance. There were no takers, and it turned out that out of the lot of us only Manny knew how to dance. Not to be deterred from his desire to get us all to these dances, he proceeded to turn our room into a dancing academy. Manny taught Pat Coyne and I how to waltz. It must have been quite a sight. Rossen, five foot two, trying to push six foot three Pat, with feet to match, around the room shouting "one two three, one two three . . .", for of course we had no music. We were also instructed in the rudiments of the quick step, though it was a long time before I dared try that on any unsuspecting female. Had I not been trapped in a Paul Jones, I never would have. He tried also to teach us the slow foxtrot to no avail. I think he'd given up on us by then, and I never did learn to do it properly.

So passed out as fit by Manny, we set off into Bridge for the next signals dance. I only dared a couple of waltzes and then only when the lights were out and a spot shone on a rotating ball giving a minimum of flickering light. Anyway, it was a change from the pictures. Army boots were not the best wear for a novice on a crowded dance floor, and I reckon any girl going to an army-run dance should have been awarded a special medal for valour.

After that we became regulars at the signals dance and quite enjoyed them. It was certainly better than loafing about in the billet. On one occasion the last waltz must have finished late, and after walking up from Bridge, we arrived at Highland Court after lights out. Still chattering, we took a shortcut through the front entrance, which was strictly for officers. As we walked up the steps, the C.O. leaned out of an upstairs window, calling, "Who's that down there?" We didn't answer. "Sentry, take those men to the guard commander and see that I have their names in the morning." Since none of us were on the pass roll and since we were late, we were officially A.W.O.L. About three days later, we were on company orders and were remanded. Eventually, on a second visit to the company office, we were admonished—the only time I was in trouble while in the army.

For New Year 1940–41, our section put on a pantomime, "Babes in the Wood." Sanders and Hylkema were the babes, and I was one of half a dozen robins who, when the babes are sleeping, cover them with leaves. In lieu of leaves, which are in short supply in January, we used empty sand bags. Sgt Rogers was mainly to blame for the script, which carried all sorts of references to people in the battalion and was really quite funny. It went quite well. Panic broke out at one point as it appeared the fairy queen had lost her clothes. We were undecided whether 'she' should go on in battle dress or underwear, but luckily, the gear was found in time. Pip Appleby, our section officer, had convulsions when he saw us 'girls'. A few nights later, we put on a repeat performance at 'A' Company in Ickham. It didn't go down so well because most of the audience were local civilians to whom the references to battalion personalities and events meant nothing.

The officers also had a New Year's ball arranged. This was held at Highland Court in the marble entrance hall, just down the big curved staircase from the landing where our room was located. The dance was not for the hoi poloi but we enjoyed the band and the vast quantities of their booze that somehow found its way up the stairs and into our quarters.

About this time, in January 1941, it was published on the Daily Routines Orders that we could apply to be transferred to the air force for air crew duties. My name went in, and I bought books in Canterbury on mathematics, since this subject, we had heard, was included in the entrance exams. At school I had never done well at math, and after all, I had left at the age of fifteen, some six years earlier.

One of the more memorable moments whilst at Bridge was another exercise that Pip arranged for our section. We were supposed to be a party taking rations and supplies up. The 'supplies' comprised a Tommy gun and an anti-tank rifle, all with magazines loaded and in their wooden cases. Quite a weight! Our route was about eleven miles, nearly all cross-country and through deep snow. Drifts in some places were chest high and we were clambering over fences and hedges just following a compass line. We were soaked in no time, and by the time we got back to Highland Court we were completely shattered. Pip had some funny idea that his section had to be the fittest and best in the battalion. There was a lot of competition between the various sections of H.Q. Company—or, at any rate, between their officers— and if, say, the signals were reported to have marched seventeen miles in four hours, Pip had us do twenty the next day.

Also at this time we did some security exercises which showed up how unaware people, even the forces were of the need for being alert. Two of our officers wandered around Canterbury for several hours dressed as German army officers without being challenged once. Our section being the one that was supposed to be trained in moving without being seen to set up O.P.s etc were often called on to test the alertness of our own units. We would be sent to steal documents from company offices, and even on one occasion were sent to steal a three tonner from the M.T. compound. This posed a problem as no one in the section had driven a vehicle of this size. I admitted to having driven a car short distances, although I had never held a licence, so I was nominated as driver. Cpl Norris, Pat, and I duly went one evening and managed to obtain a truck, starting it by rolling it down a slope. The gearbox had no synchro-mesh and was difficult. We can't have got into more than second gear all the way round to the back of Highland Court. We probably weren't very popular with the companies at that time.

We were sometimes sent to harass the companies when they were on exercises. We would creep up on bivouacked camps at crack of dawn, pushing firecrackers under the edge of the tent brailings. We were never ever caught which was just as well for us, but didn't say much for our lads chances if one morning they were set on by real enemies with more than just firecrackers.

Towards the end of January 1941, they arranged another three-day exercise for our entertainment. This was supposed to be practice in moving the battalion in convoy at night, fighting our 'battle' and returning in convoy to base.

We were on parade for the off at one o'clock in the afternoon, but it took until ten in the evening before we moved. I travelled in the battalion H.Q. truck, but we didn't get far. After eleven miles the truck broke down, and it was an hour and a half before they could get it started again.

Two miles further on we were stopped again. We had to keep our position in the convoy, and someone ahead of us was in trouble. Sgt Grey our orderly room sergeant produced a spirit stove and brewed tea. It smelt of methylated spirits, but it was wet and warm, and we were grateful. It was just as well it was dark, and we couldn't see what we were drinking.

Soon after we started moving again we had a collision with a dispatch rider. It was a very dark night and the head lamps had the wartime shrouds on them, rather like a top hat with three or four slots in the front. It was impossible to see more than a few feet ahead with them fitted. Luckily, the D.R. wasn't hurt and his bike still ridable though bent, and after the usual argument we continued, but not for long. At a small village called Halland, south west of Uckfield we broke down again.

The workshop truck was by now miles back, busy pulling trucks out of ditches and we had a long wait. Unbelievably during the night fifty eight trucks went off the road. Our lads in the workshop truck told us that they'd pulled over thirty of them back onto the road during the dark hours.

When the shops opened we were able to buy some loaves and breakfast sausage and were able to get an early cup of tea at the Cricketers Arms. Left to the army we would have starved. Despite rationing it was surprising how people usually found something 'under the counter' for us lads.

The workshop truck turned up at eleven o'clock and after losing our way in Brighton we arrived in Shoreham at two, just in time to miss dinner rations. As we arrived the battalion was just moving off again and we eventually took up position in a village not far from Arundel.

Corporal Lamming and I went looking for food. We were ravenous, and managed to find something at the local grocers shop. Then I found Sergeant Rogers. He told me that we were bedding down for the night in the local water works. When we eventually found the place it turned out to be a large building housing a good deal of machinery and boilers, already crowded with lads laying out their beds in piles of coal and dust. We didn't think much of this, and after looking around several out buildings found one with a nice large car in it.

Sgt Rogers went to the house next door to ask if we might sleep in the car, and came back with the news that we had been offered the use of their back room. We were about four in number and we sat yarning with the old couple who were our hosts. They gave us some supper and we bedded down in front of a dying fire at about ten o'clock. By eleven Pip Appleby was knocking at the door, raking us out for a recce of the approaches to the river and its bridge.

We had an enemy guarding the approaches to Arundel. They wore soft hats, we were to wear steel helmets. We went by truck to within fifty yards of a road block, dived down a side turning but couldn't get through to the river. Back on the main road where with no chance of dodging we ran into a couple of 'enemy'. They were all for taking us back to their guardroom.

"Why?" asked Pip.

"Your wearing steel helmets, you must be enemy!"

"What a load of nonsense!" said Pip "surely lots of people wear tin hats these days?" and very cleverly he managed to convince them that we were Home Guard, and even got them to tell us how to get down to the river and the bridge. We continued our recce, blundering through fields, muddy farmyards, and eventually arriving at the rendezvous for our truck back. However no truck, which meant we had to walk back several miles to our temporary H.Q. On arrival we were told to get some sleep in the local school, but we had no idea where to start looking for our blankets. It was so cold that I spent most of the remainder of the night walking around just to keep warm.

Two of our rifle companies attacked Arundel at four o'clock in the morning; I knew nothing of this; they didn't chase us out 'till six. That morning I actually got breakfast from the army, the first, in fact the only meal of the whole three days.

We climbed back wearily into our trucks at four in the afternoon and after a comparatively uneventful journey of only one hundred and ten miles arrived back at Bridge at one o'clock in the morning. Later we heard that a good part of the convoy got lost and landed up in the goods yards at Folkestone. Someone was heard to say that he was mighty glad we lived on an island—if Hitler had only known.

Another three-day exercise in February provided further entertainment. Eric Sanders and I were attached to 'D' Company. Our job was to send back information regarding the companies progress to whoever was manning the Battalion H.Q. truck. Apart from all the usual gear an infantry man has loaded on him, we also had a bicycle, telescope, and field sketching equipment. All this made 'D' Company headquarters truck very crowded and we felt they would sooner have managed without us.

We left at eleven in the evening, and by daylight half of 'D' Company's lorries had vanished. I'm not sure if they ever caught up with us. Six miles out of Eastbourne our truck ended up in a ditch and while trying to tow it out the one behind went in also.

Eventually, we reached the outskirts of Eastbourne, had breakfast, marched uphill away from the town and up onto the downs. Once we left the road the cycle was a terrible handicap. It was no lightweight model, and was carried up hills, through hedges, over ditches, and fences. We were soon miles behind the 'D' Company platoons. Luckily, just as we were wondering if we ever would see them again we ran into their Sergeant Hawkes. He was on his own, also lost, but at least knew where the company was headed. By the time we finally came up to the company, within spitting distance of the

River Cuckmere, I was dead tired, and Eric had stopped being any help miles back.

Our luck held in one respect, we were in time for another meal, and we were told we would be crossing the river at eleven o'clock that night. We tried to get some sleep, but out in the open during February, wrapped in nothing other than our gas capes it really was too cold. Eleven o'clock came and went and at twelve I went to see what was going on. I was told that our company was in reserve and were not likely to move until dawn. So Eric and I scrounged a blanket apiece, rolled up in our gas capes and settled down in the lee of a felled tree trunk.

It drizzled with rain most of the night, and it was too cold to get much sleep. I was quite relieved when five thirty came and some breakfast came up to us.

Later, Eric and I set up an O.P. with the C.O. and an artillery observation officer. This was in the middle of some bushes, and it rained, hailed and did just about everything it could to make us uncomfortable. Luckily our messages were sent back by signals to Battalion H.Q. We learnt that 'A' and 'C' Companies had crossed the river during the night using assault boats. 'A' Company managed to overturn one in midstream and nine rifles and a Bren gun were lost in the river.

As Battalion H.Q. came through, Eric and I joined on the back. We lay low until the scheme finished at about four o'clock, by which time we were at Seaford. On the way back we were involved in another collision involving a truck going in the opposite direction. It scraped right down the side of our truck from end to end. We were all flat on the floor in a trice. Only recently one of our number, Stevens, had been killed in just such an incident. We arrived back at our billets at around midnight.

Around this time I came back from leave to find that everyone had filled in forms for transfer to the R.A.F.

Most of our Battalion seemed to have put in papers, and our intelligence section had applied én bloc. Our office was in a corner of the orderly room, and a word with Sergeant Grey saw my application slipped in among the rest.

On 21 February 1941, we moved to an old reformatory school near Kingsnorth which was about a mile and a half south of Ashford. The school was a place where bad lads were sent, and it certainly was a large place. We were quartered in a huge dormitory together with signals, A.A., and the M.P.s and their prisoners. Luckily, the M.P.s and prisoners moved out as soon as they had organised a guard room and we were able to spread ourselves out a bit. Even then we envied a lot of the chaps who were out in private billets.

The school was infested with mice and all night you could hear scratching sounds and the pit-a-pat of tiny feet. Sometimes you would wake to the thud, thud, thud as someone attacked the invaders with a gym shoe. Quite a few of us had goodies sent from home stored away in kit bags or held as sustenance during those long route marches or exercises, and the little beasts would find their way into a kit bag or pocket whatever precautions were taken.

Complaints had the pioneer section on their knees nailing patches of tin over all the mouse holes. During the following night you would hear even more frantic scratching, and by the morning there were holes neatly cut at the side of the tin patches. Poison, traps, all were tried but we never did get rid of the pests.

While at Ashford we had another big church parade, marching with the band all the way to the church in Ashford, and all the way back. The C.O. and his staff arranged themselves on a traffic island in the middle of the High Street and took the salute as we all marched past. Down the Kingsnorth Road small boys ran cheering (and jeering) at our sides, dogs barked at our heels, and we wondered what all the girls were saying to one another as we passed by. We weren't sorry to hear the band break into 'The British Grenadier' for then we knew we were almost home.

The Army was always thinking up new tricks for us. Pip Appleby went on a demonstration at brigade on how to quickly break through coiled barbed wire, and naturally enough, we, his section had to be shown and then demonstrate to the rest of the battalion just how it was done. Three rolls of coiled barbed wire were stretched out, two at the bottom, the third on top making a fence about five feet high. The first two men ran at the fence and launched themselves onto it with arms crossed in front of their faces for protection. The second two ran over their mates on the ground and in the same way launched themselves at the furthest part of the fence. The rest of the platoon then ran over the four on the ground who then picked themselves up and followed. A whole platoon through in a few seconds flat, but why did I have to be one of the first two? Back in the billet I stripped off and found little splodges of blood all up the backs of my arms and down the front of my body and legs where the barbs had gone through my battle dress, but no other damage.

Another demonstration given to us at Ashford was far more entertaining! The local branch of the N.F.S. (National Fire Service) came to show us how to put out fires. A rough structure about the size of a large garden shed was knocked up on our parade ground and all sorts of inflammable material heaped inside. We were all paraded outside and after a few words from the C.O. the fire was lit and an alarm operated. Within a couple of minutes a fire engine raced into the square, bell ringing, and helmeted figures raced in all directions.

Hoses were unrolled at lightning speed and all went well until someone much too keen turned on the water before his mates were ready. The nozzle jerked out of one mans hands and snaked back and forth. After a splutter, a huge jet of water scattered everyone. Three of the firemen tried at great risk to life and limb to get the nozzle under control but it was impossible. The jet traversed the school building just as a company sergeant major came to the door and the jet caught him at chest height, knocking him back inside. Eventually, the fellow on the valve got the message and turned off the water.

On the second try, they did better, putting out the fire with great gusto. It had nearly burnt out by then anyway. Of course, as one might have known, the asphalt under the fire had melted and someone had to be brought in to make repairs.

We had been issued with a Tommy gun and of course we had to have a session on the ranges for practice. Any faint confidence I might have felt from watching gangster films was quickly dispelled when I found how diffi-cult it was to obtain any real accuracy. We were firing at about ten yards at man sized cut out targets. Firing the gun on single shot wasn't too bad, but on auto firing from the hip it was impossible to stop it from swinging vio-lently to the right and upwards. I was not impressed.

Later that day, the tale went around that someone had called out to a fellow on the firing point, who turned to reply and inadvertently pressed the trigger with the gun set on auto. Standing at the side of the range was the range Sergeant. He was wearing a tin hat and a gas mask on his chest. One of the loose shots went right through the gas mask from one side to the other. I gather he wasn't pleased. He was lucky he wasn't killed!

Shortly after this exercise, I was made responsible for our section's Tommy gun, and had to hand in my rifle and bayonet. Now I knew I wasn't a sniper any longer.

On another occasion we had a trip to the ranges to have a go with live hand grenades. We had had practice at throwing dummies many times, but this was for real. We took turns, about three at a time, to go forward to a trench which was sandbagged along the front. On command we pulled the pin out and hurled the grenade forward over the sandbags. You would have thought that there would have been plenty of incentive to throw true and long but one of our three, face clear in my memory but name long forgot-ten, brought his arm round to the side rather than over his head. The grenade shot off at an angle, hit the top edge of the sand-bags, flew up into the air and came to rest on top of the sandbags about ten yards down the trench to our left. Someone had the presence of mind to push it over beyond the sandbags, and the sergeant yelled "DOWN!!" He needn't have bothered since we were already there. It went off only a few feet from the trench and we were splattered with earth but otherwise unhurt.

Other memories of Ashford include hours of billiards and snooker played in the Y.M.C.A. at the station, and dances held in our dining hall with our band playing. Here I met a girl, Betty Diamond. I only danced a few times with her, but when the battalion eventually moved on she wanted to write. I think she regarded this as her war effort; cheering up the gallant lads with her chatty letters. I only kept in touch for a while, but our mothers started a correspondence that went on long after the war.

In the district there were quite a few Italian P.O.W.s working on the farms and Betty also knew and wrote to a few of these. I wasn't altogether in favour. I didn't see the need to do too much for their morale. They had it easy. They were provided with warm winter clothing, bicycles to get around on and did not appear to be very restricted in their movements. I wondered how our boys were faring in Italy.

During early summer 1941, the battalion moved from Ashford to New Romney. Our section was billeted in a detached house opposite a pub (I wonder which clever chap arranged that?), these being the last two build-ings on the edge of town on the road to Dymchurch.

We took over from the Hampshires, and among the things we inherited from them was a large scale hand drawn map of our area on which several areas had been shaded in red. The story went that after Dunkirk the coast-line from Hythe round to Rye was reckoned to be prime favourite for a Ger-man landing, and the whole area was mined and booby trapped. Trouble was no one at the time had foreseen the need to keep records. The map had been produced later, the red areas being minefields since discovered, usu-ally by some unfortunate sheep, finding a way through the fence, and blow-ing itself up. Unfortunately, the splattered remains were not always that of sheep. We had one or two quite needless casualties during our stay.

On one occasion a party of men were filling sandbags on the beach at Littlestone. One of them went behind a bathing hut to have a smoke out of sight of the corporal. He trod on something nasty and was blown to smithereens. Fortunately, no one else was hurt. On another occasion, while we were walking back from Hythe, a fellow saw a bungalow with a window ajar. He went to investigate and set off a booby trap under the door step. I quickly learnt only to tread in other people's footsteps.

Along the back of the beach at Littlestone and Greatstone there were sand dunes which shifted almost daily with the winds. One day, you could see rows of mines sticking out of the sand; a few days later, they would be covered, and another lot farther along would be exposed. It was all very unnerving.

On another occasion one of the companies were doing field firing in the vicinity of St Marys Bay. The troops would advance in battle order and pop up targets would suddenly appear. They would then flop down and fire. In theory the rounds should pass over open ground and out to sea, but on this occasion a stray round hit a mine and the whole field went up. We were in New Romney at the time and heard the roar and saw a huge column of smoke rising into the air. Either the mines, which were laid in a hurry, were too close or perhaps they were getting old and rusty. Both theories went the rounds.

Another unfortunate accident happened while we were at New Romney. Our corporal, 'Nobby' Norris, had been posted to one of the companies. He was checking the aim of his men in a billet. This was done using an aiming disc. The disc was about an inch and half in diameter and painted to represent a target. It had a small hole in the middle of the bull and was mounted on a wooden handle. The instructor lies on the floor looking through the hole in the bull. The pupil lies opposite with his rifle and aims at the target. It is thus easy for the instructor to see if the aim is good, if the rifle is held upright, or jerked when fired. Of course the instructor should always ensure the rifles are clear and barrels inspected before starting. Nobby couldn't have done this, for one of his lads laid down, took aim and shot him clean through the head at about two foot range.

At Littlestone there was a safe part of the beach. I'm not sure if they'd driven sheep over it, or whether it was just that no one had been killed there for a week or two. Either way the weather was hot, and they decided us lads could go bathing in this section, inside the scaffolding and wire, and in properly organised parties. We had no bathing trunks but by now were anything but shy, and went in swimming 'in the raw'. A few days of this brought a complaint from two old ladies who were apparently still ensconced in one of the houses opposite.

We normally undressed in the lee of a low wall at the back of the beach, but next morning found a row of naked males standing on top of the wall rotating their hips like belly dancers and waggling massive male members enthusiastically at the windows across the road. The Germans might not have scared the old dears into evacuation, but I reckon that we might have done the trick!

Then started a spate of cross country runs. Usually about five to seven miles long across the Romney marshes, and occasionally swimming or wading the military canal. I was never much of a runner and hated these runs, and to make matters worse on those days when there wasn't a longer run, they would make us run one or two miles before breakfast. We only wore shorts and running shoes and mosquitoes were a problem. I think they bred a special strain on the marshes. Not only were there lots of them but they seemed bigger, fiercer and altogether more vicious than I'd come across until then. We were soon covered in lumps. In our billet we used to shut all the doors and windows before lights out. Then armed with a gym slipper in either hand we prowled the whole house swatting as we went. The walls soon took on a new form of decoration. That of cream with dark brown smudges. Even so it was fairly common for one or other of us to wake in the morning with lumps over our arms or a swollen eye.

The observation post duty arranged for us was in the command centre of a battery of six inch guns on the back of the beach at Greatstone. A detached house had just about been filled with concrete. There was just space left to get in and up the stairs, where a glassed veranda made a very comfortable place to watch and log the comings and goings in the channel. An occasional shell would be lobbed at shipping from the other side and on a couple of occasions I saw the shelling of Dover. It was surprising how long the shells took to arrive. With binoculars you could see the flash on the French coast. The gunners would start counting the seconds and when they were up to about sixty, you would hear the thud, and see a column of smoke go up along the coast. We wondered who had the benefit of that lot, and wondered about the casualties. There were still quite a few civilians in Dover and with the shelling there was no warning, as there was with an air raid. I was in the command post only the once when our own battery fired it's guns, and it was deafening. No one wore ear muffs in those days.

Greatstone had a wide sandy beach and at low tide the gunners would lay out fishing lines with several hooks on each. After the tide had come in and receded again, each line would have two or three fish hooked and thrashing about wildly. Some of these came our way, were cooked in our billet and made a welcome supplement to army rations. Mostly they were flatfish, flounders, and dabs.

Despite mines, booby traps, the odd sneak raiding aircraft, and cross channel shelling, the most frightening thing around New Romney was the lady barber. Regular visits to a barber were essential if you were to stay off 'jankers', but we dreaded these visits. She would cut your hair in about two minutes flat using only a comb and an open cut throat razor. The comb was used to lift the hair which was then slashed with the razor. It's a wonder any of us had ears left; I can only suppose she'd never heard of scissors!

The miniature Romney Hythe and Dymchurch railway was still running and occasionally we would use it to get into Hythe. On one occasion the train came in, and as the engine passed we were startled to recognise the boiler suit clad figure on the footplate peering through a layer of coal dust, as Pip Appleby. He had somehow talked himself into a trip as driver. I was full of envy! I wouldn't have minded having a go myself! They actually had an armoured train standing in a siding at New Romney.

While at New Romney we were also involved in our old game of chasing imaginary spies. Just back from the sea front at Littlestone was a large brick house, the roof of which sloped up to a square flat area with a railing around it.

Reports came in of noises sounding like motors or generators, of activities on the flat roof, aerials laid out etc. I wondered sometimes if Pip Appleby or some even higher evil minded authority didn't invent these stories just to keep the lads occupied. We spent a couple of weeks prowling around the grounds of the house at night. Watching from shrubbery's in two hour stints, and from a greater distance during day light. Needless to say we didn't see anything untoward. I'm sure the real spies wouldn't behave in such an obvious way, and would be far too careful to be caught by the likes of us.

In due course the C.O. interviewed all the applicants for transfer to the R.A.F. The queue started outside his office and went right round Battalion headquarters. He certainly weeded them out all right. He had a collection of odd questions such as "Where is Madagascar?"—followed, if you didn't know the answer, by "Out!" Another question was "What is the product of $(a + b)$ with $(a + b)$?" Being on duty in our office, we waited until the queue had nearly gone before we went in. I'm sure by then he was tired of it all, and merely asked me if I had seriously thought about it and decided this was what I wanted, and having answered "yes" he wished me luck and I was in.

We knew that we still had to pass entrance exams etc, and in the meantime Sergeant Rogers gave us a quick refresher in maths and basic English. He was tremendous really. I'm sure I wouldn't have got through without his help. Eventually, word came that R.A.F. entrance examinations were imminent and the survivors of the C.O.'s thinning out, probably about forty of us, headed for Euston House, London, and an R.A.F. entrance exam. There we formed up in the foyer and were addressed by a burly and brusque warrant officer. He said, "Look here, lads, we haven't time to mess about. Anyone not serious or with doubts about their ability to pass our exam fall out now, have a day on the town, and be back here at four thirty. Nobody will be the wiser and you'll do us all a favour." About two thirds of our number fell out and made for the door.

The remainder of us had about four exams. One I remember was math, another a short essay, each lasting about twenty minutes. There were also a couple of aptitude tests—books of puzzles that needed quick and clear thinking, and there were so many that you could never finish, so that the quantity solved correctly was what mattered.

In the afternoon we had medicals, eyesight tests, colour blindness, balance, co-ordination, and more. It was a full day.

On the train Pat Coyne and I talked; neither had any real idea if we were through, although we'd clearly passed the morning session since the failures had not continued after lunch.

Several weeks went by, and out of the whole battalion, only two of us received notification that we had got our transfer, though later we saw a sergeant from one of the companies who had apparently followed a week behind us. The chap who left with me was the C.O.'s batman. I'm not sure what the C.O. thought about that.

They gave me a good send off from the section. I think it was the first time I ever got drunk—though certainly not the last! I finished up wearing a vest and socks and not much else, and in the middle of the main road through New Romney.

Next morning, clutching a rail pass in one hand and a fish paste sandwich and a piece of yellow cake in the other, we said a sad farewell to our friends and set off for Lords cricket ground at St Johns Wood in London.

CHAPTER 2

The Wide Blue Yonder

On arrival in London, they kitted us out with Air Force Blue. I remember the boots with rubber soles, which felt dreadful after army hob nails. We were divided up into squads, mainly according to the accommodation available, and were marched off to our billets. At that time thousands of recruits, all destined for air crew training, were housed in the many blocks of luxury flats in and around St Johns Wood and Regents Park. During the twelve weeks I spent there, I was in about four different blocks, two of which were Treasury Close and Bentinct House.

We ate in the restaurant in the Regents Park Zoo, and from the windows we could watch a large cage of monkeys swinging arm over arm, up and down their enclosure. The main occupation of the N.C.O.s was to keep us busy while they sorted, sifted, inoculated, vaccinated, classified, and, finally, posted us away. The means by which they did this usually comprised of P.T. (physical training) or running round Regents Park, drill in one of the side turnings, and an occasional lecture in a cinema in Swiss Cottage.

Discipline was impossible to maintain. One corporal would have a squad of about a hundred to a hundred and twenty recruits to look after.

On one occasion we were lined up in a side turning alongside Treasury Close and the roll called. Then we were told to get into P.T. gear and form up again in ten minutes. There was a tremendous row because at the end of the ten minutes there were about a dozen formed up in running shoes and shorts, the rest had gone in a side door, out the front, and away into town.

Around the side streets of St Johns Wood, there were a number of surface air raid shelters. These were brick-built structures with a thick flat concrete roof, measuring around twenty yards long, about three yards wide and eight feet high. They were built along the side of the road, with about a hundred yards between them. As the column marched past, the last two or three files would drop off behind the shelter and vanish. The roll was called each morning but I don't think anyone thought to count the numbers after that. There were a few ex-army among our squad, and for us it was a wonderland. I spent a good deal of time at home and out in the evenings with Pam Boyd dancing at the Streatham Locarno or out at the theatre. I can't remember how many times I walked the four miles from her home in Norbury to mine, caught the first train back to town, walking from Baker Street because the chances were the Red caps would be waiting at St Johns Wood station at the top of the escalator.

Sometimes, I got back late, and on a couple of occasions, an N.C.O. had been posted in the foyer. The way in then was to go to the other end of the block, along the roof and down our own staircase to bed. I was caught twice at the top of the escalators well after lights out at stations that should have been safe.

By now so many people were on 'jankers' that they had a job to think up suitable 'fatigues'. I think both occasions resulted in a couple of days 'confined to barracks' and on one occasion I had to cut the grass in front of the blocks with an ancient pair of shears.

None of the lectures were of any great interest, but we saw the most horrific film on the dangers of catching V.D. that you could imagine. Enough to put you off any thoughts about women for the duration, if not for life! This was before the advent of penicillin, and not only the diseases, but also some of the cures defied description. They must have shown us that film at least half a dozen times.

Then came the day when they had us all down for night-vision tests. We all sat around in a room for forty five minutes with dark red goggles on. At the end of this time we passed to another darkened room and took the goggles off. Dim shapes of aircraft and ships passed across a dimly lit background, and we had to guess their identity. I might have guessed at a couple. I doubt if I got them right, finding it virtually impossible. Others appeared to do better, though most seemed to find it difficult.

I left after a few disbelieving looks from those running the test but nothing was said. I thought a couple of days would see me back in the army, but as time slipped by I stopped worrying. After I'd been at St Johns Wood for eleven weeks, most of the people I'd arrived with had been posted, and I was about broke. London was costing too much for me on aircraftman's pay, so I inquired why I hadn't been posted. Looking this up, they found that I had been marked down 'Unfit for posting'—because of the night-vision test, no doubt. I had been classified as 'Observer' from my entrance exams, and that required good eyesight, especially at night. In those days bombers carried smaller crews and the observer was navigator, bomb aimer, and often captain of the aircraft.

I was re-classified to 'pilot' and a week later posted for initial training at No 2 I.T.W. in Cambridge. Apparently, it didn't matter so much if a pilot couldn't see where he was going.

At Cambridge I was billeted in Selwyn College, a red brick building on the outskirts of the town. Coming through the large gatehouse you faced a large, green quadrangle. Students' and others' quarters were built on three sides, while the dining hall and chapel stood across the green on the fourth. The student quarters were in suites of two rooms, one a bedroom, the other a study with plain table and chairs. The place had an air of tradition, the steps worn away by the passing of many a student.

The chap I shared with had come straight from university, and he ate, slept, and dreamed aeroplanes. He had the current issue of *Jane's All the World's Aircraft* and would keep me at it for hours, turning to random pages and covering all but a small part of an aircraft. I don't think I ever caught him out. At lectures he would be doodling, drawing shapes of tailplanes, or other aircraft shapes. Perhaps he should have paid more attention. He failed—on Air Force law, I think, or maybe hygiene or something equally silly. He was near tears when he heard, and I had to feel sorry for him.

The course at Cambridge lasted for eight weeks, all ground school. We studied maths, navigation, astro-navigation, Morse with buzzers and aldis lamp, aerodynamics, and as I've mentioned, Air Force law and hygiene. I suppose it was essential to know how to lay out a tented camp, and in particular the latrines, but it did seem a little unnecessary at the time, especially exams in these subjects. What was worse the lectures were held in various colleges all over Cambridge and we were marched from one to another as a squad, with a pace never equalled in the Fusiliers. I'm sure they must have worked out our programme of lectures to get the maximum marching miles per day. I don't think I had ever been fitter, even in my cycle racing days before the war.

All too soon exam time loomed. Those of us who passed were posted to Manchester, Heaton Park. The remainder, I suppose, went for bomb aimers or rear gunners. That was the threat used to egg us on, anyway.

At Heaton Park there were again thousands of air crew recruits awaiting posting. There were the usual P.T., organised games, and sickening V.D. films shown in a local cinema, livened up on one occasion when one of our number climbed onto the stage and played the cinema organ. I don't know which we enjoyed most, the playing or the row that went on when the cinema manager appeared on the scene. There were also more medicals, and dental work was hurriedly brought up to date. We were issued with packed rations—a fish paste sandwich and a rock bun this time—and entrained for goodness knows where.

The train journey eventually lasted something over two days, and those that had saved a crust or so from their sandwich were the lucky ones. The train never did stop in a station, and moved mostly at night. The navigators among us were trying to spot stars we could recognise to judge our direction. It was January and the sun was constantly hidden behind the clouds. We came to the conclusion we had to be zigzagging all over the country.

Eventually, the train arrived at what was obviously a dock area, and stopped alongside corrugated loading sheds. Word went round that we were at Avonmouth near Bristol.

We were embarked upon a Royal Mail ship, the S.S. *Highland Brigade*. I was quartered with several hundred others on a lower deck, and obviously well below water level. Two long flights of narrow stairways led to open air and I reckoned that if any emergency happened you would have to be among the first couple of dozen up in order to survive. The ship carried frozen meat in more normal times and the ceiling of our deck was covered with the refrigeration pipes. At night we slept in hammocks slung between these. There wasn't an inch to spare. Looked at from beneath, narrow ends of hammocks overlapped, so that the whole area fitted like sardines in a tin.

Below the hammocks were our mess tables. Some people preferred to sleep on the hard wood of the tables rather than fight their way up into a hammock. A visit to the 'heads' during the night, and finding your way back to your bunk beneath the sea of bulging hammocks was more by luck than judgement.

There were two ships travelling together side by side with a single destroyer as escort. The destroyer usually steamed between the two freighters, but sometimes put on speed and circled around, behind, and out in front of the freighters.

About two days out, the weather got very rough. Down below the green looking faces made me feel quite queasy, and I spent a lot of time on deck. Looking across at the other ship steaming on a parallel course to us, was quite a spectacular sight. As the ship climbed the face of a wave, it went up at a steep angle, and at the top the bows reared up practically clear of the water for about a quarter of the ships length. Then it would crash into the next hollow and the bows would disappear from sight and you would hold your breath waiting for them to reappear. I could have sworn that each time the ship would keep on going down. I wonder if from their side, we looked the same.

Our food had to be carried from a galley that was reached from the open deck. We had a rota for the rations carrying detail. While the weather was rough, the business of getting a huge billy of several gallons of hot tea along the deck and down two flights of very steep steps was fraught with danger. Some spillage of hot tea was inevitable and if you fell broken limbs were almost a certainty. Large trays of sausages and eggs were even more difficult to carry, requiring both hands to hold the tray.

I felt a bit queasy at this time, but was never really sick. On board we had a bunch of merchant seamen, part of the crew of the liner *Queen Mary*, which had been taken across the Atlantic at the outbreak of war to be out of harms way. They were on their way to fetch the liner back again. It was to be used as a troop ship throughout the rest of the war. I saw a group of these seamen, hanging over the rail retching their hearts up. I felt much better.

After two or three days, the weather abated a little. But then the engine broke down. We awoke in the morning and realised that the throbbing from the engine that we'd all got so used to, was now missing. Word went around that we had engine trouble and when we got up on deck, there we were, rolling in the swell, our companion ship gone together with the destroyer. We felt particularly vulnerable I must admit. The destroyer came back and paid a visit and went off again. This happened several times. I think our companions must have kept moving at reduced speed. We looked in at the engine room and they were working like beavers on the engine, but it was two days before that welcome throb was heard again, and we were moving once more.

The main trouble with the journey was boredom. Meals took up a lot of time, and there were boat drills, and when the weather was reasonable, we walked the decks, but this still left a lot of time with little to do. There was a saloon where some could sit, but again there wasn't a lot of room. There was however a piano, and one or two people played, mostly of the public bar standard of talent. One lunatic nearly drove me mad with a set of bagpipes, never my favourite instrument, and especially so since my London Scottish days. He knew what he was doing nevertheless and was in great demand by the Americans when we finally got to the United States.

During this time I generally found a quiet corner somewhere and wrote letters for posting later. I remember writing two of thirty-six pages each, one to my own mother and father and the other to the Pavises, old friends from my childhood.

Eventually, there was great excitement as a thin grey smudge of land appeared along the horizon, and ten days after leaving Avonmouth, we slipped into the harbour of Halifax, Nova Scotia, Canada, with the wintry sun trying hard to force a way through the cold, misty haze and with the glistening of ice in the rigging.

Having disembarked from the *Highland Brigade*, we were lined up on the dockside and detailed off straight onto a train. The train ride was of great interest, since very few of us had ever been abroad before, and the scenery was very different to anything back home.

When the train stopped for any length of time, the local ladies would come through the train with baskets of goodies which they would distribute among us, including hot drinks. Very welcome they were, too, for we were on the train all day, arriving at Moncton, New Brunswick, well after dark.

The train pulled into Moncton along a high embankment. Looking down on the town, a cheer went up all along the train. The town was all lit up. Shop windows were blazing with light, all with neon signs over them.

There were street lamps everywhere, and cars with headlamps blazing. After blacked-out wartime Britain, it was a wonderful sight, the like of which we hadn't seen for two years.

Marching from the station to the camp on the edge of town was quite an experience too. The town was still in the grip of winter, and the roads were completely coated in black shiny ice. This was heavily rutted on bends and corners, and cars would drive at speeds normal for dry roads and go round the corners in the ruts.

At one point a little girl came down the centre of the road on ice skates, shopping basket over her arm. Snow was piled along the edge of the side-walks four to five feet high. I'm afraid in our smooth, rubber-soled R.A.F. boots we were slipping and sliding everywhere. On one occasion we passed a group of ten-year-olds, all on skates, playing hockey with a tin can and sticks on the frozen area in front of a house.

Moncton camp covered a large area with several parade grounds, one of which had been flooded and frozen to make a huge skating rink. During our stay, there were speed skating events held, in which the local people took part. This was something new to watch.

We were housed in wooden two storied blocks and the first thing that struck us was the high temperature in the rooms. We were not used to sleep-ing in centrally heated rooms, and someone opened the windows. This was the wrong thing to do, of course, for the boilers turned up trying to main-tain the temperature. There was a big fuss when someone found out on the next day's inspection. However, we did get the system turned down a bit.

Moncton was a transit camp and must have had hundreds of aircrew trainees passing through on the way to various training establishments in Canada or the States, or on their way home following training. We had noth-ing to do except wait around for posting. There was no proper roster of duties, but every morning, a sergeant would go into the barrack blocks rounding up people for fatigues. We ex-army people had congregated in an upper-floor room, and when someone saw the sergeant approaching, we would wait until he was inside the downstairs door; then we'd all slide down the fire escape chute and make ourselves scarce.

On the sea trip I had become quite friendly with an Irish lad, Paddy. He turned out to be a fervent Methodist, and nothing would do but to go along to the Methodist church in Moncton. There we were made very welcome and were persuaded to stay after the service to a social evening for the young people. We chatted to a couple of girls, named Margaret and Jean, and found ourselves persuaded to go skating with them the next night. This was a crowded public rink, and the girls did a grand job of supporting us on our borrowed skates. I don't know if we would have survived without them. The friendship blossomed, and we had some good times with them, skating, tobogganing, and on a sleigh ride. The sleigh ride was quite fun.

The sleigh was not the sort you see on the Christmas cards but really a large cart on runners. There was room for about twenty, but at least forty tried to get on, usually by hauling someone out and taking their place. Luckily, the snow was soft, and no one was hurt, although it got rough at times.

On one of the tobogganing trips, we met some friends of the girls who were out skiing. So we tried to ski. They stood us up on the skis, did up the straps, put a pole in each hand, and pushed us off. The slope was level at the top, but over an edge it was almost vertical, easing after about twenty feet onto a fairly reasonable slope. We had no chance at all, of course! From the giggles we knew we were being put on, and we both ended up in a tangle at the foot of the steep section without knowing quite how we got there. They came and disentangled us amid much girlish laughter. We conned Margaret

Moncton train station.

The author outside the barracks.

into showing us how, and she also came to grief in great flurries of snow, and we felt better. I noticed that all the other girls avoided that top steep section by going round the side of it and across the easier part of the slope.

Stemming from our visit to the Methodist Church, we were also invited to another family's home on the other side of the river. They were obviously better off and picked us up in a car. The experience, our first of driving on the right and sliding round corners in the ruts, was quite unnerving. They took us out to what they called Magnetic Hill, some miles out of town in quite lovely countryside. Once on the hill, they stopped the car and took the brake off. The car apparently started to roll uphill. The Canadians insisted it

Ice skating.

was in some way due to magnetism. I couldn't see how and am still convinced it was some sort of optical illusion.

Incidentally, the Methodist minister wrote to my family telling them what a good lad I was and that I was keeping up my religion even though away from home. My mother was quite worried, apparently thinking I must have gone mad.

Both families invited us home. At Margaret and Jean's they kept talking about pumpkin pie. They couldn't believe we'd never had pumpkin pie. What sort of place was England without pumpkin pie?

Eventually, I was invited to dinner. I can't think where Paddy was—perhaps he'd succumbed to one of the various bugs going around the camp. After the main course the girl's mother came in—smiles all around—bearing what? Pumpkin pie! Well, I disgraced myself. Never had I seen such a mushy, grey, tasteless, unappetising mess. Try as I might, I couldn't force it down. It must have been a terrible let down for them, and I felt awful. Perhaps it's an acquired taste. Thank God, I've never met pumpkin pie since!

In all I was at Moncton for twelve weeks, by which time the thaw had set in. Several people were hurt crashing into snow banks on toboggans. After the initial thaw the water from the melted snow had frozen again, leaving a surface like a carpet of needles.

When the banks of snow began to thaw along the sides of the roads, the myriad rivulets of water and the thick yellow mud made getting about quite unpleasant.

We stayed at Moncton for so long because of all the illness that went around. First, Paddy caught scarlet fever, and we were put in quarantine. Then before that spell finished, someone caught mumps, and I think we ran through the whole gamut of childish illnesses, going from one spell of quarantine to another.

Eventually, we got clear of quarantine. Paddy was long gone, and I never did meet up with him again. Then I and about a dozen others who had been quarantined learned we were due to join the rest of a course already down at Clewiston in Florida.

We travelled south by train—or "trains," for there were several. The journey took three days, right down the eastern seaboard. The first stop was Boston, where we had four hours to wait for our next train. We were taken to a hotel and fed, and we had a short time to wander around the city.

I can't remember a lot; the main impression was of extremely high buildings and an incredibly noisy, elevated railway. In New York we had eight hours. We were taken to the Waldorf Hotel for breakfast. We were very impressed. Then we were let loose. Fifth Avenue and Times Square were

The author as an A.C.2 in the Royal Air Force. The white flash in his cap signifies that he was training for flying duties.

Stop over in New York on the journey south to Florida.

quite impressive, and we nearly broke our necks looking up at the buildings. In Fifth Avenue we came across a camera shop, one window piled high with second-hand cameras. Two of us bought 35mm American-made Argus cameras for a few dollars apiece and immediately loaded up with film.

We had a grand tour of Rockefeller Centre, a group of eight skyscrapers. This included a trip by lift to the very top. I was watching the floor indicator flipping over and suddenly realised it was counting in tens. The view from the top was staggering. We also went down to the underground car park ninety feet below ground and explored the underground shopping centre. You could buy all your needs and live in the centre without ever going out.

Then there was the cinema, said to be the largest in the world, and the theatre where the Rockettes were performing—dancing girls drilled to a perfection that equalled the precision of the guards, all perfectly matched in height. They were a sight to be seen.

In addition we visited a television studio and saw ourselves on tele. This was well before the days of commercial television, of course. The main thing I remember was the heat of the lamps: you could have fried if you'd stayed more than a minute or two.

New York.

We also passed through Washington without the chance to explore, and I remember a couple of hours spent at dead of night on the station at Jacksonville. As we got farther south, we saw more and more coloured people and saw the segregation we had heard of but never really thought about. Stations had 'whites only' waiting rooms and toilets, and even white and black ends to the platform, while extra 'blacks only' carriages were put on the train. The 'blacks' looked a pretty poor bunch, poor in all senses of the word. "Downtrodden" would have been a good description of their appearance.

As we progressed into Florida, we passed through vast flat swampy areas of land with great flocks of exotic birds. There was plenty to see on the journey fresh to our eyes and apart from the nights when sleep, sitting up in a carriage was pretty impossible, the journey went quite quickly.

We had left Canada, where despite the thaw, it was still quite cold, and we had been wearing our greatcoats. Getting off the train at Clewiston was like stepping into a steam bath. The temperature was in the low nineties, and it was humid. Carrying kit bags and greatcoats to a truck, we thought we might melt away.

At the camp we were quickly kitted out with American army drill and flying overalls, goggles, and other flying gear. Then, since it was Friday, we were able to go to Miami for the weekend. A truck was laid on, and we were advised to go to the Colony Hotel, which was managed by an expatriate Mancunian, Sid Burrows, who charged the lads one dollar a night for a bed in his luxury hotel. Miami was about ninety miles from the camp, but distances seemed less in America. I think the truck was put on especially for us new boys; on all future weekends we had to hitch a ride—if we could.

Our first call after booking in at the Colony was to shop around for bathing trunks. We found an open-fronted store in a side street, presided over by a friendly little Jewish gentleman, and we came out with not only trunks but also cool short-sleeved shirts and slacks. It amused us that the slacks came with the bottoms unfinished. The Jewish gentleman cut them off to length and machined the bottoms with the turn ups while you waited.

Then we finally went to the beach, which was lined with palm trees, beautiful golden sands, and sunshine. The sun was deceiving; despite the heat of its rays, a cool breeze blew off of the sea, and it didn't feel all that hot. We all got a little burned, but some of the lads met a bunch of girls on the beach and stayed much too long. They were so badly burned that they couldn't bear wearing clothes, much less a parachute harness. Back in camp they were in sick bay for several days and on the carpet in the C.O.'s office when they were fit. In the sea, the water was so warm it was unbelievable—this was March!—and we thoroughly enjoyed it.

Miami consists of two main areas: the town on the mainland and Miami Beach, which was reached by a mile-long causeway across a lagoon. The beach was a mile-wide strip running right down the coast. Apparently, not so long ago it had been a coral reef inhabited mainly by alligators. The beach was home now to expensive luxury holiday hideaways of the wealthy and equally expensive luxury hotels. The causeway had artificial islands standing just off of it. These were constructed by building a large circular wall, pumping out the sea water, and filling them in. They were large enough for a luxury home with the most beautiful gardens and were usually reached by narrow foot bridges.

Al Capone was reputed to own, and be residing on, one of these islands. We could imagine the machine guns trained on the gate at the end of the foot bridge.

A mile back on the edge of Miami town was the Hialeah race track and, beyond that, swamps. The Everglades look quite attractive in James Bond films and the like, and no doubt they have been cleaned up quite a lot since 1942. In those days they were awful. Swarms of mosquitoes made life a misery.

It was not, however, malarial—thank goodness! Snakes of all sorts abounded, from six-foot-long water moccasin and rattlesnakes down to a little green thing about a foot long for whose venom there was no known antidote. Insects came in all sizes, and most of them bit. At night bull frogs made such a racket that you had to shout to hear yourself speak, and the sound of crickets and insects of all shapes, sizes, and colours sounded like a power station running full blast. If an outside lamp was on, it would almost be blacked out by the insects flying around it.

Clewiston was just about in the middle of the Everglades, at the bottom-left-hand corner of Lake Okeechobee. The camp was eight miles farther west into the swamp from the town of Clewiston. The air field was a square with each side two miles long. A road ran down to a diamond-shaped area at its centre where all the buildings were located: living quarters, administration, lecture rooms, tennis courts, and swimming pool.

Back at camp we settled into our quarters. At that time there were two schemes under which R.A.F. people were being trained. In one of these the lads went with an American army intake to an army school and trained with them. The other was the B.F.T.S. scheme where civilian flying schools were taken over by the R.A.F. and augmented with key R.A.F. personnel. Clewiston was one of these. All the flying instructors were U.S. civilians, their chief being a flamboyant character called 'Gunner' Brink, who looked as if he was modelling himself on Douglas MacArthur. Most of the ground school instructors were also Americans. The R.A.F. personnel were a station C.O., an Adjutant, and an armaments instructor.

The three courses were running primary on the Stearman PT17, basic on a Vultee BT13A monoplane, and advanced on the AT6A, the plane we called the "Harvard." We were the seventh course to go through the place.

The centre point of our quarters was the swimming pool, up a grass bank about four feet high with the huts which were our quarters running along either side of it. The huts were long, single-storied, wooden buildings divided into rooms which held eight men each.

At either end of each room, there were two double tier beds. The two rooms were joined by a corridor down the side between the doors, while the remainder of the space was taken up by a fully tiled shower and toilet. The doors and windows were covered on the outside with fine wire mesh which did little to keep out the millions of tiny insects which were always with us. Always before going into the shower, we used the spray to wash hundreds of

Clewiston. Standing, left to right: Noel Colley, the author, 'Nobby' Clark, and Len Baker. Sitting, left to right: Ian ('Boy') Lock, Frank Pegg, Laurie Coupland, and Jock Simms.

beetles, grasshoppers, and other bugs down the drain. Before getting into bed, it was necessary to pull the bedclothes right back and brush out what looked like coarse black sand, but was in fact a dusting of tiny insects. Many of them bit. Mosquitoes were another problem. We never left a door open longer than was necessary to rush through it, and every night at lights out, all eight of us prowled around our room with a gym shoe in either hand to flatten any mosquito we could find. The walls took on an odd appearance as more and more bloody smears appeared. Even so, there was an occasional closed eye or swollen limb in the morning where we had missed one. After this nightly ritual had been completed, the Lord help any unwanted visitor who might be tempted to open the door.

None of the water from the taps was fit to drink; it all had a fetid smell, even the pool. There were machines about the place that were supposed to cool and render the water innocuous, but it still smelt foul and tasted worse, so that eventually the only water that could be drunk came in glass bottles. The pool was used quite a bit early on, but eventually, we were stopped from using it because so many people were getting fungus in their ears.

The temperature was in the nineties and dropped very little at night. It was also very humid, and we soon found that a pair of shoes put in a locker one day would be covered in green mould the next. Clothes had to be shaken well before putting them on to make certain nothing untoward was lurking within.

In due course on the Monday morning after our arrival, we dressed in our flying overalls and baseball caps, helmets and goggles in hand for 'flights'. We were allocated instructors and gathered in a group at the upwind end of the field awaiting our turn for initiation.

My instructor was a stocky, sandy-haired individual called Stubblefield, and eventually, I collected a parachute and marched out behind him to the line of PT13As. He took the plane off and flew away from the field a bit, did a few steep turns around a mucky looking pool, and climbed a bit. Then he announced, "You have a go!"

Since it was my first time even off the ground, and so far without a word of instruction, I didn't think I was doing too badly. However, my mentor suddenly shouted, "Relax! Relax! This is what you are trying to do!"

The stick whipped viciously out of my hands back into the rear-left corner of the cockpit, whacking my leg on the way. The plane reared up in front of us, and the right wing went up and over as we spun madly round and round the propeller, the stays and struts howling like banshee's.

The author on a borrowed bike at Clewiston. The pool is to the right, and the living quarters are in the background.

By then I had grabbed a firm hold on the tubular longerons running along each side of the cockpit, which was just as well for we stopped upside down and hung there for what seemed like ages before the nose dropped and I felt as if I was being crushed down into the cockpit until I might at any second go through the floor. I might add that the American safety straps consisted of just a wide band that went across your lap, with a simple catch which you knocked up to release. Hanging upside down from this felt extremely insecure, to say the least.

Once we were level again, I looked up and immediately saw his face in the mirror, grinning like a bloody Cheshire cat. I must have passed muster, for when we got down I found he was more friendly toward me, and I learnt that we had done two and a half snap rolls and a half loop—fancy!

After he got that off his chest, things were quieter, and during the following week, we did a whole series of circuits and bumps. Take off, climb, turn to port at 1,000 feet and across wind. Rate one turn onto the downwind leg, straight and level. Rate one turn to port back across the downwind end of the field, throttle back to a gliding turn onto the field, and land. Before the plane stopped rolling, open the throttle and do it all again. Then, as I became more confident, we went up to practice stalls. The stall was started from straight and level flight. Throttling back, you maintain height by easing

First days of flying at Clewiston. Left to right: Tom Whitehead, the author, and Taffy Williams.

The author and a Stearman primary trainer.

back the stick, raising the nose more and more until near the stall the controls begin to feel light. The wings are kept level by playing on the rudder, and then suddenly, you lose all control. The stick flops back, the nose drops, and the plane picks up speed. Once it regains flying speed, you can ease it out of the dive with the stick.

It may sound strange keeping the wings level with the rudder, but when already near the stall, if you lower an aileron to pick up a wing you have in effect increased the angle of attack, and increased the tendency to stall. If a wing drops and you use opposite rudder, the wing is slewed forward, picking up speed and lift. This manoeuvre was, of course, to familiarise the student with the feel of an incipient stall before letting him loose by himself. After a total of about nine hours flying time, I was deemed ready for my first solo.

I'm afraid my first solo was a mess. When Stubblefield climbed out of the front cockpit, did up the safety strap to keep it out of the way, yelled "Good luck!" over the noise of the engine, and walked away with his parachute over his shoulder, I felt a little little lonely. I'd gotten used to his grinning face in that little mirror and his head bobbing up and down in the front cockpit trying to see where I was getting to.

Wilf Tylor.

Takeoff was fine, and so was the rest of the circuit. I was told afterwards that even the landing looked fine. The trouble was that I didn't believe it. I bounced and bounced, and on about the third bounce, I took fright, opened the throttle, and took off again. I had a fleeting impression of a line of planes flashing by under the left wing, and I was told everyone ducked—I believe they all ducked in the control tower, too. I was now up again, feeling even more lonely.

Then I made the big mistake. On the crosswind leg, just as I was in the position where I should have started my gliding turn, there was another plane approaching slightly below and crossing from left to right. I suppose I must have been intent on watching him and making sure we missed one another, for I never did make that gliding turn, but landed straight ahead. A much better landing than the first, which was amazing since I was at right angles to the wind. Of course, I was not on the part of the field I should have been, which I quickly realised when straight ahead loomed a group of coloured gentlemen erecting a football goalpost. They scattered, and I avoided spilling blood, but wasn't quite able to miss the goalpost. The tip of my port wing just caught it and knocked it askew.

A. R. 'Gunner' Brink.

I still hadn't caught on to what I'd done and was a bit lost, taxiing back towards the control tower seemed a good bet. Then in the distance I saw my instructor almost running towards me, still with his parachute over his shoulder. He was hot, bothered, and very annoyed with me. He was never a very patient man and had a vocabulary of about a dozen words, all of them foul. I learnt a few particularly nasty American epithets in those few minutes, and had I not been so obviously in the wrong, I reckon we could have come to blows. Eventually, he calmed down, and when the plane had been left parked, we tried to analyse what had happened.

I was hauled up before the R.A.F. adjutant S/L Burdick and gave him my account. Apparently, my brush with the goalpost had been right opposite the windows of his office, and he said that the mess I'd made of my first solo was bad enough, but what really riled him was that I taxied back nearly as fast as I flew in.

I reckoned that it was a toss up whether or not I would be washed out, and I held my breath for a day or so. In the meantime we had a sudden storm, the field became waterlogged, and the instructors flew the planes off in clouds of spray, taking them to a sandy piece of land about five miles away. This was just an area in the wilderness, with no buildings, perimeter fence, Coke machine, or anything. We flew from here for about a week. I don't know how they got on about maintenance. Anyway, during this week, I continued with Stubblefield, performing circuits and bumps for a further couple of hours, and then I went solo with no more trouble.

So far as the storm was concerned, you could usually rely on blazing sunshine all day everyday, but a storm, when it came, could be sudden and violent. Usually, the first warning would be the wind picking up, and if you looked, you could see a black column of cloud rising up to a big anvil head. In no time at all, the wind would go round 180 degrees, the palm trees would all be bending right over, and if you were wise, you ran for shelter. The rain would beat down in solid stair rods, but half an hour later the only sign that anything had happened was a few puddles with steam rising from them. I was airborne once on basic with an instructor. On returning to the field, we found this big black column almost over the upwind edge of the field. We stooged around behind it and were able to land completely dry at the back of it on a saturated field. Those local storms moved that fast.

We did have one storm that lasted for two days and the whole camp was waterlogged. Just the concrete paths and the buildings were above the water. Again, the planes were flown off in time, and we operated from the sandy area for about two weeks.

The next manoeuvre I was taught was the spin. This started very much like the stall except that just as the stall occurred, you kicked the rudder hard over whichever direction you wished to spin, and the nose would drop and it would appear as if the earth was spinning beneath you. Opposite rudder would stop the spinning, and you then eased back out of the dive. Initially, it was enough to get out of the spin. The next trick was to stop it exactly on two and a half turns. You would start off flying, say, eastward along a canal or road and on completion you had to be flying along the canal in the opposite direction. Once shown, we practised this solo.

Then came the aerobatics. These were fun: first loops, then slow rolls, and finally combinations of each. Because of the torque produced by the propeller, it was much easier to do slow rolls to the left than to the right.

Halfway through primary, I lost Stubblefield and had a new instructor. We never did get on first-name terms, but I was sorry he went because once you got used to his limited and entirely foul vocabulary, he wasn't a bad sort. He was certainly a very good pilot and instructor, with a good deal of experience.

My new instructor was a younger man, new to instructing, prone to excitement if things looked a bit dodgy as I found out when, just before taking a passing-out session with the Chief Flying Instructor at the end of Primary, I pointed out that I had never done a roll to the right. Rolls to the right were considered more difficult in the Stearman PT17 because you were moving the plane against the torque of the engine. So up we went, and a roll to the right was demonstrated. We were upside down when the oil filler cap came off. Positioned on the cowling in front of the forward cockpit, oil blacked the screens in an instant. My instructor was bobbing up and down in the cockpit

Photo call at 5 B.F.T.S., Riddle Field, Clewiston, Florida.

in quite a state, shrieking to me to let him have it (he'd had it all along, of course!), and we glided down to a landing on the field.

It was well judged, I must admit, but he didn't inspire confidence in that sort of situation. I'd missed most of the oil being in the back cockpit. He was splattered with it, and was hopping with excitement and indignation. I had a job to prevent myself from laughing!

We practised flying in formations of three, and this was quite good fun. Then there were cross-country trips. The first of these was with an instructor. In Florida navigation was very easy; it was a big, flat, swampy area, and the few features were instantly recognisable. If you saw a road running east-west, you knew immediately which one it was since there wasn't another for fifty miles. We usually flew from one town to another, and these could be seen from a long way off. We did a period of night flying on Primary—mostly circuits—with a nighttime cross-country flight with an instructor at the end.

I don't know if my instructor had done much night flying but he was certainly very jittery about it. A degree or so off course and he would be shrieking and bobbing about in front. It was silly, too, for you could see the lights of the towns from a long way off and there was no mistaking which one it was. Anyway, we got around without incident, and I quite enjoyed the experience.

At the end of Primary, we had a passing-out trip with the C.F.I., and I think all passed. I remember a grilling on the ground before taking off, and I was asked to describe in detail the sequence of control movements in doing a slow roll, and I found some difficulty in doing this, and had to think hard and only got it right with a good few hesitations. However, once airborne I performed several near-perfect slow rolls, including my first ever to the right.

The period near the end of primary was reckoned to be the most dangerous in a pilot's life. With seventy or eighty hours of flying, over-confidence sets in, so that when mistakes were made, the skill and experience to get out of it were not always there. We had crashes, but no one from our lot was hurt. The one incident that I do remember was when Jamie McGregor landed too near a swampy area in the far northeast corner of the field. His wheels sunk into the soft ground, and he turned completely over onto his back. The plane was a bit bent, but the pilot was okay except for a few bruises. Other courses had less luck.

Low flying—which was grand fun but strictly illegal unless authorised—was the most common cause of trouble. One pair touched ground, skidded along on the plane's belly and ended half submerged in the swamp. The plane was found but not the two student pilots. It was surmised that they had tried to wade to dry ground. They could have found a deeper patch, or perhaps some of the nasties found them. There were, after all, alligators around.

I never actually saw one when I was on foot, but you could sometimes see them basking in the sun on the banks of a canal when airborne. The locals swore that they wouldn't attack a man unless provoked. I was just glad that I was never called upon to test the theory.

Someone else came back trailing telephone wire and was taken off the course and sent back up to Canada. The popular belief was that they would end up air gunners or bomb aimers. I didn't think myself that they would waste the hundred odd hours flying training. They probably were disciplined in Canada and re-posted to a flying school up there.

The only people 'washed out' on our course were during the first week or so, and two or three lacked coordination between hands and feet, and one unfortunately had a nose bleed every time he left the ground. You would have thought these things could have been easily discovered without carting them all the way to Florida.

At the end of primary, we had a few days' leave. I can't remember what we did with it. We probably went to Miami since that was the easiest place to get a ride to. People would stop for us at least. I remember on one occasion we were out near Hialeah, on the way out of Miami when a big Buick stopped and picked us up. It turned out that the people were on their way to visit friends on the outskirts of Miami, but they crammed five of us into the back seat and ended up taking us to Belle Glade about eighty miles on. Part of that road is sixty miles dead straight as if drawn with a ruler, not a building or anything at all, just a white concrete ribbon with a twenty-five-foot-wide canal on either side of it. The roads crossing the Everglades were all bordered by canals. The earth excavated from the canals is heaped in the middle to provide dry ground for the road to run along. Along this stretch of road, the Buick was doing a steady ton; in 1942 that was something. When we stopped, he telephoned his friends to say they would be a little late. Our transport wasn't always quite so luxurious as that Buick.

Then there was the time when an old chap stopped for us in a Ford of ancient vintage. We were in and rolling before we realised that he was fighting drunk. On top of this, cars of that vintage had a substantial chassis with the floor being made up of wooden boards. It made maintenance easier since you could lift a couple of boards instead of crawling underneath. On this car though it made riding in it extremely hazardous, for all the boards were missing. You could look down and see the road whizzing by underneath. I thought I might offer to drive for him, but then I realised that we were zigzagging all over the road, not only because he was drunk, but also because there was at least half a turn of play in the steering.

The Basic training course was done on a Vultee BT13A—a low-wing monoplane with fixed undercarriage, flaps, two-speed propeller, and a sin-

Two views of the Vultee BT13A basic trainer. It featured a two-speed prop and flaps.

gle Pratt and Whitney radial engine. It was incredibly noisy, especially on takeoff. All the other courses hated it when Basic was on night flying. Sleep was impossible.

Basic was a shorter course intended to lead the pupil on from the simple PT17 biplane to the more sophisticated AT6A, which had all the features of a modern fighter. I don't remember anything untoward about Basic. We did more aerobatics, instrument flying, formation, and cross-countries. By now I had taken to carrying the little camera in my overall pocket on the cross-countries and, if possible, meeting up with someone else and taking photos. This was easy when two of you were in the plane, but some of those cross-countries were solo, so that letting go of everything to line up a camera was a little difficult.

Basic was uneventful so far as flying was concerned, but one occasion during this time is worth telling. We had been on night flying, and I was down for a session that night. We had spent the afternoon in Clewiston in the local cinema; without air conditioning we sweltered. I remember the short supporting film was of a young black pianist with his trio, Nat King Cole. This was before he became commercial and 'popular'. It was a smooth, jazzy trio, and I enjoyed that film. I have no recollection at all of the big film.

We left too late, getting back to the field as night was falling. Even in those days, no one would stop to give a lift at night. We ended up walking the nine miles back to the camp. This was all right until a car came up behind us, and in its headlamps we could see hundreds of snakes slithering off the road into the canals. Then the car passed us, and we could imagine all those little heads popping up over the banks of the canal. They must move out of your way as you walk along, for we neither saw nor heard anything of them when we were in the dark, but each time a car came along, there they all were slithering off to either side of the road, hundreds and hundreds of them. It was a most unpleasant walk, and we were glad to see Riddle Field that night.

I was late for the station wagon that took us out to the bonfire, lit at the end of the flare path in the forlorn hope that it would keep away the mosquitoes, and I had no option but to walk still farther. Before going I picked up a torch from my room. A bit puny, it was better than nothing.

It was pretty dark across the field, but I could see the usual bonfire in the distance, and was heading towards it when something hit me in the middle of the forehead. It was as if someone was throwing stones, I looked around but there was no one within sight. I looked around on the ground and there was a big black beetle, at least an inch and a half long, lying at my feet. I hope he felt as dazed as I did.

Basic came to an end and the lads in my room finished a day earlier than I did. I still had a further cross-country to complete. We decided we would go to Sarasota, which was on the west side of the Florida peninsula and farther north.

We agreed the boys would set out and I would follow as soon as I could. I finished my cross country without incident and set out. Near the gates of the camp, a car came and stopped for me. It was a mid-1930s Ford, but at

Aerial shots of the Vultee.

least it had floorboards. In it was a woman, alone. She was heading for Jacksonville in the north of Florida, which was a good help on my way to Sarasota. When we got to where my route branched off westward, she asked me if I would go to Jacksonville with her. I suppose it was a good offer, but I was young, and although she was probably in her thirties, she was an old woman to me. The thought of hitchhiking all the way back from Jacksonville was enough to clinch it: I went to Sarasota! When I told my friends, they thought I must be mad. After leaving the lady and the Ford, I walked about a mile through a thickly wooded area when I came to where a large notice had been nailed to a tree: 'Danger, beware of wild hogs'. I wondered if I shouldn't have gone to Jacksonville.

I didn't see any hogs, wild or otherwise, and shortly afterwards got a lift all the way to Sarasota, where I soon found my friends all crowded into a small rowing boat out on the river. I sat on the bridge parapet and waited for them. I think we had a good weekend and obviously got back to camp, but I don't remember much about it, so there couldn't have been anything special.

We then started the Advanced course on AT6As. By now we considered ourselves quite experienced aviators, and needless to say, several incidents occurred during this period.

The flying training went as before, only more so. We flew formation, culminating in a flight of nine aircraft led by Gunner Brink. This was not looked forward to by many. Gunner was apt to spend most of the time yelling at one or another to get in closer, and the boys, especially those in the centre of the formation, had visions of the inexperienced pilot behind chewing his way through the tail with his prop.

We did more cross-countries—longer ones. It was on one of these that I ran into trouble. On the way out to the lines of planes, I saw Laurie Coupland taxiing out. I yelled to him to wait and I would meet up and take pictures. He said, "Okay, but hurry!" I suppose my cockpit drill was a bit cursory, and anyway, by the time I got out to the takeoff point, he had already been sent off by the control tower. I never did meet up with him that day.

I took off and flew the first leg up to the north. Turning south west I was half way down the second leg well over the swamplands when the engine spat a few times and stopped running. A quick look around the cockpit showed that the main tanks were dry. A switch to reserve and a quick mental calculation showed I had about fifteen minutes of flying time. On the map I saw a club flying field marked at Wauchula just about within reach. A new course was set, and in due course, to my relief, I saw the windsock and building at Wauchula. I also saw cows grazing all over the field.

I made an approach the long way of the field, this being into wind, but as I got nearer the ground I could see that I was never going to miss all the cows, so I opened up and took off again. As I pulled up the engine spat a couple of times and I quickly looked for a likely flat area ahead. However it kept going and I got around to land in a comparatively clear area, but cross wind and with not much length of runway. I got it down and taxied to the upwind end of the field and stopped the engine. All four petrol gauges were showing zero.

All the way across I had been trying to raise the field on the radio without success. The radios we had were very limited in range. One of the others on the cross country who had got petrol flew high over Wauchula and relayed my message. The airfield at Wauchula was obviously no longer in regular use, thus the cows. The grass was also somewhere near two feet high in places.

After about an hour another AT6A turned up and landed. In it was the Chief Flying Instructor and another 'advanced' instructor. The instructor was left to await a tanker to refuel the plane, and I returned to the field with the C.F.I.

As soon as we were airborne, he had me under the hood flying on instruments, even for the landing. I realised that I was on trial and was keyed up to do the best I could. Though I say it myself, I performed well, probably the most precise flying I had ever done, and the landing barely bumped as we touched and stayed down.

I was criticised by all the Americans. An interview with Gunner Brink made it all my fault. It was suggested that I should even have watched tanks being dipped to be sure. However, we had a new station commander, fresh from a light bomber squadron (from the Middle East, I believe, where he flew Blenheims). He was on my side and went into the attack on my behalf with gusto.

It appeared the planes had not been refuelled after flying the night before, but early that morning. This was bad practice because with the changes of temperature overnight condensation could form in the empty tanks, and the last thing you needed was water in the petrol. Then they were late starting the refuelling and one chap went along signing all the forms, while the bowser came along behind filling the tanks.

The form for my plane was signed up as service completed and refuelling done, but in fact somehow the bowser had missed it. So the incident did some good, since a bad practice was stopped before it could cause worse trouble.

In an interview with the Wing Commander, he told me of his sorting out of the Americans and told me that I'd done well to judge the fuel left and find a place to put down.

"I doubt you will take off again without checking the tanks." Nor did I.

Incidentally, apparently a wager emerged from friendly chaff in the instructors' mess and the Wing Commander and Gunner Brink went up to dog fight in two PT13s, and although his experience was on Blenheims, the

Wing Commander flew rings round Gunner. I wish I could remember his name!

Another incident which raised a laugh among everyone except the participants was when an instructor brought in a pupil for an instrument landing with the pupil under the hood. He simply didn't put the wheels down. Everyone watching held their breath, waiting for him to open up and go round again. No one could do anything but watch as the prop hit the ground. The plane tilted forward and then scraped along the ground on its belly with an awful metallic crashing sound and a huge cloud of dust. It must have felt awful for the chap under the hood, and I'm sure the instructor didn't know where to put himself.

Right through the flying training, we spent a certain amount of time in the Link trainer. This was a primitive form of simulator consisting of a mock up of a cockpit mounted on gimbals, with a hood which completely blacked out the cockpit. Whatever you did in the cockpit was recorded with a pen on a chart back on the instructor's desk. It was an exercise in flying courses for set times, and doing turns of certain rates to arrive correctly at a destination. It wasn't much like flying an aeroplane. For example, it wasn't stable. If you pushed the column forward, it would keep going down. An aeroplane is designed so that when you let go of the stick, it will return to level flight. The

Aerial shot of the AT6A advanced trainer. It was known in the United Kingdom as the Harvard.

An AT6A after an impromptu forced landing at the disused airfield at Wauchula.

controls were all operated pneumatically, and I was told that it was the brain-child of an organ builder called Ed Link.

I did quite well on the Link trainer. It required concentration, both to fly it and to perform the exercises, but I quite enjoyed it. A lot of chaps didn't.

The instructor was an ex-pilot named Ziler who had been badly burned in a flying accident. His whole face and top of his head looked like melted wax.

Odd patches of hair had survived which if anything made his appearance even more grotesque. He was an extremely nice person, and his wife was among the most attractive women I met in America. I admired her for sticking with him. He must have had a terrible time, and his appearance certainly took some getting used to. His hands were also burned but not so badly. They got very clever at plastic surgery during the war. I hope they were able to help him.

Someone decided we should be kept fit by doing P.T. ("physical training"—"callisthenics" in American) before breakfast. Well, the first morning, we lined up outside our huts in shorts and gym shoes. The walls of the huts were black with insects, but within a couple of minutes, the walls were their usual white, and we were black—covered with mosquitoes. They kept this up for about three mornings by which time so many people were in sick bay with bites that they had to abandon the idea.

We had plenty of sport though. A swimming gala was organised in the pool. That was before they discovered the fungus in peoples ears and blamed the pool. We also held a tennis tournament, and we had a visit from Don Budge, a leading tennis star in his day. He knocked one or two of us all over the place in a demonstration or two. What he didn't know was that a slim unassuming lad on our course had been All England Schoolboy Champion. He won all right but suddenly he found himself having to work desperately to do it.

We had a sports competition with the U.S.A.F. pupils from another Riddle owned flying school. We took them on at all the sports, including baseball (or softball) and American football and won at everything. Ours was a very competetive lot. Not that I did much, except in the swimming events.

Most weekends, we hitchhiked, usually to Miami, but occasionally West Palm Beach. In Miami we sometimes stayed at the Colony, but we found that we could also stay for a dollar a night at another hotel at the north end of the beach called the MacFadden Deauville. MacFadden was a health freak, and before the war the hotel was a health farm, to use a more modern term. The hotel had a tremendous outdoor swimming pool on its roof, with tables and seats and sunshades all round it.

At the back was its own private beach and a cabana club. We could use these facilities free of charge but had to pay for food or drinks. We had to find a downtown drugstore for these. We couldn't afford MacFadden's prices on L.A.C.'s pay of seven shillings and six pence per day. MacFadden was said to have divorced his wife because she wouldn't do a parachute jump with him; they were both in their seventies.

On one of our trips to West Palm Beach, Jock Simms and I wandered through the black part of town. This was 'over the tracks'. At the lower end of the main drag, there was a level crossing and a railway separating the white and the black parts of town. Just over the crossing was a club we used to go to. There was music and a small dance floor, and we could afford their prices. Jock and I decided to look around, though we knew we had been warned against it. We hadn't gone far before we were in an area of mud streets, wooden houses that were little more than huts, and quite a lot of poor-looking blacks loafing about, often in groups, or sitting on the steps with open doors and sometimes on their haunches against a wall. No one interfered with us, but the looks we got were far from friendly. In fact they were downright hostile, and I felt that anything could happen. Jock later said it was all he could do to stop himself breaking into a run. I, at any rate, wasn't sorry to see the level crossing loom up ahead. We didn't do it again.

On one of our trips to Miami, we found *Gone with the Wind* at the cinema. This was a four-hour film with a break in the middle, and it was a delight to sit in this cool, air-conditioned cinema. The trouble was that when we came out, it felt as if we were walking into an oven. I thought I'd die!

I also saw the English tear jerker *Mrs Miniver*, and when the cinema emptied, there was hardly a dry eye among the women. It should have drummed up a bit of sympathy for poor old England. Some of the Irish Americans, though, had little sympathy to waste on us. I was stopped several times in the street and asked why they should be dragged into our war. Look what the English did to the Irish, they said. What about the Black and Tans? Up until then, I had thought a Black and Tan was a mixture of stout and bitter!

I had a bad time in Florida, really. Being fair skinned, I always burnt easily. My nose and forehead, not covered by my flying helmet and goggles, seemed to lose a layer of skin nearly everyday. Then I had boils and particularly nasty stys. The stys kept me off of flying on two occasions. They tried several sorts of pills and tablets, without avail.

Then there was a course of injections, one a day and it went on for weeks. I used to dread going over to that sick bay. In the end the doctor said that the climate—i.e., humid heat, together with the dust always blowing around the field—just didn't suit me. By then I was getting near the end of the course, and he said that I could only sweat it out and hope things would improve when I got away.

Near the end of my stay, we came into the hurricane season. We didn't get a hurricane that year, but they took no chances. All the buildings had chains thrown over the roofs, these being double-staked. Plans were made to fly all the aircraft out at a moment's notice. Apparently, these weather systems are pretty unpredictable, and the tale was told about the hurricane the year before when the storm was forecast to pass over Clewiston and all the planes were flown to Tampa. The hurricane changed direction and missed Clewiston, and many of the planes at Tampa were badly damaged in high winds, even though they were all lashed down securely.

At their worst the hurricanes can do catastrophic damage. I saw an article once about the one which completely flattened Miami in 1929 (I think). This lifted ships out of the harbour and flung them across the six lane Biscayne Boulevard, and into the side of the skyscrapers on the far side.

Eventually we had completed our last formation, our last cross country, and checked out in the air with the C.F.I., leaving only the ground school examinations, most of us were a bit windy of these. It had been so hot and humid, even during the night, and we found it difficult to sleep.

Then during the lectures indoors, a lecturer's voice droning on, it was not only difficult to concentrate, but even to stay awake. I don't think any of us had much confidence in our ability to pass any sort of written exam so it was just as well that after flying was finished we had a few days completely free to study. We mostly lay about in groups in the sun, books all round us—all except Nobby Clark, who lay on his bed reading novels. What it is to be blessed with a

AT6As over the Everglades.

photographic memory! The exams came and went, and as far as I remember, all passed. The one way out in front, of course, was Nobby Clark.

Great excitement followed: sewing sergeant's stripes and wings onto our R.A.F. blues. Our pay went up too late to do us much good in Florida; we could have done with some of it earlier. There were farewells all round with a party or two, and we collected our passing out certificates, typical American with gold letters, big seals and ribbons, and a very nice wallet. Before we knew it, we were travelling north again.

We stopped off in New York and met a female cousin of Nobby's who helped us with our shopping for girlfriends and families. You could still get decent stockings in the States while they were unobtainable in wartime Britain, and these bought any amount of gratitude.

In Boston Jock Simms and I went off to explore. We ended up in a bar and were very nearly feted. We found the people the friendliest we had met in the States. I remember we each took half a bottle of whisky and a whole lobster back on the train. We only just made the train and then made everyone envious while we enjoyed our meal. I also bought my father a bottle of Johnny Walker, which survived all the way home, where it was gratefully received. Eventually, we were back in Moncton, and it seemed a different place in summer sunshine. We did not stay so very long this time, and there were no prolonged periods of quarantine. I did get to see Jean and her family but only once just before we left.

On the train rumour was rife that we were to embark on the *Queen Mary* or the *Queen Elizabeth*. There were those 'experts' who asserted that neither vessel could get into any Canadian port, but when we got to Halifax docks in late evening, there she was, looking immense and beautiful: the SS *Queen Elizabeth*.

The crossing home took five days. It was said it could have been done in three but for the zigging and zagging. We had no escort except for a Catalina flying boat part of the way out from Canada, and a Sunderland that met us as soon as we were within range. They were relying on the ship's speed to outpace the opposition, and an erratic course to fool any one lying in wait across our course. She would have been a prime target. Apart from the boat and crew, there were said to be 16,000 R.A.F. and Canadian army personnel on board. It was actually its first trip as a troop ship.

I was in what would have been a first-class state room. There was a built-in wardrobe, shower, and toilet, all panelled in the most beautiful walnut, but the whole space was taken up with four-tier bunks, so close you could barely squeeze between them.

Most of our time was taken up with queuing for meals. As soon as you finished one meal, it was time to join the back of the line for the next. We did walk around the decks quite a bit and thoroughly explored the ship. We were amazed to find that some people were sleeping in the empty swimming pool on straw filled palliases about eleven decks down.

We sailed up the Clyde in weak sunshine and were taken off in tenders at Greenock. Then it was straight onto a train and down to Harrogate. From there we went on leave, and it was good to see our families and friends after nearly a year away.

Course Seven—that was—Thank Heaven

In days gone by, before the war, in dear old 'civvy' street,
You once beheld some dapper chaps, of dress and figure neat.
Behold up now, those broken men—bowed down by cares and woes;
Our lot is worse than Oflag X! We hope to be P.O.s.
From far and wide, across the sea, we came—a motley crew—
And how we ever hoped to fly, the devil only knew.
Instructors' sighs; imploring eyes were raised, beseeching Heaven
To take away this bitter pill—in short, remove Course Seven.
Cross country flights amused us well, but wasn't it a pity,
When Sarasota town below turned out to be Plant city!
They rationed gas about half way through—but do not let it fool Ya,
That's not the reason why old 'Pott' forced landed at Wauchula.
We slumbered through the summer days; but was it so surprising?
We sweated all the long hot nights,
And darn this early rising!
Then, ground school for the day being done, our bodies, craving rest,
Were spurred along to greater feats, in P.T. shorts and vests.
We bounced along the ground and then took off completely crosstee
Turned traffic patterns in side out, made landings rather ropey.
With loops and rolls, chandelles and spins, we showed the world our
        powers,
Yet even then scarce dared to hope those 'Wings' would e'er be ours.
A blessed respite, our first weeks leave; the sea shores seemed to
        beckon
Miami beach with U.S. peach, is quite a place I reckon!
A certain town won some renown for four bright eyed young flyers,
While one of us—a quiet cuss—remembers well Fort Myers!
And then at last, with P.T.s past, we found a situation,
Where T.M.P. and F.F.S. caused lots of tribulation
Bombing errors hemmed us in, loop bearings we sensed dimly,
And Turton, seer among the band, saw Trenton looming grimly.
We found ourselves the senior flight, we thought about it gravely,
And though I guess we had our fears, we strove to hide them bravely,
We flew by night to Melbourne Light; we soloed in formation;
And thanks to Mr Fowler's pains, we learned Air Navigation.
We'll miss the lights, the balmy nights, the 'cokes' and 'cackleberries'
The cigarettes, mosquito nets, the little sunburn worries,
We'll miss you all, for we've had fun; and now, before we leave you,
Thanks for it all, and when YOU come, how gladly we'll receive you!

Len Baker.

Wilf Tylor.

Harry Roberts.

A high-speed train passing through West Palm Beach.

MacFadden Deauville Hotel, Miami Beach.

Wilf Taylor and Ken Brant in good company on the sands at Miami Beach.

Passing out day. Standing, left to right: Noel Colley, Nobby Clark, the author, and Len Baker. Sitting, left to right: Ian Lock, Frank Pegg, and George Williams.

Left to right: Jack Twelvetrees, Noel Colley, Len Baker, Frank Pegg, and George Williams.

Nobby Clark

Len Baker.

The author.

Saying goodbye at Clewiston.

Clewiston railway station: leaving for the return trip to Moncton.

No 5 B·F·T·S·
Royal Air Force

RIDDLE - McKAY
Aero College. Clewiston, Fla.

RIDDLE-McKAY AERO COLLEGE
RIDDLE FIELD, CLEWISTON, FLORIDA. U. S. A.

Certificate of Graduation

To all persons to whom these presents may come, Greetings:
Be It Known That

Ronald William Pottinger

has completed with honors. and high promise of credit in the Service of his King and Country.
the Primary, Basic and Advanced Phases of the Royal Air Force Flying Training conducted by
the Riddle-McKay Aero College, operators of the Number Five British Flying Training School.
Riddle Field, Clewiston, Florida. U. S. A.

In Witness Whereof we have caused this Certificate of Graduation to be signed.

FOR THE COLLEGE:

On This twenty-third day of September
in the Year of Our Lord. One
Thousand, Nine Hundred and
Forty-two

GENERAL MANAGER

FOR THE ROYAL AIR FORCE

COMMANDING OFFICER

CHAPTER 3

Into the Fray

The blackout took a good deal of getting used to, especially in Harrogate where it seemed many of the houses had a couple of steps from their front doors down to the pavement, usually with a hand rail. These were a dreadful trap for the unwary.

We spent a couple of weeks at Harrogate and were then moved to Bournemouth which was just about bursting at the seams with brand new R.A.F. sergeant pilots, home from training overseas. The few weeks here were almost a repeat of St Johns Wood; they couldn't hope to keep track of us all. They tried to keep us occupied with 'organised games'. Our crowd chose golf as likely to be the least organised of any on offer, and were left at a golf club on the outskirts of town for the day. I don't know who paid for all the lost balls and broken clubs but there were plenty of both.

In due course we were posted to No 5(P) A.F.U. Tern Hill near Market Drayton in Shropshire. Here we flew Masters and the main purpose of the course was to get us familiar with finding our way over the English countryside. After the wide open spaces of North America, England was a patchwork of hedged fields. Quite apart from the difficulty of telling which of the many roads you were following, half the time you couldn't even see the road for the trees and hedges which were overhanging it. Railroads and rivers were better if there was one going the right way but map reading at flying speed was not easy. Tern Hill had one saving grace, it was only a few miles from a sugar loaf hill called the Wrekin. You could see the Wrekin from miles away, and there, a few miles due east was Tern Hill. Nevertheless people did get lost. One I remember saw an airfield beneath him when near desperation and lobbed down to find he was at Cranwell, well south and on the other side of the country. Another went missing and was tracked by the Observer Corps heading up into the mountains of Scotland. I believe they got him down safely somewhere and eventually returned to camp.

We also flew from a satellite field at Calverley. My main memory of Calverley was of our living quarters. Wooden huts standing in a sea of mud, you needed gum boots to reach the roadway. Also from here I remember the difficulties of travel. Going on leave and standing in a packed corridor for hours on end. Of setting off for home on an illegal weekend with Nobby Clark, get-ting as far as Stafford and not being able to get any further, because there were no trains till Monday. Staying over in Stafford and going to a dance on Saturday night and setting off back to camp on Sunday. Nights spent sleeping in the Y.M.C.A. at Crewe.

The planes at Tern hill were pretty ancient, and some were in poor con-dition. I went out to one, and on doing the cockpit drill and flicking one igni-tion switch off and then the other, the drop in revs was about twice the maximum allowed. I taxied back in and when reporting the fault the fitter reckoned I was a fool. So I had him find a parachute and took him up. He came but looked a bit sick about it, and though I couldn't see his face when I tried the ignition switches, I wondered how he felt.

Anyway, we took off and got back without incident. I didn't set out to frighten him with any violent manoeuvres, but I reckoned I'd made my point without.

Within a few weeks we had finished at Tern Hill and were posted to No 56 O.T.U. at R.A.F. Tealing situated just outside Dundee. Being an opera-tional training unit they had a few Masters and early marks of the Hurricane. The Masters were used so that we could familiarise ourselves with the field and the surrounding area before we went off alone in a Hurricane.

With a single seater you had enough problems on your first flight with-out worrying about where you were getting to. You had to get it all right at first attempt, too. We spent quite a bit of time doing cockpit drill and getting familiar with its layout. Then came the first time off alone. In the Hurricane the undercarriage retract lever was on the right and you could always tell the beginners because as they changed hands to retract the undercarriage the nose would drop, and be hurriedly picked up as they changed hands. Once you got used to doing this there was no problem, but I wondered sometimes why the lever couldn't be on the left like every other aircraft that I ever flew.

The other peculiarity of the Hurricane was that it was not stable in the longitudinal axis—i.e., if you put the nose down and took your hands off, the nose would stay down, instead of the plane returning to level flight. Again it was no bother once you were used to it.

We did a fair bit of flying, practising aerobatics, some cross country, for-mation, and a fair amount of low flying. We had a set low flying area south of the Tay, and this really was good fun. There was one wooded hill with a fire break running up and over its crest. I would fly up the fire break, well below the tops of the trees, burst out over the top with the whole of the Tay estuary laid out beneath. It was breathtaking.

In another part of the area, I found a country road running pretty well straight with no telegraph poles and fenced either side with paling fences.

Even in this low flying area, we were supposed to keep above 300 feet, which was ridiculous since on operations we would have to literally clip the wave tops to keep under enemy radar. Anyway, it was so much more fun at deck level than at 300 feet. It was also much more dangerous.

After a few weeks we were moved to a satellite field at Kinnell near Arbroath, and on one low-flying exercise I met up with Bob Cole and another chap doing the same. So it was inevitable that we started tail chasing among the hills and woods of the area.

When my turn came to lead, I took them to my stretch of road and we went along it with a wing draped over either fence. Two hundred and thirty miles per hour along a country road—it was exhilarating! I realised we'd been up some time and looked at my watch to check. At that height and speed you can't afford to be distracted by anything, a lesson I learnt the hard way when my port wing tip hit the post of a five barred gate. The road had taken a bend to the right and the gate was right on the bend where I'd flown straight on and left the road.

As I hit the post there was a thump and immediately it took both hands to hold up the port wing. I climbed and flew gingerly back across the estuary any minute expecting something vital to fall off. However, I got back to the field OK, landed fast in case the port wing stalled before I was down, and tax-ied back to the park. It was lunchtime and no one was around except a cou-ple of ground crew L.A.C.s, so I went and got my own lunch. I returned to the flights to find uproar.

I was invited into the C.F.I.'s office. He was an Irishman noted for his temper, and I saw it at its best. It was some time before I was allowed to speak and by then it was obvious that the truth was going to get me nowhere, except perhaps target towing, the Far East, or the glass house for life. So I lied like a trooper, and refused to be browbeaten out of my fabricated story. Over the next few weeks I was threatened with court marshals, and all sorts of other unpleasantness, but I stuck to my story and eventually it all died down. Besides the bent aeroplane, the C.F.I. seemed more annoyed that I'd gone off to lunch without reporting the incident. I reckoned I lied better on a full stomach! I learnt later from one of the riggers that I was lucky in that the plane was one of the very early Hurricanes and had fabric covered wings. The tip of the port wing had gone, and five inches more and the aileron would have gone with it. Splintered wood was jammed in the end, and had anyone tested it, would have proved to be well seasoned gate post wood, not green tree wood as per my story. I was later told by the rigger that there was a spare wing of that type on the field, and they were able to change the wing overnight without any need for paperwork, and this was the main reason I got away with it. It was quietly covered up.

Others were not always so lucky. One chap was enjoying himself doing steep turns round Lock Leven (outside the official low flying area!). He got careless, too, dipped a wing in, cartwheeled across the lake and fortunately ended up on a shelf in shallow water about twenty yards from the shore.

He was picked up by some fishermen in a rowing boat, and they offered to bear him out that his engine failed. But he told the truth and was still awaiting court martial when we all finished our course and left. Honesty doesn't always pay.

Another incident that amused everyone except the authorities was when a pupil, trying to emulate the fighter pilots in the films, pulled his undercarriage up as soon as he left the ground. He was too eager. The plane had not properly reached flying speed, and it settled sufficiently for the prop to touch the runway. Again, it was an early Hurricane with a wooden prop, and splinters of wood came off of it looking like a Catherine wheel. As the prop got shorter, the plane settled more and the splinters got bigger until with an awful graunching sound the plane skidded along the tarmac on its belly and came to a halt. The pilot looked sheepish, the C.F.I. furious, and the plane really sad, but I think Bill Orwins gaffe was the best of all.

Bill came from Bakewell, I remember—not that that means anything. He turned up on 3 Sqdn some time after I joined. We also met up again later on in prison camp. Bill was up with a formation of twelve aircraft practising close-formation flying, led by the C.F.I. This was always a very nervy business. Flying close formation needed intense concentration. A wing man would be continuously skidding the plane in or out on the rudder to keep his wing tip overlapping the centre man, and working the throttle to keep station just about six feet behind and a foot or so below the centre man. In the centre you are aware that just behind and beneath is the next man's whirling propeller and with a small misjudgement or loss of concentration it could chop off your tail as easy as that. At the end of the session, the C.F.I. would fly the formation across the airfield to impress everyone watching, order echelon starboard—i.e., the lefthand row crosses over to the right side, the leader then peels off to port, and everyone fans out in turn so that by the time the approach is made the planes land one behind the other at about 100-yard intervals. It's very impressive, and God help anyone who spoils the show. You are all well aware that you are being judged.

For some reason, when Bill was on the approach, the caravan at the end of the runway fired a red Very light at him, and he 'poured on the coals' to go round again. He was probably too close to the plane ahead on the runway.

As his plane climbed it seemed to us on the ground as if it had lost power. It climbed incredibly slowly, and seemed to be at an impossible angle near to the stall. The airfield had three runways in the form of a triangle, and in the centre were several large oak trees. Bill turned off to port, and from where we stood it looked as if he flew right through the branches of the trees. For his next trick he mistook the runway and came in on the one that had the planes already landed and taxiing towards him. Bill must have seen them at the last moment, for with much screeching of brakes his plane stopped almost nose to nose with that of the C.F.I.'s. The C.F.I. leapt out of his plane, jumped up onto the wing of Bill's, and checked the propeller pitch lever. This, of course, was still set at 'coarse pitch'. This would have been like trying to drive a car from standstill in top gear.

I don't think our instructors thought us a good course. Certainly, the C.F.I. hinted at target towing and all sorts of other unpopular futures. It was no great surprise to find myself eventually posted to 275 Air Sea Rescue squadron on Anglesey with about nine others from my course. I often wondered where the rest went.

On arrival at R.A.F. Valley on Anglesey, I found Bob Cole and about eight others from Tealing. We were all a bit disgruntled at not being posted to a fighter squadron, but we must have been mad! The station was as comfortable a place as you could wish for in war time. The food was good, the quarters fine, and soon after we arrived, there was a station dance, which was a real wing-ding of a do. I came to the conclusion that all the best-looking W.A.A.F.s in Wales ended up at Valley. The beaches were beautiful, and you could walk straight off the end of the runway onto beautiful golden sands. With summer getting under way, what more could an airman want. On top of this the squadron maintained one flight in Ulster, where all sorts of goodies were available, long since vanished from English shops, including nylon stockings with which to tempt the girls.

The squadron flew Ansons and also kept a Walrus amphibian. We gathered that they had only tried to land the Walrus on the sea about three times, and each time they had wrecked it. It seems it was extremely hazardous to make the attempt in all but the smoothest waters.

We all went for a trip in an Anson. This also was an education after the Hurricane. It lumbered down the runway, I don't think any of us expected it to get off the ground. Once airborne the undercarriage had to be wound up by hand. I forget how many hundreds of turns on the handle. I only know it was barely raised before it was time to start putting it down again.

It was enough. We all had interviews with the C.O. and asked for transfer to fighter squadrons. He had recently come on rest from leading a fighter squadron and said.

"I wish the crowd I'd had were as keen as you lot!"

Within a couple of days we were posted in pairs to fighter squadrons. Bob Cole and I were posted from Valley on the Isle of Anglesey to West Malling towards the end of May 1943. We had no idea where West Malling was, but after asking at a travel office on Euston station, it turned out to be about six miles west of Maidstone.

Here we joined No 3 Squadron, stationed there while re-fitting from Hurricane IICs to Typhoon IBs. We met three other sergeant pilots who had joined the squadron within the previous couple of days. Rodney Dryland was a tall, fair, curly-haired lad, very boyish. Rodney survived the war, only to be killed when flying as a test pilot well after the war was over. Ken Slade-Betts was tall, dark, and handsome; he was killed just prior to my own involuntary exit from the squadron. In a 1989 issue of the 3 Squadron Association newsletter, there was an enquiry for Ken and a letter from his brother. Obviously, it's still not clear exactly what happened to him. Prior to joining 3 Squadron, Ken had been flying Defiants. The last of our number was Dickie Wingate. He had a Canadian wife who was new to England, and he was continuously fretting about how she was coping with life in wartime England and, in particular, British money. In those days it was twelve pence to the shilling and twenty shillings to the pound, of course.

Our morale took a bump when we found that we were replacements for five out of eight pilots lost on one of the squadron's first operations with Typhoons. A dive bombing raid on Poix airfield in France. On reflection it hardly seemed fair to blame the plane, since they were bounced by enemy planes over the airfield. You have to see the other chap first if you want to survive, or else be very lucky. The time between a black speck appearing out of the sun and its guns opening up is seconds only.

The squadron at that time was rather like the League of Nations. The C.O. was Belgian, S/L de Soomer, an older man. Another Belgian was Jean de Selys, nicknamed and known to all as 'The Baron'. It appeared that he was allowed to do more or less as he liked, and frequently broke the golden rule by flying off on a mission by himself. He always flew in a white overall and carried a miniature Compass camera in a pocket on his knee. The Baron, it was, who earlier had roared up and down the main street of Brussels at window level, and had shot up Gestapo headquarters in that city.

We also had three New Zealanders and a Canadian or two, not to mention two Americans, 'Lefty' Whitman and 'Buck' Feldman.

Thursday, 27 May 1943
    Today I saw an operational trip in process. The Baron and 'Rickie' (Pullen) went on a 'Rhubarb'. We watched them take off

and everyone was working out when they should get back. From time to time the C.O. phoned op's to see if there was any news of them, and finally we heard that they were on their way back separately, then a few minutes later the Baron had crossed our coast.

Bob Cole was just landing in the 'Hurri' when there was a terrific roar and the Baron literally hurtled down on the dispersal. He pulled up from about fifty feet and did about three vertical rolls until it seemed he must stall. He finished up with enough speed to rudder it into a steep turn and came whistling down at us again. This time he was still doing vertical rolls when he disappeared into cloud at about three thousand feet. When he reappeared he had wheels and flaps down and side-slipped it in to land. It was a fine show of flying.

When he taxied in the ground crews crowded around him, helping him out, carrying his parachute, he was obviously their hero at that moment. Rickie came quietly in some while later and the pair of them were taken down to Intelligence by the C.O. Apparently they bombed some lock gates, shot up some barges and a column of troops.

Bob was put in 'A' flight, commanded by MacKickan, as were Dryland and Slade-Betts, while Dickie Wingate and I were put in 'B' flight, commanded by Jack Collins. Jack was an extremely likeable man, as was his great friend F/Lt Vic Smith.

Vic Smith it was who introduced me to the Hurricane 11Cs and later the Typhoon 1B, and went through the cockpit drills.

Sunday, 30 May 1943

Got in two trips in the Hurricane, and was surprised to find that I can still fly after all this time. The first trip was in pretty misty weather and I stayed fairly close to the field. On the second one though I started by going to Worthing and flying right over Kent.

At New Romney I did a few circuits and was able to pick out all the old billets. Never thought I'd see them from that angle. At Dover I nearly had pups when I poked my head out of the 'office' and found myself looking up at barrage balloons. I got out quick!

A couple of days later, we did cockpit drill on the Typhoon, and at last they trusted us off the ground in one. Always a certain anxiety the first time off in a new aircraft. It's a single-seater, and no one can be with you—you just have to get it right first time. The Typhoon had a strong tendency, like most single-engined planes, to swing to the right on takeoff.

The prop tends to create a spiral blast down the fuselage which hits one side of the fin and rudder, and this has to be corrected on the rudder. But the Typhoon was the worst I had met, and although warned, most pilots let it get away first time off. With the Typhoon you had to start correcting almost before the swing started. Once it got away it could only be stopped by throttling back. By then it was usually too late and instead it had to be hauled off the ground, the pilot praying that nothing got in the way. Later, it became second nature to open the throttles progressively and correct early on the rudder, and I don't remember any difficulty after those early days.

Of course, once up, you could enjoy the flight in a new aeroplane. Although much faster than the Hurricane there was little sensation of speed until you looked at the airspeed indicator and realised you are travelling at close to 400 mph. Then comes time to return, and anxiety returns when you realise that you have to get down again. However, the Typhoon had a beautiful wide undercarriage, and landing was easy. You would bring it in at around a hundred on the clock, dropping to ninety or ninety-five over the fence, holding off to a perfect three-point landing.

Tuesday, 1 June 1943
Flew the worlds fastest fighter today. Swung like hell on take off and nearly went through a blister hanger. I found it hard to believe the figures I got on the clock. Cruising at 280 instead of 180 and all through, the speeds are about a hundred miles per hour faster. The landing I had been dreading I found easy, though I did have to go round twice to get my speed down.

Bob had hydraulic trouble and couldn't get his undercarriage down. I was up at the time and heard them giving advise over the R/T. Finally he got his wheels down but no flaps and came in too fast. He ground looped on the far perimeter track and his undercarriage collapsed sideways just about writing off the kite. Bob was sitting unhurt on top of the neatest pile of wreckage I've seen in years.

Sunday, 6 June 1943
Did some cine gun attacks on Bob Cole in the Hurricanes. He was supposed to fly straight and level for a while so that I could try some range estimation shots, but not Bob, He did vertical turns and even a slow roll and finished up twisting and turning at eight hundred feet over the centre of Maidstone. I soon gave up all hope

of getting a decent picture and got the film finished somehow. After that it was a dog fight at about a thousand feet, too low for my liking.

I don't remember being on any other sort of operation from West Malling. Might have been a patrol or two. Other more experienced pilots were permitted to plan, and put forward their flight plans for operations code named 'Rhubarbs'.

These would be carried out on moonlit nights, two aircraft, low level, with a two hundred and fifty pound bomb under either wing. Usually, these would be planned as a round trip. In one way, fly around a couple of set courses and times, and out by another exit. Anything interesting seen en route was fair game, but usually, the route would be planned to take in an airfield, a rail junction, or something similar. I suppose these raids had a certain nuisance value, but our losses were quite high. When the Germans flew similar raids over the southern counties, they were called 'sneak raids', and they were considered a cowardly German trick.

Low-level attacks carried a certain amount of danger to the attacker, quite apart from the irate recipients, who could be depended upon to throw everything they had at you. By then they had had a good deal of practice and were quite accurate in their aim. Tales were also told of bombs released at tree top height, bouncing on a hard surface, and being under the tail of the aircraft after the three second delay before they went off. The idea if you knew a target was coming up was to pull up before it and release the bombs

3 Sqdn at Manston, July/August 1943.

Front row, left to right: Bob Cole and Buck Feldman. Second row, left to right: Lee Sinclair, de Callatay, Jean de Selys with 'Pat', and Rickie Pullen.

The author, ground crew, and Typhoon 1B at Manston, March 1944.

Left to right: F/Lt MacKickan ('A' Flt Comm), S/L de Soomer, F/Lt Jack Collins ('B' Flt Comm), and F/O Vic Smith.

in a shallow dive, hoping they would go in and stay in. This, if it was a target of any consequence, gave the inevitable gunners a far better chance. A second run over a target was foolhardy in the extreme. Then again attacking with guns needed care, not always easy to judge at night. When pulling out after a dive the plane tends to mush out before changing direction. It is easy, even in daylight, in the excitement to leave it later than intended and many a pilot has scared the daylights out of himself in this way. I have seen aircraft damaged quite badly by debris thrown up by his own strikes, even on the practice range.

West Malling was a pleasant station, it had a well kept air. The sergeants' mess was in one double story building with a large foyer and potted plants at the foot of the stairs. There was a large dining hall, doubling as a dance hall and cinema. At that time of year (June/July) the grass was very green, trees had blossom on them, and it was a good place to be. Our planes were dispersed in an apple orchard on the far side of the airfield from all of the buildings, and over the fence behind the orchard, strawberry fields stretched for miles. They were beautifully ripe too, and would never get picked before they spoiled, so we helped the farmer out.

On one occasion we picked a large enamel bowl full and took it back to the sergeants mess. A W.A.A.F. sergeant scrounged a pudding basin full of sugar from the kitchen , and we sat around in a circle, about twenty of us, dunking strawberries in the sugar and eating them. I'm afraid cream was beyond our resources, but they were still pretty good. It amazed me that though food was in such short supply, in Kent whole orchards of fruit seemed to rot on the trees or plants for the want of someone to pick them.

We had a dance in the sergeants' mess which I remember as a good evening without anything special to note. I remember more the special mess meeting called the day of the dance, when the station warrant officer almost pleaded for good behaviour, and threatened dire consequences for any mis-demeanours brought to his notice. He said he was all in favour of everyone enjoying themselves, but anyone caught dragging W.A.A.F.s through the corridors by their hair would end in the glasshouse, followed by a Far East posting.

Next morning, one of the potted plants was spread all over the foyer and the W.O. was pretty scathing, but it got scraped up into its pot and seemed to recover quite quickly. I suspect it was used to it. I also suspect the W.O. thought he'd got off lightly.

We also went a couple of times to a dance held in a territorial army drill hall at Ditton on the road we now call the A20.

At one of these dances I danced with a really striking looking, dark haired girl in civilian dress, and asked at the end of the evening if I might walk her home. It turned out that she was a nurse, and that home was Pre-ston Hall near the British Legion Village, several miles along the A20 towards Maidstone. Still I was young and fit, and she was good looking. But the whole way, she talked of nothing else but communism, the exploitation of the work-ing classes, and, in particular, all of us young men fighting a war started by politicians. I couldn't get a word in edgewise or an arm out of place. By the time we reached the entrance to the hospital, I gladly said farewell. We didn't meet again. We moved to Manston shortly afterwards anyway.

About a week after our arrival at West Malling, we heard that to celebrate the shooting down of the thousandth Hun aircraft by fighter command, a party had been arranged at the Grosvenor Hotel in Park Lane, London. 'Sailor' Malan and others from Biggin Hill had arranged this. They per-suaded firms whose products they used—such as Rolls Royce, Hawkers, Supermarine, and Napiers—to put up money. Good thing the Germans didn't get news of this, for I think fighter command in southeast England turned up en bloc. Stop the war! We've found free booze!

We were permitted one lady visitor, and I took a neighbour's daughter, Audrey Harris. It was a good evening, except that I lost track of Audrey and found her with Dickie Wingate, looking a little flustered and dishevelled. I felt a bit bad because she was very young, and I'm sure her mother thought she was safe in my care. But among that crowd?!

It was a wonderful evening: two first-class dance bands, free drink, and free buffet, and half way through the evening, a deputation of taxi drivers was introduced from the balcony, and it was announced that they would get everyone home free when the dance was over. And they did. Audrey and I were run all the way out to Earlsfield in southwest London, and the driver wouldn't take a penny. When you remember how short petrol was at that time and how their living depended on how much of it they could get, this was really something.

We were only at West Malling for three or four weeks before we moved to Manston. I was sorry to leave really, I liked West Malling. It was a comfortable billet compared to many I'd known.

We moved from West Malling to Manston, about a mile inland from Pegwell Bay on the tip of the Isle of Thanet, on Friday, 11 June 1943

Our dispersal was a large wooden building, at the north westerly corner of the airfield. This had a partition across the centre, and in the northerly half were quartered the duty crews with their workshop. The southerly end was a loafing area for the pilots, with cupboard sized offices near the door for the C.O. and Flight Commanders.

The room was furnished with a variety of chairs, from fairly comfortable to downright tatty, and I often wondered wherever they'd been found! There was a round iron stove with metal chimney, and when the winter came we needed it.

For our comfort and amusement we had a battered old portable record player, and a tea chest full of records that we took around with us.

Every time the squadron moved, a few of these were broken; the way they were stacked in, it's a marvel any survived. I do remember there was a whole bound album of about a dozen Bob Crosby records which were favourites of mine, and I probably drove a few people, not jazz fanatics, mad playing these over and over. I wish I had them now. These were of course the old 78 rpm wax records, and would by now probably be valuable antiques. I'm sure they got as far as Holland with us, and were probably left in the depths of Germany somewhere when the war ended. We pilots spent a lot of time waiting of course. We didn't fly every day, and if we did, the average flight was around one and a half hours, so we needed something to pass the time.

The airfield was grass. Grass that is wherever it wasn't bomb craters filled with brick rubble. It was certainly a front line station and life must have been exciting during the Battle of Britain days, judging by the number of these old craters that were about. By now the Battle of Britain had been won, and apart

Manston, 5 July 1943. Back row, left to right: Rodney Dryland, McCook, Lumsden, Bob Walmesly, and Ken Slade-Betts. Front row, left to right: Dickie Wingate, Hutchinson, Chas Tidy, Bob Cole, Johnny Foster, Bob Moore, and Lefty Whitman.

Back row standing, left to right: 'Lefty' Whitman and Hutchinson. Middle row, left to right: Jean de Selys, 'Blackie' Swartze, Chas Tidy, Johnny Foster, Jack Collins with baby son, de Soomer, and 'Mac' McCook. Front row sitting, left to right: Ray Crisford, 'Buck' Feldman, the author, and 'Kibbie' Reid.

from the occasional alarms usually caused by sneak raiders, we never did have any further damage to the camp. The field was rough and 'L' shaped. The main runway ran east-west where the big concrete runway was later built. The shorter leg running northeast to southwest and starting at our northeast corner, ran quite steeply downhill to the road to Manston village which crossed

3 Sqdn dispersal at Manston, August 1943. Back row, left to right: the author, Bob Cole, Johnny Foster, and Bob Moore. Front row, left to right: Johnny Downs, LaRocque, Ray Crisford, and an unidentified pilot.

Group of pilots on readiness at Manston, 7 July 1943. Standing, left to right: Vic Smith, the author, Kibbie Reid, Dickie Wingate, and Rodney Dryland. Sitting, left to right: Hutchinson and Lumsden.

'Lefty' Whitman.

Don Butcher.

Byron Lumsden.

the field at that point, then steeply uphill to the other runway. The dip was deep enough so that planes landing would disappear from view from our dispersal, and reappear as they climbed the far slope. In a plane you would hit the road still travelling quite fast, bounce dangerously over it and be grateful for the uphill run which was all that stopped you ending up near Richborough.

Having settled the planes along the N.W. edge of the field, and settled ourselves into billets in Westgate, been issued with 'sit up and beg' bicycles for getting about the district, Bob and I discovered that a dance was on that evening at the Westcliffe Hall in Ramsgate, and we headed that way.

It was a good dance, and I was dancing with a pleasant little girl, who said

"Do you come here often!"

"No, it's the first time."

"Oh you must be from the new squadron up at the camp, number three isn't it?"

That was the beginning of my relationship with Joy, whom I called "Olga" (after Olga Pelosky the beautiful spy). It would still be several years before we married, but nevertheless, I saw a good deal of Joy from then on, sometimes at the Westcliffe, sometimes riding out on our old bicycles, and sometimes just walking. Under Ramsgate there were miles of tunnels running through the chalk. These were being used as air raid shelters, and although the worst of the German bombing raids were over, some people were still sleeping down there. Sometimes if there was an air raid and we were down near the seafront we would walk through the tunnels to the outskirts of the town, leaving only a short walk to Joy's home on the Manston Road beyond St Lawrence.

Wednesday, 16 June 1943

Laurie and Tick went out on an anti shipping patrol during the night and when we arrived at dispersal heard that Tick was missing. Later it came through that he had been picked up by what the papers called the most daring rescue of the war. He got a shell in his engine and managed to bale out OK He was picked up by a Walrus, two and a half miles from the French coast. The sea was too rough for the Walrus to take off again and they had to taxi all the way back to Dover, while Spits fought off the Fw190's overhead.

He was back on the squadron that afternoon.

Friday, 18 June 1943

Harry Moore an Australian was missing from a night intruder. He was an experienced pilot and should have known all the angles. Apparently he flew with his radio off and there was no news of him after he took off.

Friday, 25 June 1943

Did some practice bombing in my old enemy 'U'. Coming in to land I had rather a lot of drift on. Unfortunately I hit a patch of bad ground where a bomb hole had been filled in, and there was a loud bang and my starboard tyre flew past the window. I managed to stop it swinging over too much with throttle and brake and pulled up with only the wheel damaged. It was worn flat on one side where it had skidded along the ground. Did pretty well to keep it straight for I was doing a good speed when the tyre came off. We never did find the outer cover which flew past the window.

Tuesday, 29 June 1943

Tick (Sgt Ticklepenny) is really missing this time. At dusk last night they were being vectored home by Hornchurch controller and were vectored clean into Dover balloon barrage. They all got out OK except Tick who hit a cable and bought it. It certainly was a bad show.

Wednesday, 30 June 1943

Rickie Purdon, a Canadian P/O missing from an evening show. Was hit by flak over Dunkirk.

Thursday, 1 July 1943

The squadron attacked a convoy off Holland in the morning. All 'B' flight returned OK but Laurie, Benjamin and Little are missing from 'A' flight. One nineties were around and Johnny Foster and MacKickan claimed two damaged. A dinghy was seen with somebody waving in it, and two chutes were seen going down, so we hope some of them are safe. One boat left burning, others damaged.

Tuesday, 6 July 1943

Did some practice shipping attacks on Herne Bay pier. Weather was bad and we only did one attack. When I was coming in to land found that I couldn't lose my airspeed and after staggering along near the stall for it was obvious my air speed indicator was u/s. Called up on R/T and Bob called back asking control if he could bring me in. While waiting for him to take off I tried again to get the speed down but couldn't get less than 280 on the clock.

When Bob got up we came in together and he left me over the boundary with 120 mph; my A.S.I. still said 150. Got down quite safe thanks to Bob. Good old Bob! Believe he was really concerned for me and was quite touched.

At this time 609 squadron were also stationed at Manston flying Typhoons, they however were pure fighters. Apart from ground attack and escort duties they did a continuous standby during daylight hours. Two pilots in the cockpits, two kitted up, and a further two on five minutes readiness. If they were needed two red Verey lights would be fired from the control tower and the first two would immediately take off. The next two would then move into their cockpits, etc. There was always competition to get off in record time, and you would hear the bang of the Coffman starters while the Very lights were still in the air. I can't remember what the record was, but it was well inside ten seconds to get airborne. Although this duty was performed by 609 at first, they later changed over to 198 Sqdn. For a brief period 56 Squadron were also at Manston at this time.

We also took a turn when needed at readiness, and we didn't do too badly when there was a 'scramble'. At this stage of the war this was not often because of any enemy activity, usually it turned out to be an air/sea rescue trip or an unidentified aircraft which turned out to be friendly. The Luftwaffe was definitely licking it's wounds and were shy of pitting themselves against the later marks of Spitfire, the Typhoon or the Merlin engined Mustang, which definitely outclassed the current versions of the FW 190 and Me 109. (Or perhaps they were too busy fighting off American raids on their homeland.)

Wednesday, 21 July 1943
    Was on cockpit readiness for the first time. Was pouring with
    rain however and didn't stand a hope in hell of a scramble.

My first operational flight in the Typhoon was an air/sea rescue search over the sea two or three miles out from Deal. I flew number two to a New Zealand pilot Hutcheson, and I remember in those days I really felt over no mans land once we'd crossed the coast.

Thursday, 22 July 1943
    On fighter readiness all afternoon. We were scrambled on air
    sea rescue. Four Mustangs had gone out on a Rhubarb and simply
    disappeared. Jack Collins and Wingate went out first and were away
    an hour without seeing anything. Control wanted another section
    scrambled and Hutch and I went out.
    It was my first operational flight if you can call it that, and I was
    quite excited. Hutch flew at about two ninety and in poor shagged
    out 'R' I had to use plenty of revs and boost to keep up. The cloud
    base was about a thousand feet and we kept just below it. I was sur-
    prised to find how often I caught myself looking behind.
    Control vectored us on a square search, and on one leg we were
    flying about five miles off shore ,and I was very excited to see
    Dunkirk and Ostend harbours quite clearly.
    We had only been on our search a few moments when I checked
    my petrol and found my main tanks nearly empty. I called up
    Hutch and asked him to throttle back, after which I was able to
    keep up quite well.
    Once we saw a patch of water which looked as if it had been
    where a kite had gone in, but we could see no wreckage or dinghy.
    Shortly after this control came through and said that there were
    enemy planes east of us, after which I crossed over at every oppor-
    tunity just to get a good look behind. Once I saw a white painted
    buoy which I thought was a dinghy, but no luck and finally control

told us to return. We landed with an hour and five minutes ops time and was really proud of it.

At that time, all service personnel who had seen active service were awarded and allowed to wear the ribbon of the 39–43 Star. My one air/sea rescue trip was enough to qualify. Later, after the war had ended, the medal was degraded to the 39–45 Star, and there was a certain amount of ill feeling among those who qualified for the earlier version. At least that did signify that you had seen a certain amount of service.

Tuesday, 27 July 1943
On readiness all day. Got all ready for a shipping do, but a recce found a 'large convoy' to be a fleet of fishing smacks.

Saturday, 7 August 1943
On fighter readiness all day yesterday until eleven at night owing to 56 Sqdn going on a gunnery course. This morning I was on dawn readiness at five, got back to bed at nine and was raked out again at eleven. On again at dusk this evening and up at five tomorrow morning. Out of all this readiness came exactly nothing. Didn't even get airborne!

Monday, 9 August 1943.
Did thirty five minutes night flying in the Hurricane. Got out over the sea near Whitstable when a group of search lights picked me up. I panicked a bit at first, for they were right on me without any wandering around the sky first. I started talking to myself 'Now don't panic, you man, trust your instruments, they're more likely to be right than you are etc' and I kept my head deep in the cockpit and flew on instruments. However I still had a feeling that I was on my side in a vertical bank. Then suddenly I remembered that I hadn't got my I.F.F. switched on and fumbled around for the switch. Eventually I found it and after a few moments the lights went out.

Friday, 13 August 1943
Quite a lucky Friday the thirteenth for me. Bob Cole, Ken Slade-Betts, and I were promoted to flight sergeants.

Also stationed at Manston at this time was a Fleet Air Arm squadron. There was always a fair amount of friendly banter and practical joking between the F.A.A. and R.A.F. N.C.O.s. However, we had a good deal of

Bob Cole.

respect for these chaps who flew antiquated biplanes against well-armed war-ships. Their Squadron was in fact one of those that had been involved in attacking the Scharnhorst and Gneisenau pocket battleships, with devastating losses to themselves, when these ships made their escape through the Channel. They were still equipped with Swordfish and Albacores. The Albacore was slightly more modern, but both had open cockpits.

Practical jokes were being played ever more frequently as time went by, and after returning from an evening out to find all our beds 'doctored' in various ingenious ways we decided it called for retaliation in grand style. The next time our Navy friends were missing, we took the hinges off of all their doors and refitted them along the top edge. The yells and bangs as noses were bashed when they returned to find their doors swinging in from the bottom made the effort well worth while. Of course the story got about, and not everyone saw the joke. We had a lecture from the station warrant officer on the penalties for damaging Air Ministry property and the dire threats about what continued horseplay would bring.

A well-known figure from the entertainment world was a corporal on the camp, Sam Costa. He was a pianist and singer and often played lunchtime or evenings in the sergeants' mess. When a dance was arranged, he would lead an excellent three-piece band. I suppose we were lucky to have such talent so willingly available. It was the only mess I ever came across where we had music played while eating our lunch.

At this time we had two dogs on the squadron. One such dog belonged to Vic Smith. This was an Alsatian called Husky and regularly got out of hand. Usually he roamed the airfield free, and it was common to hear a

The author in an early version of the Typhoon 1B. Note the 'car door', lifting roof, and bubble over the mirror.

Jock Smith.

The author in the original 'R for Robert'.

great commotion break out, barking and shouting and on rushing to see the cause, Vic's dog would have some workman in a corner fending him off with a shovel or some tool. He seemed to have a thing about workmen, and in particular those carrying ladders. The sight of such an unfortunate was enough to make him go berserk.

At dusk each night a flarepath of smudge pots was put out. A truck loaded with these trundling down the field with two or three airman positioning the lights. Vic's Alsatian would chase down the field after them and his frantic barking could be heard all over the field until the truck vanished whence it came. One time someone found an enormous shin bone. The bone was wrapped in several layers of paper, each layer tied with string or ribbon, and ceremoniously presented to Vic as a present to his dog. It caused a lot of hilarity as the wrappings were shed, but I think the dog was only mildly interested. Maybe he was too accustomed to a diet of workmen and aircraftsmen by then.

Within a week or two of our arriving at Manston, our C.O. S/L de Soomers was posted away. Soon after, Jack Collins and then Vic Smith were also posted to other squadrons. Jack Collins became C.O. of No 245 Squadron, flying rocket Typhoons. Vic Smith went to 198 squadron. Sadly, neither survived the war. Jack Collins was killed on his last operational flight at Mortain during the push through France, and Vic Smith was flying low over the sea when he was seen to dive straight in. It was thought that his dinghy had accidentally inflated in the cockpit. The dinghy comprised the cushion of the pilot's seat and, when used, would inflate very rapidly from its high pressure CO_2 bottle. Of course, if this happened in flight, the pilot would be lifted up and pushed forward against the control column, thus causing the dive. This was just another worry most pilots had, and many carried a sheath knife pushed down their flying boot, so that if this happened, they could puncture the dinghy. That was the theory, at least. In the event I wonder if you could have got to it, or got at it quickly enough. I never did hear of anyone who actually performed this feat successfully, those that didn't manage it, weren't around to tell. I always regretted the passing of these two men in particular.

About this time we also lost Jean de Selys. Jean had been on another of his lone jaunts over Belgium and arrived back over Manston after dark. He was crossing the airfield at about 1,000 feet when he just crashed in. Everyone on the squadron was stunned. After all his exploits we really thought he was indestructible. I don't think anyone really knows what happened, but the story got around that the tail had fallen off.

This was a fairly common occurrence on the early Typhoons, but I would have thought that by this time all the 3 Squadron planes would have been the modified version. Mind you if anyone could strain the rivets on an aeroplane, The Baron would certainly be that person. On the other hand who knows what damage he might have sustained during his trip.

We were all sad to see him go, he was well liked, and a colourful character. The only one in my time on a squadron who was able to get away with his 'lone wolf'-style exploits. The rest had to conform.

Monday, 16 August 1943
   The Baron bought it during the night. Had been on an
'intruder' in the Brussels area. His tail fell off on the approach and
he hit the ground in a screaming dive, upside down. Sorry to see
him go, he was easily the best pilot on the squadron.

Thursday, 19 August 1943
   In the morning I was a pall bearer at the funeral of Jean de Selys
Longchamps, 'The Baron' to the boys. The most cut up of all was
S/L de Soomer, our C.O.

In due course his funeral was held, and I was one of his pallbearers, together with other pilots from the squadron.

It was intended to take his remains back to Belgium when his country was liberated and with this in mind the coffin was lead lined. Even with eight of us carrying it, it felt as if we would sag at the knees.

After the service in the camp chapel, he was buried in the little cemetery at Minster. Many dignitaries from the Belgium government in exile, both ladies and gentlemen attended and I believe one of these was his sister.

De Selys was only part of his name, and many of the foreign pilots flying with the R.A.F. did not use their proper names, in order to protect families still remaining in occupied Europe.

After the war, Joy and I were near Minster, and we called into the cemetery. I was sure that I knew the exact spot where the grave was, but we couldn't find it, so we presumed that, as had been intended, his remains had been disinterred and taken home.

Wednesday, 25 August 1943

Bob Barckley arrived back from the dead, with rather a thrilling tale to tell. He was attacking a train which unfortunately had some rather accurate A.A. gunners on a flak wagon. His controls were shot away, but fortunately the kite was trimmed well and hit the ground smoothly on a hill. At the top of this small rise he shot into the air again and once more landed on his belly in a field on the far side of a small village.

He wasn't hurt and managed to escape with the aid of the underground movement, to Spain and onto Gibraltar, lucky man!

None of the escapees that I ever knew talked of the help they received, the route back or the manner of their escape. They owed too much to the brave people who ran the routes and to the others still following them home.

S/L Thomas replaced de Soomer as C.O. and a period of low level operations ensued. Of these one in particular stays in the memory. I had still only been on a few operations, and these without incident, when we were sent off in the evening light to low level bomb lock gates in the Dutch islands. This would flood a good deal of reclaimed land and cause a great deal of nuisance to shipping in the channels. Vast areas of that part of Holland are below sea level, so that the effect could have been quite spectacular.

Four planes took off, a 250-pound bomb under each wing, and headed at wave top height out across the North Sea. I was flying number two to Johnny Foster and S/L Thomas led the trip. On this sort of trip it was essential to keep low to get under the German radar, and we really were down at about ten feet. It was quite common for the camera lens to get water in it from spray and the picture to be spoiled. The camera took 16mm cine film, and was mounted low in the front of the fuselage. The camera ran whenever the guns were fired, or it could be operated independently if required.

Rodney Dryland
and Bob Moore.

By the time the Dutch coast came into view, it was pretty nearly dark, and the coastline stood out only as a dark smudge along the horizon. Despite our low flying antics, it was obvious that we were expected, for suddenly searchlights shone out from either side, waving from side to side, searching for us. Then the light flak started! It was all tracer and the first I had experienced. I watched quite enchanted at first. You could see the flashes in the distance, then the pin pricks of light which seemed to float out towards us, getting larger and faster, as the tracer rounds got nearer, until it appeared that every one was coming right into the cockpit. Then finally they whizzed past like angry spiteful bees, and you realised that although they might be spectacular, they were also lethal. The firing came first from the left and while looking that way I suddenly realised it was coming from the other side also. Some shots passed above, some in front and behind, and others hit the sea short, bounced and seemed to fly over the cowling in front of my nose.

By now it was apparent that our leader had led us straight into the entrance of Flushing harbour. It was evident the present position was far too hot, and any chance of surprising the opposition at our intended target was out. By now it was quite dark and there was ten tenth's cloud at about a thousand feet. We had also lost sight of the C.O. We were just about to turn up the Ooster Schelde when the C.O. called up and said he was returning to base so we turned back too. On our way back our bombs were jettisoned into the sea, which always seemed such a terrible waste to me.

It was pretty hard to keep up with Johnny but I managed it, and just as I was about to doubt his navigational abilities land loomed up ahead and I saw the aerodrome lights. Control told us to orbit the beacon at various heights until it was our turn to land. My height was two thousand feet. How I was supposed to see the beacon through the cloud, I was too tired to fathom out. Needless to say, I stayed below cloud praying hard that I didn't collide with anyone else. I seemed to be going around that beacon for hours but at last it was my turn to land. At one stage the plane jerked convulsively and I realised I had flown through someones slipstream. Peering through the gloom, I could just make out the flames from exhaust stubs, probably thirty yards ahead. I quickly pulled up five hundred feet and hoped it was enough.

Landing was difficult. The smudge pots were very dim, no one wanted to advertise the presence of an airfield, and they were shielded so that you could only see them on your approach into wind. At the beginning of the runway were two brighter red lights but unfortunately these were not square across the runway, and so committed to my approach I found the runway going off at about thirty degrees to my left. I got it right at about my third attempt, and wasn't sorry to feel the wheels bumping over solid ground

Visiting Whirlwind of 137 Sqdn.

Vic Smith with 'Husky' and, in the background, Bob Walmesly's MG.

again. What with the first experience of light ack ack, the disappointment of an abortive trip, followed by the difficult night landing, it was certainly an experience to be remembered.

Surprisingly, no one was hit, and we all got down without mishap. Thomas wasn't always so lucky; losses were heavy on these low-level operations. He himself went missing about a week later.

Sunday, 5 September 1943
  C.O. (S/L Thomas) missing from an early morning shipping do in the Dutch islands. He flew across a ship as it blew up and crashed landed on land. He was seen to get out and set the kite alight so is not hurt apparently.

Tuesday, 7 September 1943
  Everyone is confined to camp. Something brewing, rumour says it's the second front at long last.

Manston dispersal hut. Left to right: Chas Tidy, 'Lefty' Whitman, 'Teddy' Zurakowski, Clapperton, and Buck Feldman.

Wednesday, 8 September 1943
    Something on. They have been painting two broad bands round
the wing tips with whitewash to help identification. All this was
done in a frantic hurry at dusk. 263 Sqdn have arrived with Whirlwinds—Williams and Handley are with them.

Rumour said that another Dieppe raid was planned. This seemed
unlikely after the losses sustained in the previous Canadian attempt, and
rumour wasn't always correct. Whatever it was they had in store for us was
cancelled, and everything went back to 'as you were.'

Tuesday, 14 September 1943
    While home on a 48 hr pass met Bob Cole at Victoria. He told me
that Cris and Johnny Downs are both missing from a shipping show.
Sorry about Cris, but there's a good chance they may both be safe.

Monday, 20 September 1943
    Went on a Sabre course at Napiers at Park Royal for a week.
Lived at home and had a real rest.

S/L Thomas was replaced by S/L Hawkins. Hawkins was certainly a character. A smallish dark complexioned man, he came with a reputation. He had

already been shot down over France, and evading captivity, had contacted the resistance, and was one of the first to make his way home, being passed down the route to Gibraltar. Not that he ever talked about it, but that was the story. I suppose based on his previous experiences he had all sorts of escape gear sewn into his battledress. It seemed to have pockets all over it.

Wednesday, 29 September 1943

Another Roadstead to the Dutch Islands. 'A' flight were dive bombing and we were going in low level further south, 198 were also going still further south. Blackie Schwarz was No 2 to the C.O. and Chas Tidy was three and I was four. we swept up the Ooster Schelde across Scheren and spotted some boats on our port wing. The C.O. climbed and turned so steeply that I had to pull across hard to lose ground. Saw C.O. and Blackie go in and the boats were covered in strikes. There were two boats and a tug together on one side and a large ship about a thousand tonner on the other side. We attacked the two boats first and by the time I managed to get in mine it was almost abeam. I accidentally released my bombs before I meant to and doubt if they did much damage to the boats, they were both covered with cannon strikes though. After that we milled around in circles firing at whatever turned up ahead. Once I found myself meeting another kite head on.

The tug left the two boats to their fate and started steaming madly for the shore. I caught it about half way there and all the cabin and engine in the centre of the boat seemed to go up in a sheet of flame. I felt quite sorry for whoever was on it. Probably some poor old Dutch sailor.

As we turned toward the island there was some quite accurate light flak whistling past me, once I thought it was some other kite firing at me. When the C.O. called us off, the big boat was definitely sinking and the others must have been in a bad way. I picked up Blackie and we stooged along together until we saw the C.O. having a crack at an 'E' boat. Not to be done out of any fun. I made a tight turn and beat Blackie to it. Saw strikes all over the boat and Chas who followed us in said it was well alight when he got there.

The C.O. then had a go at what we called a coaster on the report, but which we later thought must have been a ferry boat, Blackie followed him in but I was too close to get in a burst.

We then made our way out to sea, some hopeful Hun on a light gun let off a couple of rounds at us as we went, but they were very

wide. On the way out picked up Bob Moore who had got parted
from MacKickan. They were the only two of 'A' flight to get there
but had done quite well. 198 Sqdn also did pretty well.

Monday, 4 October 1943
    Lea Sinclair lost on Roadstead. Seen to crash land and believed
to be OK. Rickie Pullen our new flight commander.

The first and last operation that I flew with S/L Hawkins was one which
stays in my memory. It was another low-level attack with 250-pound bombs,
on the Sinclair oil refinery, north of Ghent in Belgium. The operation was at
squadron strength, eight aircraft setting out at wave top height via the Dutch
islands. The C.O. led 'B' flight, and I was his number two. The other two in
'B' flight were a New Zealand pilot, Byron Lumsden, and his number two
Dickie Wingate. The 'A' flight was led by Rickie Pullen, with Buck Feldman,
Canadian 'Rocky' La Rocque, and a fourth whose name escapes me.

    Nearing the Belgium coast, Lumsden broke radio silence, saying he had
hydraulic trouble and was turning back. Dickie was detailed to go back with
him. It was usual to stay in pairs. It was impossible to see immediately behind
your own tail, but as a pair you flew probably fifty yards apart and could
watch across each other's rear end. So Lumsden and Dickie turned back.
More bombs jettisoned into the sea. The rest of us continued, turning in
down the Ooster Schelde and flying inland just clearing the hedges, and
pulling up only for the bigger obstructions. On time the C.O. turned to starboard onto the second leg of the route, and we headed south.

    We were running parallel to a canal, probably a quarter of a mile to our
right, with occasional glimpses of it through poplar trees along it's banks.
Then suddenly there was the refinery on the far side of the canal.

    It needed a fairly steep turn to get round onto the target and Rickie
Pullen and 'A' flight on our left dropped some way back in the turn, so that
the C.O. with me on his right crossed the canal together, and on our own. I
was aware of light ack-ack fire crossing from our left, but I was too fully occupied to notice more. We were heading for the main building on the site, bordering the far side of the canal, and with a tall steel chimney sticking out of
its centre.

    I released the bombs halfway across the canal, and immediately had to
pull back to clear the building and bank steeply to starboard to avoid the
chimney. As I straightened out the C.O. was slightly above me, banking
slightly the opposite way to port, so that the underside of his plane was
towards me. There was a small flame and trail of smoke coming from
beneath the cockpit. I realised it would mean a forced landing and called up
to tell him he was on fire, turning at the same time towards him to see him

down OK. He continued in the shallow banked turn, slowly losing height, and without any apparent attempt to avoid it, crashed into a small copse of trees, the plane going up in a huge ball of fire. At first I was stunned at the sight, but this was followed by rage. I was still turning to port over the edge of the refinery area, and I could see the main building collapsing like a house of cards. I could also see a carpet of twinkling lights from the ack ack all along the rail sidings which bordered the canal. I dived onto these with my cannons going. Then suddenly, when the attention of all the guns turned on me, I realised how foolhardy I was being. I ran the guns along the row of rail trucks, where the ack-ack guns were mounted, opening the throttle wide and pulling straight up for the clouds, kicking first one rudder then the other. Gunners always have to aim ahead of the target, and if you are skidding sideways to the way you are pointing there is some chance you may fool them, or so I kidded myself. It seemed an age before I reached the clouds, with tracers crossing in front and on all sides of the plane, but I reached the clouds without harm, and concentrated on instruments until suddenly I broke through into bright sunshine at about three thousand feet.

I flew a course which would take me roughly towards home keeping a wary eye out for unfriendlies. I felt rather vulnerable all alone skimming the top surface of the clouds. I would have stood out well against the pure white of the sunlit cloud. Once I came down through it and was surprised to find I was still over land. Was even more surprised to see an aerodrome laid out beneath me to my left, so I popped back through the cloud again before anyone down there woke up. Eventually, I tried again, and this time, I was over sea, and I called for a homing and was directed back to Manston. 'A' flight had been down a little while. I think they had given up on me, and I was told that W/O La Rocque had bought it. He was seen to pull up to about three thousand feet and then dive straight in.

Two days later, I was called into the office, where MacKickan was with a lady who I thought at the time was S/L Hawkins wife. Since the war, I have talked to his nephew, and it appears it was his sister-in-law since he was never married. Perhaps I got it wrong or maybe memory plays tricks after so long. She wanted a detailed account of his going. She could not believe that he wouldn't be coming back through Gibraltar as he had before. It was dreadful talking to her. I hated having to destroy her hopes, but no one was coming away from that crash.

We later saw some of the cine film taken from the planes, and it was some of the most impressive I ever saw. One shot in particular was of a water tower holed by cannon shells, with water gushing out of its side.

S/L Hawkins replacement was S/L Allen Dredge. His arrival also heralded a new era for 3 Squadron. Dredge was a tall, well built man, and I liked his looks. He had previously been shot down and burnt, and had

Rickie Pullen in the later version of the Typhoon. Note the sliding canopy.

Rickie Pullen.

Bob Cole.

Bob Moore.

Dickie Wingate.

Watercolour painted by one of the ground crew at Manston around 1943. For seven shillings and sixpence, he would paint these based on a pilot's own ideas, including his personal squadron letters. Most of the pilots at that time had one done.

subsequently undergone painful skin surgery. This had been extremely well done, but still showed as two half moons under his eyes. As with Hawkins, previous experience coloured his outlook, and he immediately put into effect new rules for the boys, most of them anti-burn. No more flying with rolled up shirt sleeves however hot the weather; battledress will be worn. Flying boots will be worn, not gym shoes as of yore. Goggles will be worn especially on take off and landing. Hoods will be open and locked at takeoff and landing.

There was a good deal of grumbling; you could melt into a grease spot even in shirt sleeves with that big 2,000-horsepower Sabre engine in front of your nose. However, I think the discipline was needed, and I could see the sense of the new decrees. The one thing that ever really worried me was the thought of getting burnt.

In addition, our mode of operation changed. No more low level bombing; dive bombing from now on. I believe this change came from on high. Losses on low level trips, both the 'rhubarbs' and the squadron operations had been very heavy, and squadron leaders were not immune. Perhaps they were getting short of them! I'm not sure we were terribly enthusiastic about this change either. Low-level flying was exciting. Unfortunately, it's also dangerous.

We were sent off to practice with little smoke bombs, on a wooden raft moored off the Isle of Sheppey. I don't know if these smoke bombs would have the same trajectory as a genuine 500-pound bomb, but I wasn't impressed with our results in practice. Looking back after dropping the bomb and searching for the puff of smoke, I thought it looked quite good, but I was told later: "120 yards short", "80 yards short." I suppose a 500-pound bomb a hundred yards away would be near enough to bring down a ceiling or two, but I would have loved just one direct hit. Then started a series of dive bombing operations, often against coastal shipping, rail yards or junctions, or specific targets set for us. We would take off in pairs, would make one circuit of the airfield, later pairs turning inside the others until on the downwind leg all would be more or less in formation and course would be set out to sea. We would climb steadily, until over the target we would have gained about 8,000 feet.

The C.O. would approach to one side of the target, call up "echelon starboard" or "echelon port" and the other section would cross to stack up with the C.O. nearest the target. Then he would announce "going down now" and immediately roll over on his back and dive vertically on the target. The idea was to use the gunsight to line up with the target, pull slowly back until the target almost vanished under the nose, and release the bombs. During the dive we were in line astern and concentrating on aiming so that we would have been very vulnerable if we had been bounced by enemy aircraft, but I never knew it happen.

By the bottom of the dive we would of course be fair travelling, and I suppose that was our main protection. Depending on our target, ack ack fire could be quite heavy, but it was true that our losses were dramatically reduced, and I think that we were more effective.

The Dutch Islands were a favourite hunting ground, and when bombs were gone we were still able to shoot up barges and small ships with our cannons. 'E' boats had to be watched. They often escorted small convoys of coastal shipping.

They were heavily armed and their gunners were good. They probably had had the practice.

Monday, 1 November 1943

After a long rest from ops and seven days leave we did our first trip with our new C.O. S/L Dredge Went on a Roadstead to the Dutch islands only instead of our usual low level effort we were dive bombing. Jerry has been sending his boats up around the islands, in convoy, escorted by swarms of E boats since 3 and 198 made it their happy hunting ground.

The show went off well. We climbed as soon as we turned in the Ooster Schelde, turned north and saw a convoy of about ten coasters and a dozen or so E boats. Our dive was almost vertical and the results all the better for that. Though no direct hits were scored all the bombs fell inside a circle drawn round the boats and must have strained many of their plates, and its likely some of them sank. Reformed straight away and returned home. Was too easy.

Rumours and reports began to be bandied about, of a new weapon the Germans had. Bob Barckley returned from a night Rhubarb reporting having seen a flying object like a small plane with a long fiery tail. Ramps were being built on Gris Nez and the Pas de Calais area and aerial photos showed these with what looked like small aircraft on them. Others wrecked around the ramps and signs of explosions off of their ends.

I'm not sure that at this time we on the squadron knew exactly what was going on, but some mischief was obviously afoot. The squadron was given the job of bombing these sites. This we did up until we started refitting with the Tempest and moved to Bradwell Bay. We would take off from Manston, climbing steadily until we would be at around 8,000 feet over the target area. Our dive bombing routine would then be performed: drop bombs, level out, and re-form on the C.O., returning home still in a shallow dive and probably still doing over 400 mph back at Manston. It took thirty-five minutes for the round trip, from takeoff to touchdown, and we were each doing three of these trips a day.

If you were among the first down in the dive, you didn't see the strikes, but the tail enders could see the strikes of those ahead, and the accuracy looked quite impressive. Word came back from on high that, from photo-recon, our efforts were very effective.

It was not all good being at the tail end though. Since we followed one another down in the dive, we were very vulnerable. Air attack just didn't happen. Maybe we were too good for them; more likely, their fighters were kept busy with the big American raids over their own soil. However, it didn't take them long to move the gunners, and these were frighteningly accurate. I suppose the way we so quickly rolled on our backs and in effect reversed direction must have been difficult to predict, but by the time the tail enders were all following the same line down, they were able to get on target and we weren't without our losses.

Sunday, 7 November 1943
    Ramrod on a special constructional target at Mimogogue on Cap Gris Nez. 10/10 cloud over channel and we turned back half way over.

Wednesday, 10 November 1943

Ramrod on a special target on Griz Nez. Quite a lot of heavy flak. I was in the first section, there were twelve kites, two of whom were 195 boys who were at Manston for night intruders. I had released my bombs and as I pulled out of the dive I looked back over my shoulder and could see the following planes still in their dive. There was also a good deal of flak, and high up what looked like a huge ball of fire, tumbling over and over like a gigantic catherine wheel, leaving a trail of fire behind it. The flame was so fierce that I couldn't even be sure that it was a plane. Bob Walmesly was missing when we got back. They had been using phosphorous shells against us, so that it was only necessary to fly through the spray from them to catch fire. After the dive we just let the kite continue diving until we were well over the coast. We were still doing over 350 when we were back over Manston.

In the afternoon we had another show on a village on Cap Gris Nez called Audighen. There was 10/10 cloud over the target and we had to turn back. As it was, quite a bit of flak came up through the clouds, controlled by A.I. I suppose. Someone was getting hell over Calais, the flak was as thick as I've seen it.

Thursday 11, November 1943

In the afternoon did another show on Audighen. Was an easy show. Climbed from Lympne and dived slightly so as to have plenty of speed over target. Came in out of the sun, did an almost vertical dive and kept the nose down until well out to sea. There was no flak and I honestly don't think they realised what was happening until we were well out to sea.

Was on intruder readiness and almost got a trip. Was booked for a trip to Amiens Glisy, weather held me up until it was too late to be worth while. Taxied out to end of runway and was told to go back. Weather was so bad that no one reached their targets anyway.

Friday, 19 November 1943

Was spare on a show on another of these special targets. No one fell out so I had to drop my bombs in the sea and return. It always grieves me to see good bombs wasted like that and I never could understand why the spare shouldn't carry on and drop them somewhere where they would do more good. Heard today that these special targets are rocket guns under construction. Audighen is the headquarters of Jerrie's 'Works and Bricks' which is why it is getting so much attention.

Saturday, 20 November 1943

In morning was on a show to Audighen but had engine cuts on 'X' almost as soon as I left the ground. Had to make one circuit and land behind the last two who were taking off. They just got off in time. It was a shaky business, I had visions of myself making a belly landing in a field with bombs on.

In the afternoon we dived bombed Audighen again. Some light flak came up but not near enough to worry us. Results were pretty good again.

Sunday, 21 November 1943

Had a show on special target on the Cherbourg peninsula and started for Ford where we were to refuel. The weather was right down on the deck and we got off Deal and turned back. Landing was tricky as you could see the plane in front but that was about all. Other sections kept looming up out of the mist and it was all very nerve racking. When finally I got down the runway loomed up almost underneath me and I made an awful landing, I was thankful to be down however.

Tuesday, 23 November 1943

Another uneventful show on Audighen. Really is too easy, I suppose they'll move some heavy flak in soon and surprise us. The light stuff they have now doesn't even reach us.

Thursday, 25 November 1943

Dive bombed Audighen again, it must be a very unhealthy spot to live I should think. Returned to Ford where we refuelled and bombed up again for the Cherbourg do. I was spare, and having dumped my bombs in the sea returned to Manston.

One regular duty which no one liked was a patrol along the enemy coast, looking for shipping and reporting on the weather over the continent. Two pairs would take off and fly across to somewhere off Cap Gris Nez. One pair would fly north and the other south just off the coast peering into all the harbours, going in for a closer look if anything interesting was seen and returning to report. Usually, these trips were uneventful, but even so, we did lose people, such as Jimmy Mannion.

The weather report had to include an estimate of amount and height of cloud cover over the channel ports and sea ways. There was little point in taking a squadron of planes over if you couldn't see your target for clouds.

Nevertheless these were abortive trips, and always on the way back the bombs were jettisoned 'safe' into the sea. It seemed a terrible waste to me. Even if we lobbed them target unseen into Calais harbour, they might have done some good. I suppose the French were our friends (some of them), and I suppose indiscriminate bombing is not on. Even dropped safe, they would have given someone the job of digging them out, and any hindrance to the German war effort would have been something. I'm sure they did no good at all to the fish in mid Channel. These special targets were of course V1 launch sites being constructed.

On one of our trips Bob Cole's bombs refused to be jettisoned. We had been up at 4.30, were at intelligence by 5.00, and were airborne by 8.30. We had dive bombed a coastal battery at Hardelot with twelve aircraft. Westland Whirlwinds had bombed the same target the night before and again that morning. In the channel there were hundreds of small landing craft, some only a few miles from the enemy coast (this was the 9 September rehearsal for landings). The target was very hard to see in among sand dunes and the bombing appeared to be very haphazard. On our way back we circled over the channel hoping for some joy but Jerry wasn't playing. Coming back, Bob called up to say he had a hangup. Bob was on the radio by now, very excited —or perhaps agitated is a better word. He was told to leave the squadron and try to shake them off, but apparently, this did no good either.

Meanwhile we were approaching the coast, and when the C.O. could get a word in, he told Bob not to cross the coast until he'd got rid of the bombs.

By this time the squadron had reached Manston and had peeled off to land and I sat listening to the unfolding saga of Bob and his bombs. Apparently he'd tried everything except outside loops to lose the blessed things, and they still wouldn't move. By now Bob was worrying about the fuel situation, while the C.O. was more concerned about the possibility of nasty hard, heavy, lumps of iron falling on local friends' heads, especially if his pilot had got the switches wrong and they fell 'live'. He was ordering Bob not to cross the coast while he still had them. Sarcastically, Bob offered to bale out. There was no answer, so he made up his own mind and declared, "I'm coming in!"

About halfway down the runway was Butch's plane with two burst tyres. It had run off to the left of the runway, and already a crowd of ground crew had gathered, and were under the wing, lifting to try to get a jack under.

The Typhoon's jack was a masterpiece of design. With something difficult like a jet engine we can excel, but a simple jack is almost certain to be a disaster. The Typhoon jack was perfectly efficient once you got it located in the jack points, but it wouldn't go under with a flat tyre without about twenty bodies under the wing straining to lift the plane first.

Bob came gliding in and as he touched down, the port bomb came off and went skating along the ground. The fins came off of the back, and it started tumbling along over and over like a rugby ball, straight for Butch's aircraft. Men ran in all directions, and I put my hands over my ears. It came to rest quite peacefully about ten yards from Butch's plane and just lay there. I hadn't seen men run so fast in years, and I noticed afterwards everyone gave it a wide berth until bomb disposal had cleared it away.

I don't know what was said to Bob, I think the C.O. was probably glad the incident ended without calamity.

On another occasion I made an apparently normal landing, but after running about fifty yards, the undercarriage folded up, the nose settled, and I ground to a sudden stop, amid graunching noises, and a cloud of dust.

It seemed safer to stay where I was until everyone was down. So there was I, sitting at the beginning of the runway, looking back anxiously over my shoulder. I was grilled about my landing and was told that when the plane was lifted the legs dropped down and locked. I was told that I couldn't have made sure that they were locked properly before coming in. There were indicator lights on the dashboard, and a horn blasted in your ear if you throttled right back without the wheels down and locked, and as a 'last ditch' indication, a couple of white tipped rods showed above the wing surface, all of which I had checked.

I was sent down to see the plane towed to the hanger and find out if there was any trouble. When I got to the plane, it was standing on the grass on the far side of the perimeter track. An iron rod about one inch in diameter, with a hook either end had been attached between the bottoms of the legs, and they were just hitching it up to a tractor.

As the tractor pulled away and the plane bumped over the asphalt track, the iron rod broke, the legs folded up and the whole lot settled on it's nose again. 'Locked down!'

With so much happening it's not surprising that there was quite a lot of superstition. Canadians seemed to come and go in quick succession, and we came to look with a certain amount of pity when newly fledged Canadians joined us.

One of the 'A' flight planes was letter 'I' and this went missing with such regularity that although it was the newest plane on the squadron, no one wanted to fly it. In the end that letter was dropped in favour of another and the trouble seemed to stop.

Many pilots had their mascots, and even I always felt much safer in my own plane, letter 'R', than in any other. Yet in the end I was shot down over Germany in yes, letter 'R'. In addition, I wouldn't dream of flying without the Paisley scarf Joy had given me. I managed to keep it right through prison camp, and have it yet.

As I've already mentioned, the squadron had a variety of nationalities among it's number. We had four Belgiums, three Poles, three New Zealanders, various Canadians, two Americans and no doubt others I can't think of now. There was always a good deal of good humoured banter from which the British were usually content to remain aloof.

One day, an argument broke out in dispersal on the relative merits of this one's country and that one's country—a heated debate over which actually was 'God's country'. The loudest contenders were the New Zealanders and the Americans. We British looked on with amused tolerance—we knew!

From somewhere amongst his kit, McCook produced a New Zealand flag. This was snatched away, flying this way and that across the room, stuffed in the stove, snatched out smoking slightly, grabbed back by McCook and stuffed up the front of his battledress. The melee continued outside as Hutcheson and Lumsden hoisted McCook up onto the dispersal hut roof, where he scrambled up to the iron stove pipe chimney and proceeded to tie the flag to it.

There was quite a to do about this, with quite a lot of jeering and near brawling, as McCook slid down the roof, over the gutter and into the middle of it all.

Lefty Whitman was intent on climbing up on the roof to pull the flag down, while the New Zealanders were intent on stopping him, with Buck Feldman and others gleefully adding to the din. It really was just like a rugby scrum!

In the middle of all this Lefty vanished into the hut, came out with the shotgun we were supposed to practice skeet shooting with, and blasted a great hole, right through the centre of the flag. This made the New Zealanders really furious and the brawl became more acrimonious and raged around the dispersal most of the afternoon.

I think this was the only time I remember Buck Feldman and Lefty Whitman siding together, except in the abuse they both hurled at the U.S.A.F. whenever a plane with American markings hove into sight. Both Buck and Lefty, who had many hours of civilian flying time in the States, had been turned down by the U.S.A.F. because they did not have college educations. They crossed the border to Canada and joined the R.C.A.F. The two Americans were often bickering, which usually ended with some comic quip from Lefty. He usually got the last word in. I remember Buck once calling him, with little truth, a "fat assed bastard", and Lefty's quick reply was, "Well, I guess you can't drive a spike with a tack hammer!" I've heard this crack many times since, but in 1943 it was fresh, and everyone roared with laughter, which upset Buck even more. Another time, Buck accused him of having no ambition, and Lefty came right back with, "Sure, I've got ambition. I want to live to be a hundred and then hang for rape".

The C.O. of the squadron was allowed his own light aircraft. This was usually a Tiger Moth, but at Manston our C.O. was allocated a Miles Magister. Although the plane was normally for the C.O.'s use, it was, with his permission, used as a squadron runabout. It was used for a variety of errands, such as sending Lefty Whitman around the American bases in the locality to buy up the hard stuff, which was elsewhere in extremely short supply but necessary for making a squadron party go with a swing. I only flew the Magister twice. On the first of these occasions, I was asked to take F/O Lumsden to Gatwick. He was going on a course somewhere nearby. Gatwick was just a grass strip at the time. It's now a private flying club, a mile or two north of the modern airport.

Lumsden flew the plane there, and on landing immediately hoisted his bag out and vanished. I reported to the control tower and went back to the plane. It was the first time I had ever flown a plane not fitted with a starter. Even the Stearman PT 13 primary trainer had one. So I was not familiar with the procedure for starting with a man on the prop. This, switches off; switches on; chocks away stuff! Luckily the fitter sent to help had done it all before, and I got away with no trouble, but some little embarrassment. Back at Manston, I had no real idea of landing speed and came in much too fast. It floated along the runway for what seemed miles, and by the time it finally stalled on, I had a fair bit of drift on. I was lucky to get down without damage.

The second occasion I was asked to fly Flight Sergeant Jock Smith from Manston to Swanton Morley. The weather was not good. Solid low cloud, but said to be possible, so we took off. All went well, until we got near Faversham where we ran into patches of cloud on the deck so I decided to climb above it. This turned out to be a bad mistake for pretty soon we were flying between two layers of ten tenth's cloud and not wanting to get lost decided to go back down through it again. We struggled on hoping it would lift, but a couple of times houses and trees reached out of the gloom almost beneath our wheels. The instruments on the Magister were quite basic, not really intended for prolonged blind flying. I had to keep low to get back to flying by visual, but each time I let down we saw the tops of trees and houses suddenly appear. I had no option but to turn back. In the turn the compass started spinning and it was possible I was in a steeper turn than I intended. However, we got back to lower ground and were able to see our way back to Manston. Jock said he had never been so scared in his life, and at one time had seriously considered baling out. I told him that I had never been so scared either, and it's true that at one point I felt dangerously near panic. I can't remember what happened to Jock, but he didn't survive on the squadron long after that.

As the British war effort picked up, the large four engined bombers appeared on the scene, and the raids on Germany were increased in size so that thousand bomber raids became common. In the morning as we walked from breakfast in the mess to the dispersal, we often walked via a field, across the road from the control tower, where the nights crop of wrecks were left. This field was known to the locals as 'The Graveyard'. The number of wrecks ending up at Manston increased after the concrete runway had been built. Three thousand yards long and three hundred yards wide, it was divided into three in length , and three in width, and returning planes could land on the appropriate section according to their needs. A plane with a fire on board would be requested to land on one sector where the fire fighting equipment was waiting. A plane with wounded on board would be requested to another sector which would have medical services such as ambulances etc ready. A plane with undercarriage failure necessitating a belly landing would use a sector where crash crews and winches could drag wreckage clear.

If the weather was fine there was always a fair collection of Halifaxes and Stirlings and, later, Lancasters. Most were in a terribly bad state. Shot to ribbons, by AA fire, and fighters. We rarely saw a German fighter on our trips; they were obviously being kept back for the protection of the homeland. We saw even more of the Americans returning from their daylight raids in Flying Fortresses and Liberators.

The Liberator had a good reputation, but on two separate occasions I saw one break up over the end of the runway. I suppose the pilot would be coming in, in various states of desperation and relief at seeing safety at last. They used to come in from all directions intent on lobbing down as quickly as possible. On both of these occasions red Very Lights were fired from the control tower because there was a danger of collision, and the pilot had to open the throttles to go round again. Strangely enough, each time they were landing in a southwest to northeast direction, and were right opposite our dispersal, when a wisp of smoke could be seen from the starboard, inboard engine followed immediately by flames. The wing then folded at this engine, and the plane crashed in from about 200 feet just beyond the boundary of the field. Everyone on board was lost, and after getting back so close to safety it seemed particularly tragic. The two occasions were almost identical in the way they happened!

One morning, on our way down to dispersal, we were surprised to find a different kind of visitor: a mint condition FW 190. The story went around that the pilot had landed during the night after getting lost. Thinking that when crossing the Thames estuary he was crossing the channel, he landed at the first airfield he'd seen—Manston. There was great interest among us pilots and speculation about our chances of flying it, but it soon vanished from Manston. I imagine it was taken away for investigation into its potential.

On another occasion Bob Cole and I were called into the C.O.'s office and told to go out into the Channel and shoot down two barrage balloons reported to be drifting a few miles off the French coast. We took off and were guided on to them by the D.F. station. They were quite easy to see from some way off. They were at about a thousand feet and each was anchored by a cable to it's own pontoon float. Bob took one, and I took the other. We thought this would be great fun—one burst and the whole lot would go up in flames—but it didn't happen like that. On the first pass I thought I must have missed it, for it remained apparently unscathed. I made a second pass and took much greater care. I set the throttle steady, trimmed the aircraft so that it had neither skid nor slip, and was nicely lined up and within range before I fired.

This time, I actually saw the strikes puncturing the fabric, but still no flames and still it floated along quite unconcerned as if untouched. I stayed around some time and it was obvious that the balloon was collapsing slowly, but it was disappointing really. Since the Typhoon was loaded with armour-piercing and incendiary rounds at intervals along the belt, I can only assume the balloon was filled with some inert gas, though probably not helium. Bob had a similar experience with his balloon, and we were both amazed and disappointed that our targets didn't have a more spectacular demise.

Saturday, 18 December 1943.
    Ramrod to another rocket installation near Hesdin. There was 10/10 cloud over the target so we dive bombed Buck Sur Mer aerodrome on the way out.

Wednesday, 22 December 1943.
    Did two shows on a special target at Beauvais. On the first I was No 2 to the C.O. and it was a very good show indeed. The dive was almost vertical, I managed to keep right under his tail and all the bombs went on the target, about the best bombing I've seen. On the second I was No 2 to Lum and in the dive I overran him even with the throttle right back, and so had to pull out to one side which rather spoiled my aim. But even so wasn't too far out. Only two bombs weren't on the target area and they fell on the runway of the aerodrome next door.

The Pas de Calais was also bombed by light bombers such as Bostons, Mitchells and the like, but our raids were said to be the most effective. Mind you how effective that was is open to debate. When the V1 'Doodlebug' later appeared over the southern counties of England, they appeared in droves despite our attempts to destroy the ramps!! I believe many of the personnel and stores for the V1s were underground and the ramps probably didn't take too much to repair or re-build.

Tuesday 28, December 1943
    Squadron moved to Swanton Morley for anti-shipping duties with Beaufighters. Nobody very pleased about it.

We were moved to Swanton Morley in Norfolk about fifteen miles west from Norwich, to escort Beaufighters that were planning to carry out anti-shipping raids round the Frisian Islands.

Tuesday, 4 January 1944

Was on a fighter escort to Beaufighters in the morning with long range tanks. On take off a terrific blob of oil came back and completely blacked out my windscreen. Circled a couple of times till all the boys were off and then came in to land with my head hanging out of the window. Anyway the boys turned back owing to bad weather.

Wednesday, 5 January 1944

Roadstead off the Hook. Half way over McCook had trouble, R.T. U/S, generator afire, and U/S instruments. He turned back and I went with him. I thought he was leading the way whereas actually he had no map. By this time the visibility was down to about half a mile, and it was more by luck than judgement that we found the field. Squadron saw nothing and turned back after dropping their bombs in the sea.

Monday, 10 January 1944

Got a trip in a Mitchell of the gunnery flight. Edwards was making attacks on it for the benefit of the air gunners. Very nice after a Typhoon, to have room to move around, and not get your teeth loosened by the vibration. Eddie's attacks were pretty good but he was cold meat on most of his break aways. Once the Mitchell even got on the Tiffies tail. I was rather shaken to find how steeply they can turn too. I bet the Tiffy had a job to follow it round in some of them. On the way back Eddie formatted on us, and the pilot turned on some music on the radio. Landing seemed strange on the tricycle undercarriage and I expected there to be a terrific crash the way he brought it in. It was quite smooth actually however. It was good fun and something different to relieve the monotony. I thoroughly enjoyed the trip.

Tuesday, 11 January 1944

Did a long range escort to Beaufighters. Was just a practice show to see how we made out on petrol. Was flying No 2 to Wingate, in 'S'. When we first started off and formed up with the Beau's we both overshot by quite a bit for they were stooging along at about two twenty. At first it was pretty awful. Right down at sea level, and the old Tiffy mushing along as if it would stall any minute. Whenever Wingate turned towards me I thought I had had it and was going to spin in. After a while however I got quite used to it. Did forty minutes on each long range tank and for the last ten on each I was expecting the motor to cut. However it didn't, which kind of proves there's something in this praying racket after all. At the first turn the Beau's speeded things up to about two forty. I had to cross over on the turn and almost got mixed up with the Beau's. The extra speed made things a bit more comfortable and later when we pulled up to a thousand feet I was almost happy. The journey home was more or less uneventful. The weather showed signs of clamping down as we got farther south and all the Beau's except their leader made a dirty dive for home. I got back with about twenty gallons showing in each nose tank after two and three quarter hours flying. When they filled the kite they found that I had used a hundred and fifty eight gallons, an average of fifty eight gallons per hour, not bad going. Why we can't do these tests at a safe height and over land I really don't know. An engine cut at that height and speed and its finis, you wouldn't stand an earthly.

Wednesday, 19 January 1944

First morning with weather good enough for flying for ages. Air tests were the order of the day. I took 'R' up for an airing and was stooging along happily over Dereham when I spotted a Typhoon closing in on the port quarter, obviously wanting to play. Guessed it was Rickie, and turned steeply towards him. An aileron turn right down to the deck and a climbing turn up to about two thousand and we were on opposite sides of the turn. I had the advantage anyway, as he had long range tanks on and I didn't.

Then I saw another kite joining in the fun, and he was close on Rickie's tail when I recognised it as a Thunderbolt. As a couple of 198 Sqdn were shot up by Thunderbolts who apparently mistook them for 190's only a week or two back, I called up and told Rickie and he answered that he had seen it already. Rickie was having a job to cope with the Thunderbolt with the L.R. tanks on he couldn't out turn it and it stuck like glue to his tail. I was following on the Thunderbolts tail until over the drome I was in a very tight turn when the seat went down with a crash and by the time I had got it up I had lost them.

Had settled down to a nice comfortable stooge again when suddenly I spotted the Thunderbolt coming after me again. I whipped into a turn towards him, but neither of us seemed to be able to out turn the other, I think that had I used about ten degrees of flap I could have out turned him easily enough, as it was I was a little better then holding my own. I found that by following an aileron turn by a really steep climbing turn I could leave him miles behind and could certainly have got away from him any time I liked. We finally broke it up and I came in to land. I really enjoyed the trip, I think we could do with a lot more practice at dog fighting and a trip like that certainly does you a world of good.

Friday, 21 January 1944

Did what was supposed to be a roadstead, with six bombers and six long range fighters. I flew No2 to Ken. Ken had trouble in getting his door shut and we were almost late taking off, still we caught up OK Swept for about twenty miles, off the Dutch coast north of Ijmuiden without seeing any shipping other than a fishing fleet so the boys unloaded their cargo on the steel works at Ijmuiden with pretty good results. While the boys were doing their stuff we were supposed to sweep inland behind them. For some reason however Mc turned out to sea.

It was funny to sit up there and watch someone else doing the graft. there was quite a bit of flak, very wild at first, then a concentrated barrage over the target which was quite wasted because the boys were well away by that time, and finally some quite accurate heavy stuff followed us about three miles out to sea. I think we must have caught them pretty well napping. Most of the bombers arrived back with next to nothing in the tanks, which made it unpleasant for them as it was also for me, for I flew out, and home, looking directly into the sun.

On the way out I had a good look at the target and it certainly wasn't too healthy a spot. I didn't see a single bomb burst outside the target, and huge columns of smoke and steam were coming from some of the buildings, so though it wasn't successful as a Roadstead, we did do some damage to something this time.

Thursday, February 3 1944

My first day back from nine days leave. Was on early morning show. Took off at eight fifteen with navigation lights on, eight bombers and four long range fighters. Blackie Schwarz had trouble with the L.R. tanks and had to force land on Horsham St Faiths pumping the primer to keep the engine going. Switched nav' lights off as we crossed the coast. I was flying in the C.O.'S section No2 to

Lum and found I was kept pretty busy on the throttle to keep with him. About ten miles from the enemy coast we started climbing and I had to use pretty high revs and boost to keep up with the C.O. Had visions of the petrol draining away in buckets. Did a couple of orbits over the islands looking for targets and saw a few old barges. Then the C.O. turned out again and bombed a concentration of barges in the entrance to a canal. I wasn't quite sure what he was going after as my R.T. was a bit duff and I didn't hear all that was said. However once in the dive it was pretty obvious as the barges were the only possible target. One of Lum's bombs hung up and fell off some while afterwards. As we were crossing the coast on the way out quite a bit of accurate flak came up near Lum and I, not many of the others even saw any though.

About twenty miles out on the way back someone screamed, "mayday, mayday" over the R.T. and a few seconds later Chas Tidy came through to say that Green H had ditched. The whole squadron did an orbit but saw nothing of green section and not having petrol to spare carried on home. I had already had my engine cut when my petrol gauge said thirty gallons in each tank so I didn't trust the gauge and was rather worried about the petrol situation. The remaining two of green section who had long range tanks on however stayed over the spot where the plane went in until we were almost home, sending 'Maydays'. When we got back found it was Johnny Earle who had gone in. When Chas and Ken got back they said he had clouds of brown smoke pouring from his engine. They saw him go in and apparently he made a good landing and the plane floated with the tail high in the air for about ten seconds. Something flew off when it hit and they thought at first that it was Johnny, later though there was a L.R. tank floating around and they thought it was probably that. Bloody bad luck, for such a piffling target too.

The camp at Swanton Morley was pretty isolated, and it's inhabitants generally pretty starchy compared to those on the average fighter station. We were in trouble from the start. The other squadron stationed there were flying Mitchells, and we N.C.O's saw little of them. Our officers met them in the officers' mess of course, and quickly put up a whole heap of 'blacks'.

The officers' cook used to bake a large iced cake once a week. Our lot were early turning up at the mess and sliced off all four sides and the top of the cake before the bomber boys got there. Their C.O. used to make a habit of standing back to the fire warming himself with a few of his cronies around him, but those of 3 Squadron not on readiness were again able to get there first. I gather he was quite put out.

One night, they had a mess do, when the officers were permitted to invite their N.C.O. colleagues for an evening at the bar. It wasn't long before soda siphons were being hosed around. I suppose the joke palls a little when you have to buy your own uniforms. Anyway the evening came to an abrupt end when four of our number were caught rolling a barrel of beer out of the back entrance of the officers mess, and a running battle with soda siphons ensued all the way down the road to our own billet. I'm sure that we won, but rank will always count; we had to give the barrel back and apologise.

Ken Slade-Betts, normally the nicest and quietest of chaps, used to go berserk when drunk and that night he was stinking! I remember that when he was finally coaxed away from the officers mess by the subtle means of insult followed by retreat in the desired direction, he went around the room tipping the beds upside down on their occupants. Having eventually coaxed him to bed, and with things settling down, he would leap out of bed with a roar, and it would all start over again.

Our room was in one wing of an 'H' block. There was a dividing wall across the centre of the cross bar of the H. and on the far side of the wall lived the W.A.A.F.s. They were ruled by a fearsome female who, dead on lights out, flung over the main switch for the whole block. This was not appreciated by us, but was suffered until one night Bob Cole was caught in a late bath. With a towel round his waist, he stormed down the stairs, dripping soap suds all the way, out of the building and round the road, into the W.A.A.F.'s entrance and up the stairs amid girlish squeals (of terror? I doubt it!), and slammed over the switch and stormed out to finish his bath. The lights stayed on—that night and in the future. The battle axe must have decided against war and put the individual room switches off. The main switch stayed on.

On several occasions we were in trouble over missing the R.A.F. transport back to camp. West Dereham was the nearest small town where there was the odd pub, cafe, and the occasional local shop. Twice we got stranded. There were a good many American bases in Norfolk and none of the local people would open their doors after dark. They seemed to be terrified. One night, we were advised through a letter box to try the local police station, but I think the cells were full already. They suggested an army unit nearby where we not only got a bed, but also a good breakfast in the sergeants mess.

We were also stranded twice in Norwich. The first time was not Bob's fault —pretty unusual! The station bus could not get back to camp because a real pea souper fog came down. I doubt you could see more than four to six feet.

It was very cold in the bus and Bob and I decided we would try to find somewhere to stay. We were soon lost and when we found an hotel sign we opened a door and went in. The door led straight onto an uncarpeted stair-case, and at the top an open door to the right showed a room where it appeared the hotel waiters rested, changed etc. There were a couple of old arm chairs, a gas fire, and a row of waiters coats hanging on hooks. What more could a cold and weary airman want! We lit the fire, bedded down in the armchairs, and slept. When we awoke it was after daybreak. We put every-thing back the way we'd found it, and quietly left. I often wondered who was responsible for locking up at night in that hotel. We were grateful to him for missing the servants' entrance that night.

It was still foggy, and we found the bus more by luck than anything, and got back to camp. It was still too foggy for flying.

The second occasion was certainly down to Bob. By now he had met a local girl. We decided we would go to a dance in a hall called the Hercules and Sampson, and you had to start queuing up early to get in. Bob thought he would try and see his girl meantime while I held his place in the queue.

Eventually, after probably an hour, the door opened, the queue started moving and I reached the pay desk. I let people behind go in front and when I was almost giving up altogether, Bob turned up. He'd seen his girl, who was on fire duty with a friend at a school way out at the edge of town. Bob had arranged for us to go back and see them, so we never did get into the dance.

The school where the girls were fire watching was at least four miles away and by the time we got there I was already more concerned with getting back for our transport than in getting to know some strange girl. Eventually, I managed to convince Bob we were going to be in trouble if we didn't leave, and we started back. As we approached a road junction we saw our bus head-ing towards us, but it turned along the other road and by the time we got to the corner, the red rear lamps were disappearing in the distance.

Back in Norwich we queued at the bus station, tried for a taxi and a hire car, all to no avail. It was too late for the buses, and the others weren't inter-ested in using precious petrol going out of town when there were plenty of customers for local runs.

It was decided that Bob would find and book us a bed in the Y.M.C.A. while I phoned the squadron office and told the sad tale. Getting through wasn't easy, and Bob was back by the time I had finished phoning having accomplished his mission. We were told we were both down for an operation early next morning, and we'd better get back as soon as we could.

That done, we headed back to the Y.M.C.A. only to find it locked up for the night. Much banging at the door produced foul language from those trying to sleep, but someone did come to the door but couldn't unlock it.

While we were standing undecided on our next move, an American sol-dier came along. He, like us, was also stranded.

The front of the hostel was a shop front, the glass shop window having been painted over and above what would have been the nameboard, making a good-sized ledge.

Bob persuaded us to lift him until he could reach and pull himself up onto this ledge. He was sitting there getting his breath back when two policeman rode slowly by on bicycles. I don't think they even noticed him. Bob was able with a certain amount of violence and noise to raise the window above him, knock down the blackout board behind it and get into the room. However, that room was also locked.

Eventually, I went up with Bob pulling and the American pushing. We then hauled the yank up on a blanket, his boots banging against the glass shop window. In the room was a single bed, all made up, and we tossed for who slept on the floor. I was pleased to lose. Blankets and greatcoats were shared out and we settled down for the night.

Next morning, we went out the way we came in, climbing out of the window and dropping from the ledge to the pavement. Dusting ourselves down we went, unwashed and unshaven, in the front entrance to claim the breakfast we'd paid for.

We found a bus and were walking up the road towards the camp entrance, when the squadron came in overhead from the operation which we should have been on. We weren't very popular and had a very one sided interview with Allen Dredge our squadron C.O. We were confined to the camp and had to man the squadron office at nights for a week. This meant sleeping next to the telephone, and if the weather was suitable for flying, we were likely to be disturbed early with news of the morning operation—not too severe a punishment, really. No doubt, the rest was good for us. We got more sleep than when we had evenings out in Norwich.

All this may sound as if life in Norfolk was all laughs and light-hearted fun. Some relief was certainly needed from the operational flying, which was no fun at all.

For the trips, the Typhoons were fitted with a long-range tank under either wing. These gave about an extra forty-five minutes flying at cruising speeds. They had no gauges so that you didn't know how much fuel was left in them. A fuel-control cock was fitted so that you could change over to main tanks. This was gauged purely on a time basis. It was usual on an operation to jettison the tanks as soon as you switched to main tanks to reduce drag and get the last bit of endurance. If you ran the long-range tanks dry, the first intimation of this would be when the engine quit and the prop just windmilled round. By the time you'd changed tanks, petrol had come through, and the engine fired again, a minute could slip by—which is fine, if you've plenty of height or have sufficient speed to gain height, but when escorting the Beaufighters, we were at wavetop height to get under enemy radar and down to 180 mph to stay with them. If the drop tanks ran dry before time was up, two things were certain. One, you were in the sea, and two, at that time of year, you would be lucky to last five minutes.

As usual, it was okay for the formation leader, but the poor blighter out on the edge of the flight would be pumping the throttle like mad to keep station and using a lot of fuel. We lost several in the sea; none through enemy action. Faces come to mind, but I can't put names to any of them except McCook. McCook was a New Zealand Flight Sergeant. Quite experienced and very capable, he had been made responsible for our safety equipment: parachutes, Mae Wests, and dinghies. He was conscientious in ensuring these were in top condition: CO_2 bottles changed, lamp batteries in Mae Wests, etc., but a fat lot of good any of these were to him in the end.

Tuesday, 8 February 1944

Large boat reported in Den Helder and we went out to bomb it. There was a pretty strong wind blowing and we made landfall a little south. Lum and I just about caught up in time for the dive and I'm afraid I didn't see the ships at all. I gave up looking and dropped my bombs when I saw Lums go. There was quite a bit of flak but they didn't wake up until we were well on the way out and then it was all well behind us. Arrived back with quite a small amount of petrol left. Eight galls in one tank and ten in the other, not enough for my liking.

In the afternoon we went out again on the same job. My boost gauge wasn't working but I didn't bother much until we were about twenty miles out to sea, then I noticed it was dripping petrol and I turned back. Actually they tell me that very little could have leaked. The boys met with a warm reception this time, and the flak shook them. On the way back Clapperton had trouble with his engine and just managed to get it going in time to stay out of the drink. Hindley stayed with him leaving Moore and McCook on their own. Next thing was that Mac called up saying his fuel pressure warning light was on. Moore saw he was slowing down and he then called up saying that he was baling out. At that moment he disappeared into a rain storm. Moore did an orbit and as he came round saw Macs plane spinning down from above him. It hit the sea and he saw it burning for about ten seconds. He stayed there until relieved by Spits. Mac went in only twenty miles off of Lowestoft but no sign of him was seen till dark. After dark they still had out Mosquitoes Wellingtons and launches. A Wimpy reported that

it had seen a light and was going down to have a look at it, that was
the last they heard of it. Though a launch was only five miles away
they didn't manage to pick up anyone from the Wimpy nor did
they see the light. At first light four of the boys went out and
searched the area but without result and we had to give up. Even if
he was picked up now he would be in a pretty bad way. Later there
was another trip to Den Helder which was abortive due to bad
weather and we turned back about half way over.

It was pretty heartbreaking for the rest of the flight. Fuel was so short we
couldn't stay with any of these unfortunates for any time. Usually, one would
be detailed to climb and fly one circle above him while transmitting so that
the shore stations could get a fix. Not one was ever found, much less saved.

This went on for several weeks without our ever seeing anything to attack,
ship or plane, and it all seemed rather pointless. Despite the high jinx, morale
was suffering and after one particular incident reached an all time low.

It was the usual thing, the weather pretty murky, stooging along with the
Beaufighters barely above the waves, when out of the grey appeared a collection of coasters and smaller vessels. We were on them too quickly to go
straight in, and the Beaufighters climbed. A few shots of tracer came up at
us, making it apparent that the smaller boats were 'E' boats. I thought the
Beaufighters were climbing to attack, but it soon became apparent that they
were shaken and in complete disarray. I thought for a moment there was
going to be a collision. However, they reformed, but instead of attacking,
turned for home.

To say we were outraged would be an understatement. What were we
doing, risking our necks out there if not to attack shipping? Allen Dredge
was furious and I understand that on landing he immediately phoned group
headquarters stating that he would not escort the Beaufighters anymore.
True or not, we didn't!

We flew a few more operations while waiting decisions from above, but
these were dive bombing raids on the island of Texel and on the steelworks
at Ijmuiden in Holland. Both of these could just be reached without long
range tanks and four planes would carry bombs while four others escorted
with tanks on. If attacked the bombers had no fuel to stay and fight, whereas
the others would shed their tanks and fight off any opposition.

We never were intercepted but received a hot welcome from the flak,
especially from Texel. I was on two or three of these trips always with bombs.
These were more the sort of trip we were used to and immediately morale
picked up. We lost no one in the sea and though we were hardly a thousand
bomber raid, we hoped we caused annoyance to someone.

Friday, 11 February 1944

Up early for a show but the weather was pretty bad. Took off lunch time for the usual Den Helder bus run. I was one of the fighter escort. However there was a small patch of cloud over the target and the boys didn't bomb.

Saturday, 12 February 1944

Once again were up early for the Den Helder bus run, but it was cancelled when we were in the cockpits. Did it at four thirty.

Sunday, 13 February 1944

Did an early show on shipping at the Hook. Did some really good bombing for a change. There was one large boat and two small ones about half it's size.

Scored a direct hit on the large one and near misses, and near missed on the smaller ones. Got them all Cat III. I personally thought the large one at least a Cat II.

Then without warning we returned to Manston.

Monday, 14 February 1944

The squadron moved back to Manston. Everyone happy.

Tuesday, 15 February 1944

Panic show in afternoon. Withdrawal cover to Mosquitoes with 198. Got as far as Lympne and were recalled.

Sunday, 20 February 1944

Had a Ranger all worked out and took off, MacKickan leading. Got almost to the Dutch islands and he decided weather was no good. I think we could have got through the gaps myself. We swept down the coast to Calais and came home without seeing a thing.

In the afternoon a Liberator was in distress and trying to land when 198 were taking off on a show. It had to go round again and one engine started to smoke. Then when it was just north of the field the starboard wing just broke off at the root and it crashed in flames. The second one I've seen do that. It made me feel rather sick.

Wednesday, 23 February 1944

Boys did a show on shipping in Zeebrugge. Flt Sgt Fudala, a Pole was seen to be in trouble and baled out at the bottom of the dive.

We escorted many of the shorter range bomber raids carried out by twin engine bombers of the U.S.A.F. Mitchells, Bostons and Maurauders.

Thursday, 24 February 1944

In morning did a fighter umbrella at 15000 feet over Bostons and Mitchells, with 198 Sqdn. Went in at Le Touquet, to Cambrai to Ault and out at the mouth of the Somme. There was something reported at Gris Nez and we headed up the coast after it. When we got there found nothing and the controller had the nerve to tell us that it was a stale plot he had left on the board.

In the afternoon did a Ranger. Went to the Islands on the deck and climbed to six thousand to cross in. Went in down the Ooster Schelde where we parted company with 198 who were going to Eindhoven. The idea behind this show was to catch any Hun fighters coming back to their bases from the Fortress shows.

Dived down onto the deck and flew along in line abreast, five of us. I didn't have too happy a time. I had an oil leak which had covered the windshield. We were flying into sun and I couldn't see a thing forward and had to judge my height from the others. Once I was badly shaken when a windmill sail whistled past under the wing.

I was surprised to see how lifeless things seemed. I don't know if every one had gone to earth but I didn't see more than a dozen people all the way, no vehicles except a couple of hay carts, and a couple of trains which were very tempting but are taboo these days. (There was a ban on attacking trains from Dec 43 to May 44.) We went round Antwerp and Brussels without seeing a thing, and I thought we were going to get back without firing our guns. Then about ten miles east of Mons the boys spotted a plane. I first spotted it about a mile off and we passed clean beneath it without it seeing us apparently. It was a twin engine thing with twin fins and rudders and lots of dihedral on the tailplane. I recognised it as a French type but couldn't name it. C.O. ordered us to drop our jettison tanks and we broke off to attack. I followed the C.O. in a steep turn to starboard and saw the C.O. attack but no strikes. I attacked from about ten degrees off the port astern. Saw two others almost abreast of me and opened fire early to make sure of getting in a shot. As I broke I saw strikes all over the fuselage and starboard mainplane. I could have closed in much closer but the other two were getting too close for my liking. I broke to port and followed the C.O. round to the right. Saw him dive on the wreckage of the plane on the ground and I also made an attack. Then we climbed and reformed. Climbed to about six thousand feet again and went out between Ostend and Zeebrugge. Surprisingly enough we didn't get fired at, all the way around, though we flew over Bruges at about four thou'. The plane turned out to be a L.E.O.45 and Dryland Bob Cole and I shared it. Bob followed me in and says the starboard engine was on fire after my attack. There was a celebration in the 'Cherry Brandy' at Sarre that night.

Around this time we received the news gladly that we were to be re-equipped with the new Tempest V.

The Tempest was derived from the Typhoon and had several significant changes. The main improvement was a new thin elliptical wing although this meant that less fuel could be carried in it's tanks. To overcome this the engine was moved forward and a fuel tank mounted in the fuselage between the fire wall and the oil tank. The Tempest also sported a new undercarriage, spring tab ailerons to improve the roll rate and an increase in both horizontal and vertical tail surfaces, the latter by an addition of a fillet between the fin and fuselage, to compensate for the longer nose.

All these changes resulted in an aircraft that was far more manoeuvrable and had a greater rate of climb than the Typhoon. Below 20,000 feet, it was faster than the Spitfire XIV, Mustang III, Bf109G, and the Fw190A. Altogether, a very formidable aeroplane.

February, 28 1944

Today were told that we were to be the first squadron to be equipped with Tempests. The first two arrived in the afternoon and the C.O. took one up. Seems to be a good kite and certainly has a terrific rate of climb.

Thursday, 2 March 1944

Got my first trip in a Tempest and boy what an aeroplane. I found I could turn comfortably at 150 mph and it seemed to be turning on it's wing tip. The rate of climb was way above anything I had dreamed of. Needs rather more trimming than the Typhoon.

In the afternoon we went on a show escorting Marauders. I was No 2 to the C.O. Took off with 609 and 198 and picked the Marauders up off the French coast and they crossed in right over Dieppe. Two Marauders were hacked down before they even got over enemy territory. For a while it was all quite simple, we were guarding the rear box of bombers and as they were flying a straight course it was easy enough to weave gently and stay with them.

When we got to the target area however they didn't seem to be able to find the target though we went over it several times. It became hard to follow them then and we had to cross over so frequently that I lost all sense of direction.

We split up into sections and I was left on my own with the C.O. This suited me fine as I was able to cross over at will and there weren't so many other planes trying to use the same bit of sky as I was.

After turning circles for quite a while the Marauders dropped their bombs on St Quentin a peaceful looking French town a good thirty miles from the rail targets they were supposed to bomb. One bomb hit a gasometer but apart from that I don't think they did much damage to any military target, most of them fell in the centre of the town. I should think they must have wiped out half the civil population.

We escorted them home and when in sight of our coast left them, reformed and turned for home. When I tried to put my wheels down to land nothing would happen. I went round again and called up telling the C.O. After kicking the emergency release pedals and pumping for what seemed ages I managed to get the wheels down. One came down long before the other and all the while the plane skidded and slewed along almost sideways, however I finally got both wheels locked down. Then came the task of getting down the flaps, already I was cross wind on the approach and although I pumped like a madman I still only had about forty degrees down by the time I got down on the ground. However I landed O.K. and by using more brake than usual managed to pull up before reaching the planes parked at the far end of the field.

Apparently I had been flying all the while with my tail wheel and one wheel flap down. Though several people had called up to tell me I hadn't heard.

We didn't stay long at Manston and before we left we had a squadron farewell party in the camp cinema. Joy was one of two civilians there, and on the way home I showed her the Tempest and asked what she could see different. The obvious thing in the dark was the silhouette of the four bladed prop. Our Typhoons had three blades. Joy still swears that I tried to coax her into the cockpit and take her for a ride. Actually, I thought she might like to see what the 'office' looked like and maybe sit in it. I wasn't *that* drunk! I rode with Joy on our bicycles back to Ramsgate and Joy knew that we were leaving, and every now and again there would be a burst of tears, and her arms would go round my neck. Coping with two ancient bicycles and a weeping girl after a very liquid party took more driving skill than piloting a Typhoon at rooftop height.

Monday, 6 March 1944

Though we were due to move this morning it didn't stop them sending us on a show. I didn't feel up to it after several farewell parties in a row, so didn't go. The boys were escorting Marauders I believe and were bounced by two Me109's who came down on them in a screaming dive, took a quick squirt at them half rolled and went on down in another great screaming dive before anyone could do anything about it. Nobody saw them apparently until it was too late to break, Wingate got the hell out of it by half rolling and going down into cloud, Edwards was badly shot up but wasn't hurt himself and belly landed back at Manston. Chas Tidy had to bale out I'm sorry to say; a good friend, I'm really sorry it was him and hope he got away with it OK

In the afternoon we moved to Bradwell Bay. There was a shambles on take off owing to Dick Wingate not knowing his proper position. Four took off in the first 'three' and me on my own in the second. Bradwell seems to be miles from anywhere and not a bright sort of dump. Had hardly landed when they started getting out a night flying programme.

Bradwell Bay was an airfield on the south shore of the River Blackwater estuary, with Denge Flats just off the eastern end of the aerodrome. Soft oozy mud on two sides, much of it quick sands, and very dangerous for anyone unfortunate enough to wander onto it.

Tuesday, 7 March 1944

Was on night flying. It was pretty misty and I only stayed up for fifteen minutes.

Monday, 20 March 1944

Took Bob Cole to Horsham St Faith near Norwich in the Tiger Moth. Arrived there quite safely and uneventfully, except for some nifty low flying which got us rather lost, and a few 'beat ups' on land army wenches etc.

Just as we arrived there, bad weather set in and I had to wait a short while before I could take off again. I just managed to get off before some really bad weather loomed up, and set course for home. Reached about five miles north of Colchester when there was a splutter a bang and the engine stopped. Was the first time I had ever flown a Tiger Moth and I had a vague idea that the endurance was four hours, but it certainly seemed as if it was out of gas.

I picked a suitable farmer's field and made a nice approach. When I got down near it however, I realised that it wasn't nearly so good as it looked from higher up and that I was landing up a steep hill.

However as I levelled out the engine picked up again and with a sigh of relief I climbed away. About another five miles further on there was another splutter and a bang and the performance was repeated. In fact it was repeated about five times before I finally saw an aerodrome looming up in the distance. Another twice and I was over the aerodrome and managed to scrape in over the top of a Thunderbolt which was also out of gas parked at the end of the runway. Turned out to be Birch, a Yankee drome still under construction, and of course they didn't have a drop of petrol suitable for the Moth on the place. So I had to phone for some to be sent along. The yanks were highly amused at the Tiger, one strolled up, kicked one of the wheels and said 'Where ya'll get this thing Bud, d'ya make it yessel?'

Later that morning a van arrived with Cpl Clark and another bloke with some petrol. By the time we had filled her up it was almost dark so I decided to stay the night with Nobby and send the van back with the other bloke. I tried to taxi the crate nearer to the huts which were all over on the far side of the drome. It was a cross wind and a very long runway and I found that by keep using the throttle to keep it straight I was working up a pretty fair speed and couldn't slow down for every time I closed the throttle it swung violently into wind. Finally when nearly run out of runway, I just had to slow down, and ran off of the runway into the wind. We were so tired we didn't even look for damage, just turned it into wind and pegged it down.

We did pretty well there, drawing our rations of tobacco and chocolate in the P.X. and cooking our own breakfast, eggs and steak in the hut next morning. Then we took off and flew home. Had only about ten miles to go, I reckon another pint of petrol and I would have got right home.

While at Bradwell we had the first of a series of incidents where propellers went into fully fine pitch, usually during take off. The propeller pitch control was driven by engine oil pressure, and at that time it was not known for certain whether the prop oil seals failed, with loss of pressure to the prop allowing it to go to fully fine and of course starving the engine bearings of oil, or whether the engine bearings failed first, with reduced pressure causing the prop to go fully fine. The revs would then go off the clock before you had a chance to close the throttle. It was like driving a car at full throttle in bottom gear with no oil in the engine. The first time this happened, was to a Polish flight sergeant, Stan Domanski. He was taking off when there was a very high pitched scream from the engine. He got it down okay on the first available runway, had stopped, and was just getting his parachute out of the cockpit when the lot went up in flames. Obviously grossly overheated, he was lucky to be out of it in time. It burned so intensely that all the foam on the station wouldn't put it out.

The aeroplanes of that time burnt fiercely. The fuel was bad enough, but much of the actual structure of the plane was made from light alloys containing magnesium. Once this got hot enough it would burn with an intense white light. Magnesium of course, was the material used by the early photographers for their flash photography.

Twice I have seen planes alight on the ground, with molten metal running away from them in rivulets which burned with this intense white light. In each case all the foam on the station was used with no effect, and flying had to be cancelled and planes diverted until further supplies could be obtained.

An instruction was issued from group that the squadron was to practice taking off, and forming up at night. D-Day was drawing close and they wanted air cover over the beachhead from first light. Until then it was usual for day fighter squadrons to fly only on moonlit nights, but this order was to be regardless of this.

Wednesday, 22 March 1944

Took 'X' up for an air test in the morning (Typhoon R8895). Seemed to be flying well, except that there was a little vibration above 3000 revs.

Due for night flying, but were delayed from getting off due to an air raid. Finally got permission and took off at midnight. Was very dark with practically no horizon and I swung slightly. I was just beyond the perimeter track with my wheels up, and settling down to climb on instruments when there was a terrific thump from the front of the plane and the whole kite started to vibrate so much that I couldn't read any of the instruments, and I expected the engine to fall out any minute. I thought that I must have allowed the kite to sink slightly and hit something on the ground damaging the propeller. I was prepared to buy it on the spot and remember that I was surprised when the kite continued through air and not

earth. I throttled back slightly and found that at about a third of
the way back the vibration fell off quite a bit, however I still
couldn't read any instruments they were so blurred.

Seemed I was in for a prang of some sort so I wound back the
hood, tightened my straps and called on the R.T. to say that I was
in trouble and was coming straight in. Like lightning various possi-
bilities flashed through my brain. The kite was not climbing and
felt near the stall, already it seemed doubtful that I would make the
flarepath. I thought about force landing on the far bank of the
river, but remembered that there were far too many houses spread
around that I wouldn't be able to see. This made me think the
same applied to the drome side of the bank. Even if I made the
field it was going to be a mighty low approach and any houses or
trees in the way were going to get their tops taken off with pretty
certain results for yours truly. Almost better odds on the ditching.

I was about half way round the circuit by now and about midstream. I was calling up to tell them that I might have to ditch
when the kite hit the water. I was thrown violently forward and a
solid silver wall of water came back over the front of the kite, the
windshield kept most of it from me. I managed to get my left arm
across the front of the windshield and pushed with all my might,
even so my head banged against my arm and it's lucky for me that I
got it up there in time.

The kite slewed from side to side and came to rest with the tail
out of the water and the level of the water about halfway up the
wings. The port mainplane started burning about half way out,
probably either the long range tank or ammo going up. That
scared me for the first time, I didn't like the idea of getting
burned.

I always have said that it is impossible to get unstrapped in the
time a Tiffy stays afloat and for the second time in a few seconds I
was dead in my own estimation. In a frenzy of despair however I
got the oxygen tube undone with one twist, amazing how I managed to twist it the right way first time for it came apart. I had the
new type of harness and was glad of it for the first time since I've
been using it. It came undone with one simple little flick. I then
felt myself floating out of the cockpit and realised that the kite
must have sunk, though I had felt no cold shock of immersion. I
kicked and struggled to make sure that I was free of everything and
my struggling must have pulled out the R.T. lead which I hadn't
already done and in about two or three strokes I broke the surface.

There my first instinct was to tear the oxygen mask off of my face, I couldn't breathe freely in it. I clawed it under my chin, and in doing so swallowed the only mouthful of the whole trip. Then I fumbled for the lever of my Mai West and found everything except it. I got my fingers tangled in the tapes, I ripped off my fluorescent pack (accidentally) and finally pulled the lever, nothing happened, pulled it several times more cursing the bloke who was supposed to have changed the bottle less than a week ago, and finally realised that it had either blown up in the crash or wasn't going to work.

By that time I was beginning to feel the cold and wasn't thinking all too clearly I'm afraid. It dawned on me that I ought to get my dinghy out and that I still had my chute making it difficult for me to keep my head above water, so I turned the release disc and banged it with one hand, while I held the side of the dinghy pack with the other. The chute came off and I shook the dinghy free from the chute. I tore the top cover off and the dinghy fell out into my arms in a floppy mass. This made things difficult for I had to work my way round the thing to find the bottle which inflated it. I swear I went round that thing a dozen times before I found it. I was ready to weep in desperation when I thought of the idea of gathering it in armfuls and feeling for the solid lump of the bottle. This I did and almost immediately felt the bottle, and working my way through the folds of rubber with one hand I held the bottle in the other. At last I managed to get my hands on the thing itself and by that time was having difficulty in keeping my head above water. I hadn't the patience to waste on the safety pin, and gave the knob a terrific wrench and safety pin or no the dinghy blew up, boy was I relieved.

Luckily I remembered my gen about turning the knob slowly and though there was force behind my wrench I didn't go wildly at it and only turned it part of the way on to begin with. Strangely the dinghy was the right way up, but there was some cord or other right across the centre of it dividing it into two parts, and I hung on to one side of the dinghy with one arm while I tried to disentangle this cord with the other. Working it out now it could only be my dog lead, an attachment which joins your Mai West to your dinghy, for when I found I couldn't move the cord, I was getting so exhausted that I had to climb onto the dinghy for a rest. I don't remember ever getting that cord off so as I moved round the dinghy to climb in I expect that did the trick. I hoisted myself in by the rubber handles and lay on the thing as I'd arrived, face down, for a while, while I got my breath back.

I was beginning by now to feel really cold and was shaking a bit and at first started paddling, more to keep warm than in any hope of reaching shore. The search light canopy was up over the drome so I could see which direction I had to go, I seemed an awful long way from the shore. A bright light was searching back and forth across the water from about two miles west of me and several times it played on me and I waved frantically. A Mosquito flew down the river with two landing lamps on but he missed me by quite a bit. I was shaking with the cold by now and started baling out with the cup on the end of a piece of string. I kept searching for the dinghy cover which I knew should be around somewhere but every piece of string I hauled in seemed to end at this blasted baling cup. I then remembered the torch on my Mai West and managed to get that out, but I couldn't remember how to get it to work, nor could I see in the dark. I banged and scraped the two halves together and finally it lit, I've still no idea how it is supposed to go.

Then I tried to get inside my Mai West after the signal cartridges I had there, but with the wet tapes and shaking hands I couldn't get it undone. In fiddling with the tapes though I came across my whistle tied to the end of one of them and sat there with my whistle clenched in my teeth, blowing for all I was worth at every breath and waving my torch around in one hand while baling out with the other.

Again the Mosquito came around and this time his lights went right over me. The light that had been playing across the water went out and I cursed thinking they had given up. By this time I was really feeling the cold and daren't stop moving I shivered so, and yet my arms felt like lumps of lead from my exertions.

Then the light started flashing across the water again and seemed to be nearer. Every time it shone on me I waved frantically and almost wept when it carried on without stopping. I was about dead beat and almost ready to lie back and give up when the light flashed on me wavered a bit near me then stopped on me. I could have cried with relief. Soon I heard the thumping of engines and soon the long black motor launch loomed up and some one steered me to the stern with a boat hook. It was all I could do to hang onto a hand from each and be lifted aboard, I hadn't the strength to lift my flying boots even.

They took me below and took my clothes off and gave me a rub down with rough towels. The dry clothes they found me were a queer rig, but at least were warm. Long seamans woollen pants and vest, a very tattered pair of dungarees, a pair of long grey socks, badly in need of darning, and a couple of duffel coats.

I sat in the galley in front of a fire, drinking hot cocoa, and it was fully an hour before I stopped shivering. I was on the naval launch 'Reda', the skipper had been on deck and heard the plane crash, they were then about two miles away. They had stopped the engine and listening to my whistle and found me in that way. Their job was to tour up and down the Blackwater taking the temperature of the water. That night it was thirty seven degrees F. They took me to Brightlingsea naval base where they rushed me off to sick bay and stuck me to bed with about fifteen blankets, half a dozen hot water bottles and an electric fire.

It was a long time before I could sleep, I kept thinking of what had happened, and the more I thought the more miraculous seemed my escape. Only a few fellows have ever ditched a Typhoon in daylight and got away with it, for me to have done it at night and got away without a scratch seemed impossible, yet I had. I prayed that night.

Thursday, 23 March 1944

After walking through Brightlingsea, still in my strange attire, to the Navy's mess, I had breakfast and later they took me back to Bradwell in a launch. It was a very fine morning and I sat at the back drinking tea and thoroughly enjoyed the trip. On the way Bob Cole and Bob Barckley shot the launch up in the Tiger Moth. They were out looking for my plane and had spotted my ruddy complexion on the boat.

Mac, Doc and Jock Smith formed a reception committee on the bank and seemed over joyed to see me, especially without splints or bandages.

Till that afternoon I felt fit as a fiddle. Then I developed ear ache, and next morning was taken to sick bay suffering from cold and exposure, and an inflamed ear drum. Spent ten days in sick bay where I was very much like a caged tiger. Then I paid three visits to an ear, nose and throat specialist at Uxbridge and after twelve days sick leave was able to start flying again.

While in sick bay I was visited by an expert from Napiers, and after listening to my story, suggested that the cause of the engine trouble could have been failure of one bank of valve gear, or it could have been loss of oil pressure allowing the propeller pitch to go into fully fine. People on the ground reported hearing a high-pitched scream from the engine which would favour the latter theory, and we had a spate of this happening around that time.

Anyway the plane was said to be in forty fathoms of water and they were not going to try to recover it.

Wednesday, 5 April 1944

With Stan Domanski I had to take my log book to see W/Cdr Aitkin the station C.O. After wondering what it was all about I received a green endorsement reading F/Sgt Pottinger is commended by A.O.C.85 group for showing coolness and resource during accident on night of 22 March 1944 ref etc. Didn't appreciate the wording very much. I don't think the old boy realised how cool I really was.

Thursday 20 April 1944

Got my first trip since the ditching. Was very shaky. Took a Tempest up and swung clean off the runway on take off. Must admit that I didn't trust the thing at all.

In the evening I did readiness in the air with Jimmy Mannion as my number two. Were told to go to Orfordness on A.S.R. Had no map, and no idea where Orfordness was, and were recalled before things got really difficult.

Saturday 22 April 1944

Was scrambled at dusk on an air sea rescue trip. Rose was my No2. Went up the coast to Felixstowe passing over a convoy complete with balloons in the murk. Maurice swears they fired at us, I was too busy watching instruments to bother about what was going on outside. It was very hazy, besides being almost dark. From Felixstowe they vectored us out to about sixty miles from the coast, by which time it was too dark to see very much at all. We hung around as long as we could trying to get in touch with the Walrus who's radio was apparently u/s and then headed home. The vectoring was pretty good and brought us slap over the drome. I was pretty proud of my instrument flying too.

The airfield had three runways, triangular in layout, the main one running east/west. What I remember of the buildings they were all single storey wood and asbestos, looking very temporary; they are probably still standing today.

With us on the airfield was a Mosquito squadron, and I believe that these were night fighters. The Mosquito was a fine looking aeroplane, and performed well. It had already earned itself quite a reputation. However, they were made of moulded plywood, and I saw some of them after they had been shot up. A bullet made a neat round hole on the outside, but as it left on the inside it took out a chunk of splintered wood sometimes the size of a saucer, and this flew in all directions. I remember one morning seeing one that had managed to get back. It was peppered with holes, and inside, the bottom was literally covered in blood soaked wood chips. The whole inside was splattered with gore. In a metal plane most of the shots would have gone right through and unless it met anything vital on the way, would not have caused too much concern. But all those flying wood chips could tear a chap into little pieces.

Another strange episode was when one night a Mosquito ran off of the end of the runway. It never did leave the ground properly, and vanished into the darkness skidding across the mud. An airman and a W.A.A.F. were snogging quietly just off of the airfield and saw it happen. I suppose they thought someone else must know, or perhaps they'd just got to the interesting bit. Either way they didn't report it until next morning when the aircraft was still missing. It was found sitting out on the mud, flying boots on the wing, but no trace of the two man crew. It was assumed that they had tried to wade ashore and gone down in the mud. It was strange really, after all, they had a radio and flares. I suppose it looked too easy to get ashore, and they didn't realise the dangers.

Slowly the new Tempests were ferried in and the Typhoons went. My letter 'R's engine had completed its 240 flying hours which was considered fantastic; fifty hours was the norm. at that time for the Napier Sabre engine. I was told they were taking it back to the makers to investigate and find out what the difference was. I reckoned it was the driver.

I can't remember too much about operations from Bradwell, I suppose we weren't there all that long, and I was in sick bay a good part of that. I do remember that some of the German fighters were coming over at high altitude dropping anti-personnel bombs and continuing their dive at high speed back whence they came. We did readiness in an old caravan at the end of the runway, but by the time we got into our aircraft, started up, and got airborne we never did get near them. Then we had the whole squadron on readiness, sitting in our planes, warmed up ready to go. I remember a couple of take-offs, but we still had no luck.

Bradwell Bay was one of a very few stations equipped with F.I.D.O. This was a system for assisting planes to get down when fog descended over the country. It was installed at half a dozen stations up and down the east coast to assist returning bombers or any others caught out in fog. Bradwell Bay was one station and the new runway at Manston was similarly equipped. I never saw the one in action at Manston, but that at Bradwell was used two or three times during our stay. The system comprised pipelines laid along either side of the runway for perhaps a third of its length, with jets at intervals through which petrol was pumped. Once lit the flames were probably two to three feet high and the heat sufficient to clear fog up to about a hundred feet above the runway which gave sufficient visibility for a safe touch down. The glow would also be seen from some way off even above the mush which helped the pilot to home on the station.

One filthy night we were in the sergeants' mess, when over the Tanoy the crash tender, fire crew and blood wagon were put on alert for a plane coming in with an engine on fire. The story told afterwards was that the plane stopped at the downwind end of the runway, and the ambulance arrived on the scene first. To the driver's consternation the four-man crew of the aeroplane were walking towards him speaking German! With amazing presence of mind the driver whipped off his cap with it's R.A.F. badge, opened the rear door of the ambulance, into which the visitors climbed without a word. He then locked the door on them and drove straight to the guard room. Meanwhile the fire on the engine had been put out, and the plane towed off the runway. It was a Ju 88!

During our time at Bradwell Bay, we had three Polish pilots on the squadron. One of them, Stan Domanski owned a car, a maroon Citroën, a model I believe they called the 'Light 15'.

Stan talked Bob Cole into buying a half share in the car for twenty pounds. This he duly did. Then it seemed the car wasn't running too well and their heads were buried under the bonnet. The experts decided that the cylinder head gasket was blown, and this was confirmed when the squadron moved to Newchurch and Bob and Stan elected to travel by car rather than fly. Luckily, there were enough pilots to enable them to do this. Late in the day, Citroën and crew turned up and it came out that they had had to stop every few miles and knock on house doors to beg water to put in the radiator. As they drove in, it was obvious that the white cloud emitting from their exhaust was steam not smoke.

The only place they could trace a new gasket was at a Citroën works in Acton, West London. Bob was able to get a days leave and travel to London and collect the gasket.

Bob and Stan fitted the gasket themselves, and it was a pity they didn't call in expert advise for they installed the gasket upside down so that the cutouts were all in the wrong places, and when they had finished, more water than ever leaked into the cylinders. Off came the cylinder head again, and the mistake pointed out to them and it was refitted the right way round. However, the gasket had been compressed in all the wrong places and it still leaked, although it was better.

Bob did use the car. He was stuck late one night near Ashford station trying to start the car without much success, when out of the station walked an A.T.S. girl. She made some saucy remarks about tatty old cars, or maybe it was about their equally useless owners. Bob said, 'Well, you have a go then', which she did with success. She drove Bob as far as her billet at Chartham— a long way off of his route to Newchurch. She was, of course, a transport driver and was used to dealing with recalcitrant 30-hundredweight Bedfords. Thus started the beautiful friendship that ended in marriage after the war.

The Citroën was always difficult to start, no doubt due to the water still getting where it shouldn't and eventually they took the head off again. By this time the flying bombs had started coming over and we were either flying or on readiness at all hours. So the car was left with the head off for quite a while before they got back to it. By this time the bores had gone rusty. They tried pouring petrol into the open bores and turned the engine over on the handle. Unfortunately, the dogs on the handle were worn, and it slipped with skinned knuckles as a result. At which point someone pressed the starter. Of course, there was a spark somewhere, and the whole thing caught fire. They were pretty smart with an extinguisher, but not before all the wiring in the engine compartment was a charred, blackened mess.

The bonnet was put back on, and that's how it stayed until the squadron left Newchurch. They had no way of moving the car, so they had no alternative but to accept the transport officer's (he was staying!) offer of five pounds as it stood.

Having fully re-equipped the squadron with Tempests, and with a few hours of familiarisation at Bradwell Bay, we were moved to Newchurch on Romney Marshes. We were joined by 486 New Zealand Squadron, and Wing Commander Roland Beamont arrived to lead the No 150 Tempest Wing. A little later we were joined by 56 Squadron who still had Typhoons. They were re-equipped with Spitfires as an interim measure, since there were no Tempests available for them. The Spit was said to handle more like a Tempest than the Typhoon. Certainly, there must have been a good deal of difference between the Typhoon and the Spitfire. One Australian pilot got into a 'dog-fight' with some American Thunderbolts based nearby (only fun, of course!), used the same amount of beef on the control column of his Spit that he was used to using on his Typhoon and tore both wings off. The Typhoon was a strong aircraft alright, as was proved time and time again carrying bombs, and later rockets, but it took muscle to obtain the last bit of manoeuvrability.

Newchurch was preparation for things to come. Conditions were as near as they could be to the sort of airfield we might use after the invasion of France. We lived under canvas, six of us N.C.O.s to a ridge tent. Our mess tent was a marquee and this was where briefing before and after a 'show' took place. The airfield itself was 'L' shaped and comprised several farmers' fields with hedges down and Sommerfeld tracking laid on the rough ground. This tracking was made up of steel plates and made a pretty good runway on almost any sort of ground. However, it was not so smooth as the concrete runways of Bradwell Bay as I found out to my cost, but more of that later.

Our planes were dispersed at the north end of the longest runway, and there was a farm cottage that we used as our dispersal quarters. Workshops were set up in out- buildings at the back.

Many of our off duty excursions took us into Folkestone, and this was the scene of many riotous, not to say rowdy evenings. The dances at the Majestic Hotel were a favourite spot, and the Queens Hotel. It became the custom to bring back trophies from these expeditions, and our cottage was decorated with these. Someone painted a pub sign for it which was hung up outside calling it 'The Gotsum Inn'. The sign from a static water tank was stood in a bucket of water and someone dragged an illuminated A.A. sign back onto our truck, among loud protests from those who could only expect an even more uncomfortable ride in the back than usual. Another hotel lost a sign advertising 'Crabs and lobsters served in season'. And we grumble about the high spirits of the young today.

Strangely, these evening sessions were usually more rowdy when things were bad, such as when we lost a pilot. One such occasion I'll always remember was when we lost Jimmy Mannion. He hardly looked old enough to ride a bike, much less fly a Tempest. He played the most wonderful jazz piano, and I can picture him now sitting at a piano in a pub on the marshes, four pints lined up on top of the piano, playing 'Body and Soul', dreamy eyed, and everyone else clustered around completely enthralled.

Jimmy and a Polish pilot called Zurakowski took off into the blue on a recce along the French coast, and just disappeared. When the war in Europe was over, and I returned from prisoner of war camp, there was at Cosford a board listing air crew who they would like news of. Jimmy headed the list. As far as I'm aware nobody ever discovered what became of them.

After one of these dodgy evening sessions, my flight commander Van Lierde and Lefty Whitman ended up in one of the many dykes which run alongside the roads, draining the marshes in that part of the world. Van had a Ford 10 soft top. A pretty rare car even then. In immaculate condition, the apple of his eye! They were driving back from the pub, obviously in a 'happy' state. Van said.

"Look, Lefty, 350 on the clock, no hands!"

The next thing Leftie remembered was being upside down under water. The road had turned, and Van hadn't! Neither were any the worse, except for the algae in their hair, and the stains of ditch water, which joined those of beer on their best blue uniforms.

Wednesday, 3 May 1944

Was on the first operational sortie to be flown by Tempests. A wing sweep to Mardyck, Lille, Armentieres, Berch. On take off one undercarriage light stayed on, but after pulling the undercarriage down and up several times I ignored it and chased after the rest of the squadron. We saw nothing as was usual on these sweeps, but I was amazed to see what large areas of country along the Belgium coast had been flooded.

Van weaved violently from the minute we crossed in until we were half way back across the channel and made it very difficult for Teddy and I. I was on the inside next to the C.O.'s section and once he weaved so far towards them that I found myself among them and was lucky not to collide with Buck.

Monday, 8 May 1944

Went on leave. When I went to the orderly room to collect my pass C.O. suggested that I should go in for a commission. Didn't give him a definite answer as I wasn't really too keen on the idea.

I found that Bob Cole had also been approached, and he also was happy as an N.C.O. By now we had both reached the rank of Warrant Officer, the highest non commissioned rank, and our standing was good in the sergeants mess. To become the most junior of the officers mess was not all that attractive. Maybe we just lacked ambition! About a week later the C.O. had the pair of us in his office, and demanded to know why he had not received our applications. He said that we by now had gained quite a bit of operational experience, whereas he had several newly joined officers with none. He was not going to have N.C.O.s leading officers around the sky, so we'd better be sure our papers were on his desk tomorrow morning. They were, and in due course Bob and I received our commissions.

Tuesday, 16 May 1944

Bad weather all day. In evening had to stand by in sergeants' mess. Rain was leaking through the marquee and we sat in about three groups round oil stoves in about the only three places where the rain wasn't coming in.

Wednesday, 17 May 1944

A good day for the squadron. In the morning McCullock landed short in the ditch at the beginning of the runway and completely wrote off the kite without hurting himself. Van's engine cut on take off. Bailey and I did some formation with Teddy and during some tail chasing Bailey's throttle jammed shut and he just made an airfield called Deanlands near Lewes. Kite was again a complete write off and Bailey banged his head, not seriously hurt though.

Wednesday, 24 May 1944

Four of us went to Manston to refuel for a Ranger. Met Hutch there who is now on 137 with Tiffies.

Refuelled and took off on Ranger. Had to climb through cloud to nine thousand feet and how I hung onto Eddie I don't know, but somehow all four were together when we broke cloud at the top. Over there the cloud had broken up but it was still very hazy. We went down on the deck and flew round the back of Brussels without seeing anything at all. I fired at a factory on the way over, but as I passed over the top it looked derelict. At one small village they opened up with M.G. fire but didn't get near us.

When Wiggy started to climb he didn't give us time to get in close after a turn with the result we were all separated. The other three met up again at the top but not I. I came home on my own, crossing out in a screaming dive at seven thousand feet. Some hopeful types started firing with light stuff but didn't get near me.

Sunday, 28 May 1944

Scrambled on shipping recce from Gris Nez to Ostend. Bailey was my No2. Went up as far as Zeebrugge but only saw a few odd fishing boats. Came back down the coast to Calais and set course for home crossing in at Folkestone quite proud of my navigation, it was better than I thought it would be, quite hazy too.

Newchurch being so near the coast, as with Manston, had a fair number of planes returning in trouble of some sort, and landing at the first friendly place they saw. Most mornings there were one or two strangers on the field, two of which stick in my memory as the sort of thing that tended to make the majority of pilots fatalistic, and maybe superstitious.

One of these was an American Thunderbolt which landed after dark towards our end of the runway. He obviously had come in too high or too fast and overshot the end of the airfield. Now, across that end of the runway ran a dyke, maybe some ten to fifteen feet wide. More or less in line with the runway was a small bridge over the dyke, intended to allow farm carts and farm machinery to get from one field to another. The pilot, with tail down, and in the dark, couldn't possible have seen the bridge, and pure good fortune must have carried him over it. Looking at it in the light of day, it was almost unbelievable. In fact it was only with difficulty that the plane was towed back over the bridge with a tractor.

The other occasion was a Marauder which tried to land in the other direction, along the short leg of the 'L'. The approach from this direction was over a minor country road, bordered again by the inevitable dyke. The pilot had landed short, and the plane lay with its wings in the bottom of the dyke, the nose at an angle up one bank and the rear part of the fuselage and tail at the opposite angle up the nearer bank.

It must have decelerated from about 100 mph to zero in just a few short feet, yet apart from minor cuts and bruises the crew escaped unhurt. Perhaps they'd done the required amount of praying while nursing a sick aeroplane back home, perhaps Lady Luck decided to be on their side, maybe rubbing that rabbits foot did the trick, or maybe it just wasn't their time yet.

In the early days at Newchurch, most of our work was in patrols or sweeps, the latter usually at squadron strength, and being aimed at the enemy rail, road, and sea lines of communication. Bombs would have been useful for this sort of work, but nine up to twelve aircraft each with four 20mm Hispano cannons were a considerable weight of fire power, and any target found, was left in a pretty sorry state.

Trains were a favourite find. There were no diesel or electric trains in the Western Europe area at the time which we were able to reach, and the steam locomotives made quite an impressive sight when the boiler burst among great clouds of steam. I often felt quite sorry for the drivers and their crews who would have been French, Belgium, or Dutch, possibly working under duress. A wrecked train of course put that line out of action, for at least a few hours, with resultant disruption to timetables, and an adverse effect on morale of any of the travellers.

All this time there was a continuous build up to the event everyone knew had to come soon, the second Front, the invasion of Europe. Newchurch was good training for living and flying from temporary airfields. On many of our trips we would land at a different airfield on our return. Maybe Ford, Tangmere, or Thorney Island. There we would be re-fuelled, re-armed, and any troubles sorted out before returning to Newchurch. This gave us good practice, and of course enabled ground crews to get more familiar with aircraft other than those of their own squadron. This could be fascinating, especially when as on one occasion I had to show the fitters how to undo the fasteners on the engine cowlings. I think they would have used crowbars rather than give up, if I hadn't arrived on the scene.

We were still having a good deal of trouble with oil leaks around the propeller seals, and on one trip spots of oil were coming back almost from take off. We were returning to Thorney Island, and by the time we arrived there my windscreen might as well have been frosted glass. I couldn't see anything at all forwards. We flew over the airfield in pansy formation, snapped into echelon starboard and peeled off to land, just to show off to those below how a real fighter squadron did it.

On those sort of landings you came in quite close together, probably three planes on the runway at any one time, but with visibility the way it was I left a bigger gap. I got quite low, mainly due to the difficulty of seeing forward, and had to put on throttle to reach the beginning of the runway. I remember flying up the sandy beach at about ten feet, and the relief when the end of the runway loomed up more or less in my line of flight.

I couldn't lock my harness, but came in standing up on the upper rudder pedals, with my backside about half way up the back of the seat, peering over the top and around the side of the screen. At 100 mph there was quite a breeze, of course!

After landing we quickly re-fuelled, re-armed, and the screen was cleaned, but they couldn't do anything about the seals. This usually entailed changing the propeller. In fact at this time it was quite a common sight to see low-loader lorries—'Queen Marys' (after the ship, not the lady) they called them—tearing round the winding country roads of the Romney Marshes with half a dozen propellers on board.

The seals must have been getting worse, because by the time we got to Newchurch, I was in just the same sort of difficulty, with zero forward visibility. As I made my approach, I realised that a flight of Typhoons was taxiing out to take off and were zig- zagging all the way down the right side of the runway. My judgement was not so good on this occasion. It was as if I was drawn to that side of the runway, and I landed much closer than was comfortable to the taxiing aircraft. There were some irritable comments about this, but when the state of the aircraft was seen I was forgiven and considered lucky to get down without worse mishap. The whole flight was risky, for had the seals broken down suddenly and completely, as had happened on at least three previous occasions, then I would indeed have been in dire trouble.

Monday, 29 May 1944

Had an exercise to see how the airfields could cope with various squadrons coming in for refuel and re-arm.

We did an uneventful fighter sweep at ten thousand feet and returned to Thorney Island. Sweep was in the Lille area and apart from a little flak from Lille itself was just a formation practice. 'R' being a good kite had been pinched by the flight commander, leaving me to fly 'W' with oil streaming back from the prop, so that half way round I couldn't see a thing forward.

I spent most of the trip pumping the de-icer to try to wash the oil off, but it didn't work. Landed at Thorney Island in a long creeping approach over the water and up the beach. Not able to see Stan in front of me half the while and didn't see the runway till I was crossing the perimeter track. I was very lucky to get down safely.

When our kites had been refuelled we took off again for Newchurch. Even on that short trip my windshield oiled over so badly that I couldn't see through it and landed on the right of the runway nearly writing off a Tiffy which was taxiing out. I didn't even know it was there until it flashed past my wing tip.

Van started to bawl me out when he landed but when he saw my screen apologised.

Tuesday, 30 May 1944

Was on early morning readiness at 3.45 a.m. Later in day did a fighter sweep. We were due to go down to Paris but bad weather prevented us.

We crossed in at Cayeux and flew across Abbeville to Amiens, collecting a little flak from somewhere near Poix and came out near Le Havre. On one turn Scratch Adcock had an engine cut as he was crossing over and lost so much ground that I thought we had lost him altogether.

Undercarriages seem to have caused several of my most exciting moments and I suppose the following must come high among these. Soon after arriving at Newchurch I was returning from a patrol, just myself and a number two. I came in to land, made what seemed a normal landing, rolled about fifty yards when the port wing dipped, the plane spun round in its own length, the hood slammed shut, I banged first one side of the cockpit then the other, and then all was quiet and still.

The hood must have twisted it's rails because it was firmly jammed shut. No amount of pulling, shaking or cussing would move it. I was trapped! A crowbar was fitted inside the cockpit on clips along the side of a floor board. It was quite impossible to reach it from a sitting position inside the cockpit. Someone from 486 Squadron fetched one from another plane and eventually, after about ten minutes, I was free!

Sitting inside the plane, I had felt quite okay—probably a couple of fair-sized bruises on each shoulder, but otherwise unscathed. However, when I stepped down out of the plane and saw it's condition I felt quite ill! The engine had left it's mountings, and with it's propeller, blades bent all this and that away, was sitting dejected looking a couple of hundred yards down the runway. The fuel pipe's broken end was still pouring aircraft fuel, which was bubbling and steaming on the hot engine mountings. The one thing I never did like much was the thought of being burnt! The fuselage was broken behind the cockpit and at right angles to the front of the plane, broken again in front of the tail which hung down towards the ground.

Both undercarriage legs were gone, and the plane sat more or less level on two short stumps. It hadn't done the runway tracking much good either, and from the damage it could be seen that the port leg had broken, the plane had swung round on this stump at around 95 mph. The other leg had broken on the way. No wonder I had been thrown about a bit.

Our senior engineering officer was a Wing Commander and ex-pilot. You would have thought he would have been sympathetic, but he wasn't. He was most irate at what had been done to his lovely new aeroplane and accused me of ground looping it. Fortunately, several people saw the landing and vouched for the fact that it was perfectly normal. In particular, the crew of the control caravan (there was no tower at Newchurch) that was located at the end of the runway within a few yards of my touch down. A ground loop generally involves digging one wing tip in and miraculously there wasn't a scratch on either wing.

Both undercarriage legs were sent to Farnborough for investigation and after some weeks I was called into Allen Dredge's office and told that a report had been received which stated that both legs had fatigue cracks which had been there some time, and that the breaks were in the opposite direction to that which would occur from a heavy landing. No one else said a word, no apology from humbled Wing C.O.s, whose bloody aeroplane had so nearly killed me. As a result of the report, all the Tempests on the two squadrons were subjected to a careful inspection of their undercarriages, and five others were found with cracked legs. A modification was made on the legs with great speed and I never did hear of any further cracks of this sort.

Eventually the invasion of Europe took place and we did our share of beachhead patrols, without so far as I was concerned very much of interest happening. We certainly saw nothing of any enemy aircraft and had little time to study what was going on below.

As soon as the beach head was established and airfields laid we were expecting to move over into France, although priority would obviously go to the squadrons of rocket firing Typhoons which were to give close support to the army with such devastating effect.

Then something happened which changed our role completely. The first 'Doodlebug' came over.

At the time we were doing readiness from first light. Two in the cockpits ready to go, and two kitted out ready to run from the dispersal. I was on one morning and just arriving at the dispersal in a truck, at about 3.30 am when we heard a strange burping noise, and a dark shadow flitted across the still dark sky, quite low and with a long fiery tail behind it. I'm afraid that first time of seeing one, we just stood and stared until someone shouted.

'Flying bombs, lets get up there after them!'

That ended any chance of joining in the second front. The Tempest was the fastest plane in operation at that time, and at the sort of height they came over, so that we were held back at Newchurch to chase them.

Usually they came in waves, at around a thousand feet, and travelling at about 350 mph. They varied, and the best of them we were hard pressed to catch, others were more easy. In the early days we had the field to ourselves. Lefty Whitman chased one right into the outskirts of London, shot it down, only to see it hit a block of flats. After that we were told to leave them alone once they were over the suburbs. After all they might possibly pass right over London and fall in open country beyond. It was soon made impossible to chase them far into London because a dense balloon barrage was put around the southern and eastern approaches. It was frustrating to be almost within range of one only to see it chug merrily on through the balloons. I don't know how many the balloons did bring down, but it was amazing how many V1s we watched pass through quite unscathed.

From an hour before dawn, until an hour after dusk, we maintained two aircraft in the air, two at immediate readiness, and two at five min. If an alert came these took off. If the Doodlebugs were detected in any numbers, every-thing flyable took off.

The area around Romney Marshes and in to Ashford was literally pep-pered with the craters made by these things. One early morning, I was on readiness and had just left for dispersal, when one came down only about thirty yards from our tent. Fortunately, between it and the tent there was a ditch with raised banks, and this deflected much of the blast upwards. Never-theless, the tent was split from end to end and the late sleepers shaken out of their beds.

Eventually, a three-mile-wide band along the coastline was given over to AA guns, and any other device that might prove effective. We were allowed the space between the guns and the balloons, or the area over the sea. We were more or less obliged to stick to this area, but any gun whether in the area or not had a go. In particular the Americans who were stationed at other airfields on Romney Marshes, and had plenty of ammunition, most of which seemed to be aimed at the following aircraft rather than the Doodle-bug. Maurice Rose flying my 'R' for Robert, had half inch shells through the wing, which meant the wing being changed. Strange to say, it was never so fast after that change.

Our own gunners too, were not allowing sufficient deflection and initially their success rate wasn't all that good, which frustrated us, because we also had greater difficulty in shooting them down in the brief time allowed us. However, the gunners had plenty of opportunity for practice and eventually, when provided with proximity fuses, were doing extremely well. Even we were forced to admit it!

The main difficulty I found was in seeing the Doodlebug. To gain a speed advantage we usually patrolled above their usual height and with their small size and khaki colour it was not easy to see them against the ground beneath. I was officially credited with six and a half shot down. Not very many compared with some others. I think there was one pilot claimed sixty odd, but I believe the plane was specially equipped. Several on 3 Squadron scored in the twenties and up to thirty. I realised later that my eyesight was not as good as it should have been, but of course, I was not going to risk being thrown off the squadron by saying so.

My half a kill was probably made up of several parts of Doodlebugs. It was amazing how you could shoot one down, with so far as you could see an otherwise empty sky, and yet you would find yourself sharing it with two other pilots who both reckoned they had got it. Mind you, it must have been a terrible job keeping track of it all, with so many coming over at once, but it could also be frustrating for us!

The people controlling us would give courses to steer to pick up a Doodlebug, but of course had quite often little idea of the conditions in the air. On one early morning myself and a No 2 were up on patrol and there were huge black cumulus clouds everywhere. We were out over the sea and were continually being guided into the heart of a really fierce thunderstorm. It was black as night, apart from which the rain lashed down so that visibility was nil. I had no alternative but to keep my eyes in the cockpit and fly back the way we had come on instruments. My No 2's eyes would have been glued to me flying formation, so that the chances of either of us seeing V1's were zero. But each time, we got out of the murk, and were given a fresh course to steer we found ourselves headed straight back into it again. The whole patrol was a complete waste of time. If there were any Doodlebugs around, we certainly didn't see them.

Another time, I was directed out to sea when there was low cloud down on the deck all along the coast. The only way through was by flying down the valley and out over Hastings. It was like flying down a tunnel, hills on either side and cloud above my head, and not knowing if the tunnel might be blocked. Again we saw no Doodlebugs, and then came the difficulty of finding a way back in.

Certain episodes stick in the memory. On one occasion I was flying No 2 to F/O Kosh, and we and a third pilot were all chasing after the same Doodlebug. I was in the middle and slightly below and behind the other two. As soon as I was within reasonable distance I gave it a good burst and was gratified to see large lumps fly off and the thing go into a nose dive. I was later complimented on my shooting but told I should have let my No 1 have first whack! I'm afraid my home was in London and I was only interested in stopping the 'Doodlebugs', never mind the niceties!

W/O Reid shot one down over Romney Marshes near Ham and it landed on a farmhouse, the only building for miles. It killed the old couple in the house. Reid was terribly upset.

One day I was down amongst the tents when one came over quite high and flew in large circles over our part of Kent. Probably it was hit, or possibly there was a fault in it's guidance system. Anyway, you can imagine the scramble for cover every time it came overhead, and the almost audible sighs of relief when it passed over. Then it didn't re-appear so presumably it had come down somewhere else.

It was on a Doodlebug patrol with F/Sgt Everson as my No 2, when I had yet another undercarriage failure.

We were at a height of around 3000 ft somewhere behind Eastbourne. On this occasion, we had been guided onto an oncoming V1. Suddenly I saw it way beneath us, travelling in almost the opposite direction. I rolled the plane onto it's back and dropped into a half loop, meanwhile trying to keep my eye on the Doodlebug. They were not at all easy to see against the ground. I was near vertical and, travelling at somewhere near 500 mph when the plane suddenly and violently dipped downwards and under, trying to do an inverted loop. I throttled back, and heaved back on the control column. It took all my strength with my feet raised onto the upper pedals to pull the plane slowly back into more or less level flight, and a more reasonable speed. By then I had seen that the undercarriage light for the port leg was showing red.

My No 2 had stayed with me, he should really have gone after the Doodlebug, but maybe he didn't see it. He confirmed that the port leg was in fact down and swinging loose.

Back at base the advise which came over the air was tremendous in quantity, and varied in content. Land with wheels up, land with wheels down.

It wouldn't be raised, neither would it lock down. It just swung loosely beneath the aircraft.

I myself was uncertain how to play the scene, wheels up would possibly be safer for me, but would almost certainly write off the aircraft. Wheels

The author, just after commissioning, August 1944.

The author and Joy.

down it could collapse on the port side with the possibility of a high speed ground loop with even more dire results.

Someone had fetched our boss, Wing Commander Roland Beamont, and he settled things by telling me to come in wheels down. I remember circling, uneasily, but too busy to be afraid. On the approach I yanked my safety straps as hard as I could, and made sure the hood was securely locked open. I didn't fancy being trapped in the cockpit again. The landing must have been the best ever. It really greased on, ran for a couple of hundred yards straight and then slowly turned left, despite all my frantic efforts on the right brake and judicious bursts of the throttle. It ended up about fifty yards off the runway, and at right angles to it, as if it had turned it's back on the whole sorry scene.

As I climbed out, everyone came running up, congratulations and smiles everywhere. Beamont congratulated me on the landing, and bawled me out for not knocking the switches off as soon as I touched down. In fact with my straps so tight I couldn't reach the switches, and in any case the engine was a good deal of use in keeping the plane straight after touchdown. My flight commander also bawled me out for not flying around longer to get rid of more fuel. Should I have cared, I hadn't even a scratch.

So far as the plane was concerned, it was still in one piece. However, the small strut which had broken, had swung down during the landing and gone through the wing. This meant that the wing had to be changed. A pity because otherwise there would have been no damage except the strut which caused all the excitement.

The Tempest Wing and their successes against the V1 were making the news. Of course any good news was a boost to the general public's moral, so the press were invited down to Newchurch for the day.

I didn't see much of them but I think they talked to anyone who was around at the time. Some of the European pilots, who still had families across the Channel, were not too keen on the publicity and made themselves scarce while the news hawks were around. As usual, what they didn't hear, they made up. In particular several pilots acquired nicknames which none of us had ever heard, and a good deal of amusement was had by all.

Around that time we also had a visit from the famous writer, Ernest Hemingway. He had come over from America as a war correspondent to cover the D-Day landings. I think he spent most time in the officer's mess, and talked to Roland Beamont and others. He did come out to dispersal where some of us, in a variety of states of 'readiness', were sitting in a group on the grass. From what I can remember he didn't take part in any conversation with the group. I recall it was a comparatively quiet time without a lot of activity.

The Air Officer Commanding, Air Vice Marshall Harry Broadhurst also paid us a visit, and took up a Tempest to try out his new super plane. Unfortunately the Sabre engine played up with it's old tricks. After sputtering and coughing on take off, he was glad to get down on earth again safely.

Then we started doing night patrols, and I didn't like that at all. A fighter is not like a larger plane where things happen comparatively slowly. Without any sort of a reference you can be upside down before you know it, unless you keep your head inside the cockpit, and glue your eyes to the instruments, and then you aren't going to see many Doodlebugs.

To assist us, searchlights at intervals along the coast would be arranged in pairs. One with it's beam vertical, the other with it's beam elevated to about 45 degrees and pointing out to sea. A single plane would patrol between two of the vertical beams, flying figure of eights, turning out towards the sea at either end. The searchlights helped in that you knew where you were, but the light did nothing for your night vision.

On the first of these night patrols (30 July 1944), I was directed onto a V1. I could see the flame from the rear of it's engine from some way off, and turned to come up behind it, adjusting the trim of the aeroplane as I did. You can't shoot accurately if the plane is skidding or slipping all over the sky. It's difficult to judge distance at night, but as soon as I thought I was near enough I gave it a long burst of fire. It's fuel caught fire and the whole thing went up in a sheet of flame.

I pulled up to avoid flying through the flames, but was pretty well blinded by the explosion. The last thing I saw as I ducked my head into the 'office' to look at my instruments, was the grey shape of yet another plane which pulled up from beneath me passing within fifty feet on my port side and a little ahead, and then vanished into the night.

My thought as I went onto instruments was 'How many more moths round this particular flame?' I flew on instruments for a few minutes to let my sight recover a little, and an anxious few minutes it was too! Then I set a course for my friendly searchlight, and resumed patrol. I only had a momentary glimpse of the other aircraft, but I was fairly certain it was a Mosquito. However the next day I was told I had shared the kill with a Spitfire of 91 Squadron.

Friday, 1 September 1944
    Did one patrol in the morning with Adams who was suffering
    from a hangover so we patrolled separately. Got horribly cheesed
    and tried a few aerobatics to pass the time away. C.O. asked me for
    a list of trips and claims, the boys say for a gong, I doubt it myself.

In the afternoon had a lecture on V2 the long range rocket. Amazing the amount of gen they have collected about it already.

Sunday, 3 September 1944
Patrol in the morning with Adams, Hastings to Rye. In the afternoon we were patrolling Ashford to Canterbury. Before returning to base I beat up Joy's and Addie came down too, so if she was in she certainly heard us. Flew back to Newchurch on the deck.

Thursday, 7 September 1944
Weather was pretty duff and they released us about lunch time. Bob and I went to Hawkinge for a bath and afterwards to flicks in Folkestone. Met the rest of the gang in Bobbies afterwards. When the dance finished, had a sign hunt and a good haul.

Friday, 8 September 1944
My commission came through, also Bob Cole's backdated to the 6th July. Celebrated the event by being on a charge for a dirty tent in the morning.

Apart from the general mess in the tent, Bob was keeping a spare wheel from his car in there, and had made a bed from an old gate, complete with fittings, so that he didn't have to sleep on the floor.

Sunday, 10 September 1944
Did a show to Rotterdam area again. This time it was a wing show, splitting into squadrons when there. I was number two to our new flight commander F/L Sparrow. On take off the Wing Co did his usual tight circuit and I had to use full revs and boost for about five minutes to catch up.
Bert Bailey who was Red 4 turned back at the Dutch Islands having trouble with one of his long range tanks.
Could see nothing of V2 targets but we shot up two trains and sundry barges at Leiden and Katwijk. I didn't manage to get at the trains but got one large barge at Leiden and six tied up at wharfs at Katwijk on the way out.
On the lakes there were dozens of small sailing boats. They were a wonderful sight with their white sails gleaming in the sunlight. I expect they all held German officers and their popsies but we left them alone.

On the way out I saw the odd bit of machine gun and rifle fire and somebody must have scored a lucky hit on Orwin's kite. As we were climbing away about a mile off shore he started streaming smoke and called up saying he was heading back to shore. He slowly lost height and made quite a nice ditching about a quarter of a mile off shore. He called up saying he was OK before he got out and the kite sank in a few seconds. Clapperton flew low over him and he was last seen swimming for the shore in his Mai West, so he should be all right.

In the shambles we got split up rather badly and three of us came back with 486.

Monday, 11 September 1944

Did another wing show in the Rotterdam and the Hague area. We were to stay up as cover while the Wing Co with 486 went down to have a look at suspected V2 sites. They didn't spot any sites but went down on a train.

We then spotted a train all of our own and the Wing Co gave us permission to go down on it. We had to dive from eight thousand feet and I couldn't slow down enough to get out of the C.O.'s and Teddies way and couldn't fire. Everyone else did and it was left with clouds of steam coming from it and burning furiously.

Both squadrons then headed south followed by the odd spot of flak. McKenzie called up that he was hit and started heading for the emergency landing strip at Brussels, later it turned out that a strut had broken on his undercarriage in the dive.

Then we spotted another train and this time I dropped well back to make sure of having a crack. The C.O. stopped it between two houses and Teddy was too close to fire. I got in a long burst and scored strikes all over the engine. Some flak gunners on the train opened up on me and I broke so violently that I lost the two ahead. Apparently the flak got so hot that everyone else broke without firing. I did one circuit and the C.O. called up and said rejoin over Schowen. I headed that way and picked up a gaggle of other planes on the way. As we passed Overflakkee there was another train steaming merrily along and the whole mob went down on it. I was almost the last down and already it was burning and almost hidden beneath clouds of smoke and steam.

The C.O. and Teddy Sparrow had met up with Mc and were escorting him home. We formed up into something near a formation and headed back too. Wing got four trains destroyed in all.

Tuesday, 12 September 1944

Did a show in The Hague area. An armed recce with four air-craft, Teddy Sparrow leading. We spent quite a while looking at the woods north of The Hague. Just as we were approaching The Hague I spotted a V2 at about three thousand feet. Looked like a doodle bug going vertically upwards. At the time I thought it was an Me163 rocket job and kept my eyes glued on it. At about ten thousand feet it started leaving a vapour trail and the others could see it. Finally it disappeared into the sun at something over twenty thousand feet. I fully expected it to come whistling down out of the sun and kept a good look out behind. It wasn't till later I thought of it being a V2. After searching the woods pretty thoroughly for any sites without any luck we headed north looking for a train Clapperton had pranged that morning but couldn't find it.

As we turned out to sea we got showers of light and heavy flak. We set course straight for home and what an awful lot of sea we seemed to cross before crossing in at N. Foreland.

Wednesday, 13 September 1944

Did an early show beating up some woods north of The Hague suspected of hiding a V2 site. Wing Co was heading our squadron. Was rather hazy and didn't spot target until last moment and went down in a very steep dive pulling out at something over five hundred miles per hour and firing all the way across the wood. Personally I saw nothing at all to pick on, but some of the boys on my left got bursts in on a house with tents pitched all round it. S/L Wigglesworth was leading the section behind ours and blew something up on the ground, blowing himself up with it. Davies who was flying behind him nearly finished on his back too. I didn't see him go in but saw the cloud of smoke and his plane still burning on the ground. We did an orbit to starboard and went straight back to base.

Sunday, 17 September 1944

We did anti flak on the airborne invasion of Holland. We were over there quarter of an hour before the gliders started arriving, and had a couple of flak positions to deal with along the river W of Nijmegen. We couldn't find any guns nor did they open fire on us though we offered them a tempting target by stooging along round in small circles over the place they were supposed to be. Finally we beat up some barges which looked as if they might have the odd

gun aboard but even this didn't provoke them into showing themselves. Got three barges Cat III.

Monday, 18 September 1944
    More reinforcements were being dropped in Holland and again
we did anti flak for them. This time we were a little later and flew
up and down the line of gliders and tugs waiting for the guns to
open up. One lot got really unfriendly along the river bank and we
went down and sprayed them with our cannon which subdued
them somewhat. Bert Bailey lost us in the haze and after looking
for us for some while he set off home on his own.
    As we came home Overflakkee lived up to its name and let loose
at us. We couldn't see where it came from and hadn't the petrol to
mess around so came home.

Wednesday, 20 September 1944
    We were due to move to Matlaske. Having seen the trucks off
with all our kit aboard the weather clamped and stayed clamped all
day. Went to Hawkinge for lunch and in the afternoon flew to
Manston where we found ourselves billets and I promptly headed
for Ramsgate, and Joy.

Friday, 22 September 1944
    Six of us headed by the Wing Co tried to get through to Mat-
laske. By the time we reached Leysdown we were nipping over trees
with next to no forward visibility and we turned back. Did I cheer.

Saturday, 23 September 1944
    Weather took a turn for the better (or worse according to how
you look at it) and we all set out for Matlaske. Seemed an awfully
small drome on a terrific hill. Thank goodness we landed up the
hill.

Matlaske was by way of being a transit camp. We were only there a matter of days.
    During this time Bob and I had only recently been commissioned, and
had had no time to spend our fifty pounds officer's kit allowance. All we had
was our Warrant Officer's side caps, and our badges of rank on our battledress.
    I was ordered to take a long week end in London to get myself a uni-
form. An Australian, 'Scratch' Adcock, was in a similar plight, and we were
loaned the squadron Auster to speed the trip.

Sunday, 24 September 1944

Scratch Adcock and I bound all day and finally borrowed an Auster to get to London and get some uniform. I was supposed to be flying the thing but our first take off was a sort of joint effort.

We tore across the field with me trying to heave it off the deck by pulling back the throttle and pushing forward the stick. They are on opposite sides to normal kites. Anyway between us we got it off.

The weather got steadily worse and I had quite a struggle to keep the kite right way up. The stick was always in one corner or the other.

We were soon hanging onto a railway line at about two hundred feet and then it started raining. The front panels, none too clear when we started, soon looked like frosted glass with the rain over them and it was most unpleasant peering out of the side windows and praying that nothing got in the way. At one point we ran into some Halifaxes taking off and had an even more worrying time for a while.

Finally when we cleared a factory chimney at Ely by about twenty feet and weren't too sure how much petrol we had, we spotted an aerodrome and decided to lob down.

As we had no A.S.I. except some Heath Robinson effort out on the wing, landing was a rather tricky business and we stalled in from about five feet, breaking a wire on the undercarriage.

So as we were too late to finish our journey that night we left the kite to be repaired and went on by rail. The aerodrome was Witch-ford, a Lancaster satellite not marked on our map even.

Tuesday, 26 September 1944

Having done our shopping Scratch, and I met at Liverpool Street and after training to Cambridge and scrounging a ride to Witchford we set off again in the Auster.

This time we remembered to put down some flap and made quite a good take off. Journey was uneventful. Except for sundry aerobatics to get out of the way of various Libs and things who all showed a marked tendency to fly straight through us.

We arrived bang on Matlaske and did a reasonable landing. Bob Cole and Bert Bailey landed in the Tiger Moth after dark with about a spoonful of petrol left.

First news we heard was that the squadron was due to go over-seas any minute.

Preparations were made for our move across the channel, and when the day came, our ground crews, their gear, together with Rocky the Labrador, were packed into Dakotas and left for Grimbergen, just a mile or two north of Brussels. We were to follow later in the day with the Tempests.

Thursday, 28 September 1944

Were up at four thirty for the move overseas. All the ground crews went in Dakotas and shortly after the last one had taken off we got ready to leave. At the last minute 'R' developed a coolant leak and Johnny Foster took my place in the formation. I was due to leave with Chas Tidy later.

They only had to tighten a hose connection on my kite so that we took off right behind the rest. I had packed my small kit, hat a pair of shoes and one or two items of kit in the sliding hood and after take off found they had shifted and jammed the hood. However I was prepared to carry on with it open, but when after half a circuit Chas's engine cut badly and he went in to land I thought I might as well too.

Later when Chas's kite had been seen to, and my kit stowed away in the gun panels we took off again with Torpy who also had turned back with a cutting engine. We had to go via North Foreland, Gravelines to Brussels.

I was leading and flew at about five thousand feet until nearly to the French coast when I had to come down to less than a thousand feet below cloud. Crossed in about a mile north of Gravelines and I turned and set course over the town. After that I must admit I was pretty well lost until we reached Denge. Passed south of Ghent a little north of track and on E.T.A. was over Aalst. The canal running north confused me rather and I did an orbit to make sure. Half way round I realised the town wasn't nearly big enough for Brussels and realised my mistake. Flew on and saw Brussels looming up. Was looking around for the drome when I suddenly spotted it beneath my nose, almost covered with Dakotas, Tempests and the Mustang wing we were taking over from.

The aerodrome had only one runway but was not nearly as bad as we had been led to expect. We found ourselves billeted in a large Chateau not tents, and the food was many times better than 150 wing had provided. Grapes and peaches were plentiful.

That evening we visited Brussels and found it a very gay city indeed. There seemed to be no great shortage of anything. Everyone seemed quite well dressed, the women made up. There was

plenty of beer wines and spirits, and no shortage of glasses. When
the Germans had been there dancing had been 'Verboten' and
they seemed to be trying to make up for lost time. Every cafe had
it's small band and they danced on every available inch of floor
space, even between the tables. Everybody seemed very friendly and
would talk to you on the slightest encouragement. A lot of the kids
wore British army badges sewn on their sleeves and almost everyone had a collection of flags of the United Nations on their lapels.

Later I heard that although you could buy all manner of things
impossible to get at home, such as fountain pens, watches, scent,
films and cameras, they were short of food and one family I talked
to in Grimbergen hadn't eaten meat for three months.

Grimbergen was a small grass aerodrome. The officers' mess being in a
quite imposing Chateau a few miles away. There was an air of urgency about
the whole set up. Quite a few pilots joined the squadron around this time,
and there was little time for introductions so that it was difficult to determine
who was ours and who was visiting. There were always lots of people, half of
whom I didn't know, and who seemed to appear and disappear at a giddy
rate. Food came from the army 'D' ration packs. Each pack consisted of half
brown stew and the other curry. If curry was on, you could smell it a mile
away, and I immediately lost my appetite. Otherwise, it was surprisingly good.

At this time it was not so very long after the fiasco of the bridges, Arnhem and Nijmegen. There had been a big push north in an attempt to
relieve our troops at the bridges. Brussels had only been liberated a matter
of days and the finger of territory held by the allies was only a mile wide in
places a few miles north of Brussels.

Friday, 29 September 1944

Did a show in the morning, a squadron patrol over the Arnhem
and Nijmegen bridges. Apparently these airborne types have captured them whole and now they are afraid the Hun will try to bomb
them, so we are doing a standing patrol over them all the while.
Show was quite uneventful. In the afternoon we did a similar show
only this time the weather was right on the deck. We had been
milling around the bridges on the deck for a while when control
told us that something might be coming up from the east and to go
in that direction.

We had been stooging about over the Hun lines for a while
when they decided to get all unfriendly and sent showers of light
flak up at us, which at about six hundred feet isn't very pleasant. I

went right down on the deck. Half way round a turn someone went down in flames and hit the ground with a terrific explosion. Later found out it was Clapperton. Frank Reid who was flying behind him saw direct hits on his engine and he caught fire and baled out. I didn't see a chute but others did and we hope to see him again soon, he was just about inside the Hun lines and might make it back with luck.

We soon decided that it was too hot around there and moved farther along towards the bridge where the main danger was from Spits who kept looming out of the rain in an alarming manner.

Soon set course for base and on landing found two other kites with holes in them.

Saturday, 30 September 1944

Did another squadron patrol over Nijmegen bridge quite uneventful. We have now lost Arnhem bridge owing to the army not reaching the airborne boys in time, so we now have to concentrate on the Nijmegen bridge which is still in our hands. 56 Sqdn got three destroyed and two probables in a mix up with 109's. Williams of 486 got a 190.

Brussels was still in a state of euphoria, with people celebrating their freedom and crowding the streets, bars, and dances. We had Jeeps allocated to the squadron and would use these to go into Brussels for the evenings.

The square in front of the Gare du Nord was crowded with parked Jeeps with various insignias on them, and it was fairly usual to find your Jeep gone when you got back to where it had been left. Nothing daunted, you jumped into the next one and drove off. Some people took to removing the rotor arm and taking it with them, which didn't achieve much since all the rotor arms were the same, and by now people carried a spare in their pocket anyway!

Someone acquired an open top Mercedes at this time, and several Lugers appeared which were acquired on forays up nearer the front.

We flew fairly regular patrols over the bridges at Arnhem and Nijmegen, but if any enemy planes were about they steered well clear of us. None were sighted on any of the trips I was on. We also did sweeps across the twin rivers of Meuse and Rhine and into Germany. "Armed recces" they called them. These were like the night rhubarbs, in that a route was planned but with no definite target. You just beat up anything that opportunity put in your way. Trains were a favourite target and any road transport was fair game. Boats on rivers, or just anything to create havoc and generally harass the enemy. Flying into Germany was satisfying. You felt you were hitting the enemy where it mattered, in his own back yard.

We were only at Grimbergen for a matter of days before moving north to Volkel in Holland.

At this time the front line was extended into a long spearhead up towards the bridges at Arnhem and Nijmegen, where there had been a frantic attempt to relieve our airborne troops holed up there. This was for a good part of it's length about four miles wide. Volkel was in this narrow strip with enemy troops not far off of the perimeter boundary.

The squadron flew up in two formations, the C.O. led the first, Spike Umbers the second. I was in the second formation which took off perhaps fifteen minutes after the first. I was second plane back on the starboard side. I don't know where Spike Umbers thought we were, but he had us fly up in close formation; nine aircraft wing tip to wing tip, nose to tail crossing the airfield at less than 1000 ft must have been a stirring sight. The German troops thought so. W/O Reid was shot down by light AA fire almost within the airfield circuit. I had to sit about forty feet away and watch him struggling to get out of the cockpit with flames all around him and not able to do a thing to help. Frank Reid was married with a young family.

He had been a pilot before the start of the war, and had the Air Force Medal, the equivalent of the D.F.M. but awarded in peacetime.

Sunday, 1 October 1944

Moved from Grimbergen to Volkel in Holland. Weather was dull all morning and when we did get off had to fly most of the way at less than a thousand feet.

About five miles south east of Volkel the Hun got unfriendly and Frank Reid was shot down by light flak, I saw a couple of red streaks go by and looked back. Frank who was on the other section, number four, was already on fire. He pulled up slightly then went down quite steeply. At about two hundred feet something flew off and I thought he had got out. Somebody else later said it was only his hood, in any case no chute opened.

We flew onto the drome and did a very tight circuit. The aerodrome is one mass of bomb craters I don't think you could walk fifty yards in any direction without falling down one. All the buildings that we didn't bomb were demolished by the Hun before he left, it's an awful shambles. One runway has been repaired and the perimeter track is OK if you steer carefully between craters, wreckage and a large bomb which still lies in the middle of it with a large flag on it.

Are billeted in the school house in the village. No kit arrived for us and we slept on the floor with one blanket apiece. I was too cold to sleep much.

Chateau at Grimbergen used for officers quarters.

Bob Cole, 'Rocky', and a Tempest V at Volkel, November 1944.

Volkel, November/December 1944. Back row, left to right: unknown, Maurice Rose, and 'Mac' Mckenzie. Centre row, left to right: 'Scratch' Adcock (in forage cap), Johnny Foster, Ted Sparrow, unknown, and Chas Tidy. Front row, left to right: 'Enoch', Bob Cole, McCullock, and Bert Bailey.

'Scratch' Adcock.

The author and his
Tempest at Volkel,
late 1944.

Volkel was a large airfield. All the runways and miles of perimeter tracks
were brick laid. The place was a regular maze. It had been heavily bombed
during its German occupation (I believe 3 Sqdn had a go at it on one occasion!), and the craters hurriedly filled in with brick rubble causing quite a
hazard to aircraft and jeep. The planes were dispersed within the shattered,
roofless walls of bombed airfield buildings, and we had a wooden hut as our
dispersal quarters. Our ground crew lived and had their workshop in a similar wooden hut built among the ruins and the aircraft.

Our first billet was in a school in Volkel village. Clean but empty. Just
walls with our camp beds within them. We didn't stay long enough to make
it more like home. Within a couple of days we moved to Uden, a slightly

larger village about four miles north of the airfield. Here we were billeted in the seminary. Some of the students were still there. God knows how they had survived a German occupation. We ragged them rather, I suppose it seemed wrong that these apparently able bodied young men should have been left alone when so many of their countrymen had been marched off to forced labour or worse. We were better off in Uden, having reasonable quarters, with showers and a decent dining room.

Travel between billet and work was by squadron jeep, and these were sometimes grossly overcrowded, and in fact it became a bit of a competition to see how many you could cram aboard. The jeep would trundle along, the driver hardly able to see for bodies clinging across the screen and with arms and legs sticking out on all sides. This was moderated suddenly when the driver of one of these jeeps didn't quite give enough clearance when passing a parked truck, and someone's knee cap was cracked on the rear corner as we passed.

Kibbie Reid.

Bert Bailey.

The little town of Uden had only recently been 'liberated' and they'd had a rough time under the Germans. Most clothing was home made. The men had shirts made from the blue and white striped material used for bedding ticks in those days. Most of the women wore blouses, scarves etc made from parachute material so conveniently delivered by our troops at the time of Arnhem a short while previously.

It was still common to see parachutes hung up in the more inaccessible parts of trees, and the countryside was littered with the broken wrecks of the plywood gliders, landed in the most impossible of places and attitudes. One wondered what state the occupants must have been in when they got out, if they did at all.

In Uden a little girl used to lie out in an iron bedstead actually on the pavement outside the house. Well wrapped up, for by now the weather was bright but quite cold. She had been wounded when the Germans fired on a crowd before moving out. Actually she made a heart rending picture, and in fact she made the front page of one of the London daily newspapers.

Most of the locals rode battered antique bicycles and they hadn't been able to get tyres for them for years. These they improvised by cutting strips from old car tyres and wiring them on. This gave a hard ride and it sounded more as if they were riding on the rims as they came rattling by. Kibby Reid, back for a second tour, had a jeep pack up on the road, and walked for help. By the time they got back to it, the jeep was sitting on bricks, and all four wheels were missing. I wonder whose bikes those tyres ended up on? They probably fetched a fortune on the black market!

Slowly we got to know people, and a local family used to do my washing for me. Language was a difficulty, in Uden there were very few English speakers. I remember on one leave I told my mother about this Dutch family and how little they had, and she baked a fruit cake, (no mean feat for we had rationing too!) and I took this back for them. I think they were usually lucky to get bread, never mind cake!.

Monday, 2 October 1944
   Did another patrol over Nijmegen. Saw an Me262 and two 109s
   way above us and started to climb after them but couldn't get near.

Wednesday, 4 October 1944
   An uneventful squadron patrol over Arnhem and Nijmegen
   with the Wing Co leading. Spent most of the trip dodging Spits
   who didn't seem to be able to make up their minds whether we
   were friendly or not. Spent most of the trip above cloud and the
   Wing Co didn't seem too sure of the way down again. Got down
   without much petrol after many small circles.

On one train busting operation we lost our boss, Wing Commander Beamont. I was not on this operation, but apparently they found a train and commenced to beat it up, only to see large numbers of uniformed figures pouring out of it. It was a troop train. The Tempests then went up and down the line strafing with great glee. They must have created havoc, and terror even among the survivors. Later I was twice on the receiving end of strafing attacks, and apart from anything else the noise numbs the senses. Instinct takes over, and the natural reaction is to hide under anything, however useless, even bedclothes. But there must have been seasoned troops among those on the train, for they shot back, and Beamont was hit in the engine and had to force land quite close to the scene. I met Beamont later in prison camp and he told me that he wasn't able to get far from the plane before the troops arrived. He hid in a ditch, but they knew he couldn't be far away and begun spraying the ditches and hedges with machine gun fire. He came out with his hands up when he knew the game was up. I suppose you couldn't expect them to be all that friendly.

Thursday, 12 October 1944

Took off on an escort job, but my wheels didn't retract fully and I had to return to base.

In the afternoon the Wing Co (Beamont) led the squadron on an armed recce. They beat up a troop train and left two engines and about five coaches burning merrily. Soon afterwards however the Wing Co's kite was seen to be streaming coolant and he force landed. Called up when he was down to say he was OK He was well inside Germany so he doesn't stand a very good chance of getting back.

Friday, 13 October 1944

Started the day with a patrol of four a/c at twenty thousand feet over Nijmegen and Arnhem. Spent most of the trip chasing a bunch of unidentified a/c about the sky. They turned out to be Rocket Tiffies when we finally caught them.

In the afternoon did a patrol with Dryland over the aerodrome. Bob Cole made a name for himself by shooting down an Me262. after chasing it nearly to Aachen. Lucky blighter!

The Germans were repeating the tactics they used at Bradwell Bay. Their Me262 jets would come over at great height. Over the airfield they would go into a dive releasing canisters of anti personnel bombs. They would then take off for home at great speed. The canisters came down on parachutes, and opened when they were low over the airfield, scattering small bomblets over a large area. These would lie unexploded on the ground until they were dis-turbed, when they would easily take off an arm or a leg.

We had tried readiness to take off after them, lying in wait for them to on their way home, all without any luck at all. They really had the better of us until Bob, while airborne, saw one on its way back to base. He was able to keep it in sight until the German thought he was safe, and throttled back allowing Bob to catch up and shoot him down. This did wonders for our moral, and we hoped it had the opposite effect on that of the Germans.

Tuesday, 17 October 1944

Two patrols over base with Teddy Sparrow Weather wasn't too bad on the first, but the second was at dusk in very duff weather. There was a beautiful fire just north of the aerodrome, and artillery flashes to the S.E. looked dangerously close, almost in the circuit.

Wednesday, 18 October 1944

Today is the fifth anniversary of my leaving civvy street. Five
bloody long years, when the hell will it finish.

Friday, 20 October 1944

Did a patrol with W/C Wray, from Volkel to Grave. Of course, just
because I was going with the Wing Co I couldn't get 'R' started. Took
the combined efforts of two fitters, myself and some fifteen cartridges before it finally consented to run. Luckily it didn't matter as a
bunch of Spits were coming in and we had to wait for them anyway.
Patrol was quite uneventful, except for chasing one or two friendlies.
The only excitement was when we met Spike and his No2 head on.

Saturday, 21 October 1944

On an early patrol the boys met up with three Me 262's but
couldn't get near enough for a shot at them. At dusk I was on a
patrol of six aircraft over Nijmegen. Was very hazy up to about
eight thousand feet and at eighteen where we were, the forward
visibility was about a mile. Did some crafty formation and turn
abouts except once when Butch who was leading said '180 degree
starboard' and turned port. By the time we returned to land it was
getting pretty dark and I thought Butch did pretty well to find the
drome. The inside of my hood and windshield had misted over, as
if the vis wasn't bad enough and hung on like grim death to the
plane in front. Butch made the mistake of making a fairly wide circuit and I couldn't see the runway. I blindly followed the bloke
ahead but when at about three hundred feet I could see the aerodrome buildings going by beneath me but no sign of the runway I
poured on the coals and went round again doing a tight circuit so
that I could see the runway all the while and got down safely. Certainly was a dicey do though.

In the evening we went to a concert given by some Canadian
Army types. We went in a jeep with no lights except a bicycle lamp
which I held out at the side. That also was a dicey do!

Sunday, 22 October 1944

Was on another patrol with six aircraft. 'R' had been flown meanwhile by Hindley who had let it oil up badly. On the perimeter track
I ran the engine up to clear it and it started cutting badly.

I was going to turn back then but decided to give it a chance. On
the runway I ran it up to 3000 revs and it was OK so I took off with it.

Everything was OK till I started to throttle back and then it started cutting like blazes so I just completed the circuit and landed. As I was coming in they fired a red at me and called up telling me that Spits were taking off on the other runway. I told them I was coming in Spits or no. They fired more reds at the other end of the runway and stopped the Spits till I was clear. It was rather a good thing that they did for they were taking off down wind and I would have met them head on instead of only at the intersection.

We were still having a good deal of trouble with the engine oiling up. The Napier Sabre didn't really like idling. It was far happier when we were chasing V1s at full bore when serviceability was the best ever. At Volkel there were miles of brick laid perimeter tracks. The ground off of the tracks was soft, as Joe Hindley found to his cost when he ran off the perimeter track and the plane tipped up on its nose.

This meant that you had to taxi slowly and with a good deal of care. This in turn meant that unburned oil collected around the sleeve valves of the engine, and when you opened up for take off, great blobs of oil came back from the exhausts. At best obscuring the windscreen, at worst causing the engine to cut.

One day, I and others were near the end of the runway when a Tempest taking off had the engine cut. It ran off the end of the runway quite near to where we were. It charged across the perimeter and onto a potato field, where it continued for about fifty yards before turning completely over on it's back.

People ran in all directions, and we found the pilot, still conscious, hanging upside down in his straps. The top of the canopy was smashed and he was too near the ground to drag out. We all got under a wing in an attempt to lift the plane enough to drag him out. I'm told a bulldozer came and got under the wing to help. This is possible, although I don't remember it. We did get him out, and by now an ambulance had arrived. I remember him walking to it unaided, and quite unconcerned, one arm torn off, the stump and sleeve shredded and bloody. He was a French pilot, Major Vaissier of 274 Sqdn, and I met him later in Brussels. He had recovered, but less one arm, and was talking enthusiastically about getting back to flying. I wonder if he ever did.

While we were struggling to lift the plane, another Tempest repeated the performance about thirty yards to our right. This one, probably going slower, didn't go right over but stayed on it's nose, almost vertical with the fuselage broken behind the cockpit and hanging down behind. The pilot of this one, Warrant Officer Torpy of 3 Sqdn, at least came away unscathed.

This sort of occurrence was becoming far too regular, and it was decided that we should in future taxi with a fitter or rigger on the wing signalling how we should steer, so as to avoid the slow zig zagging procession out to the end of the runway. This certainly did speed things up, we were able to taxi quite fast, but I wouldn't have wanted to be one of those sat on a perfectly smooth wing tip, no hand holds at all, on an extremely bumpy perimeter, with a fair chance of falling into the whirling prop, or breaking your neck if you fell off.

Saturday 28 October 1944
    After another good three day clamp the sun broke through.
Did one patrol at dawn with Bert Bailey as my number two over
Eindhoven. Was uneventful but gave me a chance to have a good

Kibbie Reid:
target practice.

McKenzie.

The author chopping wood.

McKenzie.

Ted Sparrow.

Joe Hindley's 'black'.

look around the area. Missed the drome on the way back and finished up at Grave, did better at second attempt.

On the second trip I was spare and practised aerobatics over the
drome for half an hour or so before landing. Was surprised how
good they are after all this while too. Third trip was a patrol as
number two to our supernumerary Squadron Leader Cock. We
were over Nijmegen and after watching one of our other sections

get quite a bit of flak from our unfriendly neighbours in the Reich-wald Forest were surprised when we got some flak from just south east of Nijmegen. Don't know for sure but I think it must have been coming from our own lines.

There were plenty of signs of the battle below. There usually are plenty of flashes to be seen, and it was quite impressive. They were laying a huge smoke screen over most of Nijmegen and there were several fires burning in the town and just around.

Sunday, 29 October 1944

Started the day with a patrol with Scratch, at S'Hertogenbosch. Bob was on a patrol later, saw a kite leaving twin trails and gave chase. Caught it at 26000 feet, got closer and fortunately recog-nised it as a Mosquito before he fired.

Thursday, 2 November 1944

Were doing squadron standby at the end of the runway, the idea being that when any Me 262's were reported we toddled off to their aerodrome and waited for them to return. We had hardly got out to the runway before we were scrambled. Despite the fact that the erk was putting more cartridges in my starter it wasn't a bad scramble except that in the rush he didn't turn my oxygen on.

I took off with straps hanging loose and my R.T. lead in a hell of a tangle round my neck. After struggling for what seemed hours to get my oxygen on in the cockpit I found it was still turned off at the bottle. By that time we were already at 10000 feet and still going up so I thought I'd better return. As it happened they were all recalled anyway so I didn't miss much.

In the afternoon I flew on an armed recce with six aircraft. Joe Hindley turned back soon after take off. Went to Dordrecht where Rodney and Maurice Rose went down to have a look at the bridge where they'd seen puffs of smoke. There was nothing there but quite a lot of medium flak was hurled at us, while Rodney and Maurice got their share of light. Rodney stayed on the deck for a while and we missed them altogether. Finally saw them when they went down again to have a go at a couple of tanks which were already burned out anyway when they got down. Formed up and stooged on towards Arnhem over a layer of cloud.

The others were scrambled from the end of the runway while we were airborne and were bounced by God knows what, nobody even saw them. Butch was badly shot up, had holes all over his kite and the leads shot away from one bank of cylinders. While staggering home on his own passed four Me 262's going the other direction so close he could see the crosses on their sides. Fortunately for him they didn't see him!

Saturday, 4 November 1944

Did a freelance patrol with Doug Worley as my No2. Didn't see a thing. Later did a patrol over Helmond with a new bloke, Wright. His flying was rather frightening, he slipped from one side to the other so often I never knew where to look for him. However he saw two kites that I didn't so I can't say much.

Me 262 dropped A.P. bombs in afternoon and injured 31 blokes on 121 wing on the other side of the drome.

Monday, 6 November 1944

Patrol from Helmond to Deurne with Wright. A couple of bombs dropped on the aerodrome during the afternoon, we are getting quite good at hitting the deck now.

Friday, 10 November 1944

Yesterday Butch and I planned a Rhubarb, but owing to weather and standby at the end of the runway we weren't able to get off. This morning the weather looked about right and so we got off smartly before it had time to clear up. The C.O. had told us to do it at 6000 feet but at about Grave the weather got pretty poor so we stayed on the deck, which suited us fine.

The first leg was to Amersfoort and after steering a rather erratic course we arrived there OK. Butch went on one side of the town and I the other and so low were we that I lost sight of him completely for a few minutes.

Soon we hit the Zuiderzee and turned right and flew along it's shore. We passed over a line of railway carriages near Amersfoort but decided to leave them alone. Further up we passed over a shrub covered stretch of country and saw some large camouflaged areas on one stretch made to look like a golf course.

We had been flying right on the deck when we suddenly found ourselves flying down into an inlet with three minesweepers in it and a cluster of small boats around them. It was too late to turn away and so I went as low as I could over them to make it harder for the gunners, and actually passed between the masts of two of them. Butch said afterwards he saw rather wild light flak follow us but I didn't.

Resulting damage to Butch's Tempest after the 'rhubarb' of 10 November 1944.

Further along there were some barges and a tug all going
through some locks which I would have liked to have had a go at
but Butch said it wasn't worth it. Went up as far as the inlet south
west of Meppen where we ran into some rain and turned south
again. South of Zwolle I saw a car ahead and fired a short burst at it
before it disappeared behind a house. Was a grey painted car with
some badge or emblem painted on the door.

We turned to have another look at it and it had stopped in the
side of the road, we didn't fire at it again.

As we passed Harderwijk where the minesweepers were Butch
said he was going to have a go, and turned starboard. I couldn't get
round fast enough and lost sight of him.

As I was turning onto the boats he called up and said he was hit
and I tried to find him so losing the boats as well. He said he was
heading 210 so I steered that course too. Then he said he was
going to climb for a homing but in a few minutes called again and
said he couldn't climb, so I went up at full bore to 6000 feet and
got a homing. 'Kenway' were very faint indeed and by the time I
heard them I was over cloud and had hardly turned when through
a break in the cloud I saw Rotterdam with it's docks and everything. Turned onto 125 degrees and told Butch to do the likewise.
I then had to dive down to get beneath a large cumuli nimbus
cloud and could only just hear control again. Gradually as I got
nearer it got louder, and I finally could contact Desmond our
home station direct.

Soon I came to S'Hertogenbosch and then base. I met up with
Butch and he had a large hole through his tail and a large lump
missing from his wing tip. He managed to get it down OK with no
brake pressure and left it parked at the side of the runway. Not
really a profitable trip but I enjoyed it. There's something about
skimming just above the deck which really gets you.

At dusk did a free-lance patrol with Wright. He saw a parachute
go down somewhere on the far side of the Reichwald Forest but we
were unable to pinpoint it very successfully.

Among our ground crew who had flown out from Matlaske to Grimbergen by Dakota, was Rockie, a red Labrador belonging to a girl friend of Bob
Barckley's. Bob was returning home tour expired, and it was a question of
how Rockie could be returned to his rightful owner.

Also at that time each squadron had been allocated an Auster as C.O.'s
runabout. Many had been straying over eager German gunners, and made

easy targets. They also were to be returned to the U.K. Bob Cole was due for leave, and what better way to travel home than by Auster. He also offered to take Rockie as passenger.

As he was about to climb into the Auster to leave, someone said, 'What happens if he gets difficult half way over?' Bob patted the revolver holster he was wearing, and in which he carried his father's World War I Webley .45, an enormous cannon, and said "I'll shoot him, open the door, and push him out!"

In the event Rockie sat quite contentedly at Bob's side. They landed at Hawkinge where they were met by a pretty W.A.A.F. who gave her dog a rapturous welcome, and Bob flew on to Hendon where he delivered the Auster.

We had fairly regular leave from Holland, usually this entailed taking a truck to Eindhoven where there was a regular run by Dakota to Northolt Aerodrome west of London. Then by bus to Haymarket where a transit office had been set up. From Haymarket you found your own way, reporting back forty-eight hours later for the return trip.

Once at Eindhoven we were taxiing out for takeoff in a Dakota when someone noticed that the wooden blocks, used to lock the ailerons when the aircraft was parked, were still in place. Frantic yelling at the 'clots' in the front office brought the plane to a halt while they removed the offending blocks. One would hope these would have been noticed during a cockpit check; anything strange should have been spotted before we left the parking bay.

Then on another occasion there was fog at Northolt. It really was thick, and all the pilots aboard were really biting their nails and looking most uncomfortable. Also on board were about half a dozen army officers. These 'Pongo's' were chirpy as crickets, blissfully unaware of the situation we were in. We got down OK which was a tremendous effort on the part of the pilot, and in fact the Station Commander at Northolt came out in his car to personally congratulate him. This was of course without the sophisticated blind approach aids we think nothing of these days.

By now Dickie Wingate had left the squadron 'Tour Expired'. In fact the five of us that had been posted to 3 Sqdn together had all been tour expired but were asked to stay on. A tour was eighteen months on a squadron or two hundred operational hours, whichever came first. We had been asked to stay on however until the latter had expired. Dickie on the other hand was worried about his Canadian wife who was about to have a baby and was allowed to leave. Perhaps the rest of us four should have left too!

Bob Cole was shot down on 7 November 1944. I was not on that trip, but apparently the squadron made a sweep across an airfield they were attacking. Bob saw a truck and went back on his own for a second go. He was hit by ground fire and fortunately had enough speed to climb and bale out. He was subsequently taken prisoner.

Rodney Dryland was hit by flak and had to make a false landing just behind enemy lines. He was picked up by an American patrol who had been shooting at anything that moved. He finished the patrol with them in their jeep before returning to our lines.

Ken Slade-Betts, was not so fortunate. As it turned out he was killed on 29 December 1944 although I was not aware of it at the time. I was on leave and returned to the squadron late on New Year's Eve. I was shot down the next day and nobody had told me about Ken.

CHAPTER 4

In the Bag

Christmas 1944 came and I was due for seven days of leave. I hitched a ride on a truck to Eindhoven and from there flew by Dakota to Northolt. Then on by bus to Haymarket where we wished all a "Merry Christmas" and headed for our respective homes.

It was a good Christmas, the time being shared between my own home and Joy's. It was even better when I found I couldn't get back due to bad weather grounding our air transport. Each day there would be a gathering at the Haymarket office only to be told "No flying today, come again tomorrow!"

This went on for about three days, and eventually we found ourselves in a bus on our way to Dover. We spent the night in army barracks situated on the outskirts of the town above Buckland. Next morning, it was back on the bus to Folkestone, where in the harbour we boarded an air/sea rescue launch.

Once out of the harbour and up to speed it was a pretty bumpy ride and down below decks with no view out, it wasn't long before most of us felt sea sick. Sitting there looking at all those green sickly faces wasn't helping me much, so I made my way up to a passage along the starboard side of the boat where I could see what was going on. I could also look into the driving compartment which I found interesting, and I quickly felt much better. The boat steered from buoy to buoy, and eventually into Ostend harbour.

Here it was obvious that no one wanted to know us, and another 3 Squadron pilot, Bert Bailey, and I set about cadging lifts back in the general direction of Volkel. These rides were generally in army trucks, and I remember driving alongside canals and over bridges in Bruges before ending up in Brussels at around early evening time. A visit to the R.T.O.'s office found us a bed for the night, and we then had an evening out on the town. Some of the initial euphoria had died down, but Brussels was still a lively old place. All the bars were busting at the seams with our troops and their Belgium girl friends. Even so it was impossible to sit with a beer for more than a few minutes before a frowzy, tired looking girl sat at your side, hand on your knee, demanding "Buy me a drink Tommie!" Bert reckoned you could catch a dose of anything for a few francs, and I had to agree. We had a comparatively early night.

The new francs incidentally had been issued by the military authorities, thus rendering any old currency worthless. Civilians and local people could change a reasonable amount of old for new, but this, as was intended, put black marketeers, brothel keepers and criminals, in a panic. Our troops were of course paid in the new francs and were continually pestered by shifty looking men and well set up middle aged ladies offering ten old francs for one new. I don't know what use they thought they were to us, and I doubt they got many takers—or much sympathy either.

Next morning, we resumed our marathon hitch hike northwards and arrived back at our billet in Uden at around nine o'clock in the evening. In the officers' mess we found a New Year's party in a well-advanced state. Already the floor was well awash with beer, and ties, where worn, were mostly cut off at about three inches below the knot.

We beat a hasty retreat, making our excuses. We were both completely shattered from our journey and went to bed only to be awoken by the drunken mob at a minute or two before midnight and dragged down in our pyjamas to see in the New Year. Pyjama legs rolled up to avoid the damp underfoot, we managed to negotiate "Auld Lang Syne" without physical damage, and escaped back to bed as soon as we decently could. Arriving cold sober in the middle of a party like that is no good at all—you have to be pretty far gone to find it even remotely funny!

At the crack of dawn, I was awoken by McKenzie, a Tasmanian pilot, saying, 'Ron, I feel like death itself, could you take my place on this morning's op!' So obliging old Ron hurried to dress and run downstairs to the waiting jeep. At dispersal I found the end of my tour on operations had been made official, and in telling me this the C.O. 'Jimmy' Thiele said, 'You don't need to fly again, I'll put you down as spare plane!' So in due course, I taxied out behind the others. They all took off without any problems, and I taxied back along to dispersal.

I had been back a little while, had stowed my gear, and was outside talking to some of our ground crew when we heard cannon fire from across the airfield. It was obvious that we were under attack, and as we stood there, a Fw 190 roared towards us at about fifty feet, with guns blazing. Everyone raced for cover into a wooden hut used as quarters by the ground crews on duty. I don't know what protection we thought wood would provide against cannon fire. None of us had been subjected to low level strafing at such close quarters before and the action was purely instinctive.

A rifle was standing up against the wall just inside the door of the hut and I grabbed it and raced outside again. However, nothing else came close enough for me to fire at, and I never did think to find out if it was loaded anyway.

That morning, the Germans had attacked our airfields in force. I suppose they thought we'd all be in bed nursing hangovers. In fact the Tempest wing was airborne and were quickly recalled. No 3 Squadron had been first off and arrived back to catch Me109s. They scored two kills but were short of ammunition, No 56 and 486 squadrons had only just taken off and had no such problems. No 486 arrived back over Volkel in a few minutes while the attack was going on and shot down several planes for no losses to themselves. The wing scored a total of eight destroyed, one probable and four damaged.

Volkel was practically untouched, but during the morning planes from Eindhoven and other airfields landed, and stories quickly spread about considerable damage and loss of aircraft at these fields. Some were unusable due to wrecked aircraft and smoke drifting across the runways.

Long afterwards I learned that this was an all out attack, code named 'Operation Bodenplatte', by the Germans to smash the allied airforces and their bases. However the Germans lost over two hundred planes, all in the air so that inevitably pilots were lost with them. The allies lost one hundred and twenty two planes, mostly on the ground so that only six pilots were killed. Among the German pilots were many experienced fighter leaders whom they could ill afford to lose.

Later that morning, according to my log book, I flew a patrol between base and Emmerich. It must have been uneventful for I can't remember a thing about it. After the C.O.'s words that morning I suppose I should have pointed out that I was 'Tour Expired' but my flight commander was on leave and I don't think that anyone else except the C.O. and I realised it. Anyway I didn't argue, just got on with it. The same thing happened after lunch when, again, I found myself down for another operation, and I just got on and flew it. This time, though, I really shouldn't have.

The afternoon op was an armed recce of eight planes into Germany around the vicinity of Paderborn. We had beaten up a couple of trains and then found one that was stationary. The idea was always to put the engine out of action so that the whole train was stranded.

While strafing the engine, I had a run away gun, and I remember going all the way down the train with the gun still going. You couldn't waste it. At the far end of the train, there was a signal box, so I let the gun run itself out on that. We then reformed and climbed to about eight thousand feet and set course for home, stooging along in open formation as you did over enemy territories. Suddenly, there were black puffs around us and then a huge bang, so loud I could hear it inside the plane. If you could hear it above the noise of a two thousand horse power Sabre engine situated just in front of your nose, it had to be damn close. The next thing I knew there was oil coming back all over the nose and windshield. First a few spots, then lots, so I realised

I had been hit. Obviously without oil the engine was going to overheat, so having seen one or two planes burst into flames in the air, I closely watched the already rising temperature gauge. We knew roughly how hot you could let it get, and it became obvious that I wasn't going to get home.

There were two recognised ways of bailing out. One was to tip the plane on it's back and drop out, the other was to hold the stick well back and trim the plane forward. Then you push the stick forward and shoot out of the cockpit. I didn't really like the idea of the latter, so I decided to tip it on it's back and go out that way.

I had already pulled the canopy jettison lever, which also jettisons a panel in the right hand side of the cockpit, and with the thought of getting burnt, I had already undone the harness, so as to get out fast. As I started to roll the plane I found myself falling into the hole in the cockpit side left by the panel. The parachute jammed so that I couldn't get out and I couldn't get back in.

The plane meanwhile had gone into a dive, and I was eventually whipped out like a piece of paper. I remember seeing the green, blue, green, blue of earth and sky, alternating as I tumbled over and over, but there was no real sensation of falling. I had gone out with my hand already on the handle of the rip cord and I found myself yanking on it long after the jerk as the chute opened Then suddenly everything became deathly quiet and peaceful. I looked up at the canopy with some relief. I never did believe these things were infallible, nor that I would ever find the nerve to use one. Bob Cole and I had discussed the prospect, and I had always said I would stay with the plane and try to set it down if possible. When faced with the prospect of burning, I didn't give it a second thought.

After leaving the plane I didn't see what became of it, and in fact I later learned that Don Butcher returned and circled me; I didn't see him either. Within two days he was able to visit my parents and tell them that he had seen me hanging in my parachute, apparently well and unhurt. This must have been a great relief to them. Meanwhile the harness had come down and pinned my left arm to my side so that I couldn't move it.

Having been pulled out of bed that morning in a hurry, I still had a wallet in my pocket so I spent my time coming down getting rid of all the bits of paper that might be of any use to the Germans. I kept the wallet, this having been given to me when I 'passed out' in Clewiston, Florida. I needn't have bothered, it vanished at the first search.

It is easy to think you are just hanging there, you don't seem to be moving, but of course when you get lower you realise that the ground is coming up quite fast and the last few feet, it rushes up. They told us in training that a parachute landing was equivalent to jumping off of a twenty foot wall.

I could see that I was coming down in a small wood by the railway. By this time I was going backwards and I couldn't turn myself because of my trapped arm. But as it happened, I fell through the branches, the chute getting caught up in the tree tops. So the actual seat of the parachute must have stopped about two feet, six inches off of the ground.

I released the harness and ran off through the woods. It was quite a dense wood of young trees, rectangular in shape, bordered on the north by a railway, and about half a mile by a quarter of a mile in size with otherwise open country all around. I came to the end of the wood and was about to emerge from the trees onto a path when a soldier came by on a bicycle. He had his rifle off his shoulder, resting across the handlebars. He didn't see me, so I ducked back into the wood. I made my way up to the top edge of the wood and came out by the railway. Looking along the railway, I could see a gang of people working. I didn't realise at the time, but they were probably displaced persons and might have helped me. I made off again into the wood and came out into a small clearing, only to be confronted by a group of school children on the other side. I ran back the way I had come, but they followed me. As I ran, they ran, when I walked, they walked, they just stayed a safe distance behind me and of course some of them had gone off to bring the soldier back.

When he caught up with me, he kept demanding "papier, papier". I didn't have much in the way of papers, so I was searched. The only weapon that I was carrying was a forces jack knife. I was then taken to a signal box by the railway. I was shut in the lower part of the building below the actual signal box for about three hours. People came and looked through the window, all the kids were intrigued to see this foreigner. I was in quite a mess being covered from the waist up in engine oil. I must have been a terrible sight. Eventually, a Luftwaffe sergeant came along from the local town (this being Dülman, I found out after the war) and walked the two miles back into town.

They had their H.Q. in what was a lock up shop. It had been gutted and had trestled tables and chairs across it. I was offered a seat and while I was waiting the sergeant tried to talk to me. He told me of his family in Aachen and how they had suffered during the war. He told me how his brother had been sent to the Eastern Front and they hadn't heard from him for so long. He showed me pictures of Hitler that he kept in the front of his wallet and I asked him what he thought of Hitler now the invasion had come. He said that he thought Hitler had some way of helping them. Of course, they had been promised the secret weapons—doodle bugs, V2s, etc.—and were expecting others. It was really quite difficult to talk to him because he spoke so little English. He then went over the road and came back with his girlfriend. She gave us some black bread and salami type meat, and a pot of coffee, which was very decent of her.

Long after dark, I was taken through the town to the local gaol. The sergeant gave me what bread he had left. The cell I was put in was about three feet wide by about eight feet long. The bed was a board affair that let down from the wall on chains with a sack of straw to sleep on and no pillow. The cell had a small window about one foot square which you could just see out of if you stood on the bed. Looking out of this window your eyes were at ground level.

I was a real curiosity. The door would be flung open and a group of people would crowd into the opening. Their leader, often dressed in uniform, would rant and carry on in German, and the phrase "frau und kinder" was in frequent use, from which I gathered I was being called a murderer of women and children. Then they would point at me with two fingers, as if shooting, and say, "Kaputt, Kaputt". I expected to be dragged out and put against a wall any minute.

On the second day the door opened, and this time there were just two of them. A portly Prussian-looking man in his fifties, dressed very smartly in a light chestnut brown uniform, accompanied by a weedy-looking character in civilian dress. The portly one motioned me into the corridor and started the usual women and children rant, and when I didn't respond, he started to hit me about the head. I warded off most of the blows with my arms, and he undid the flap of his pistol holster. The weedy one grabbed me from behind, and the blows continued. Luckily, my arms were still free, and I was again able to take most of the blows on my forearms. I think he got out of breath quite quickly and I was pushed back into my cell. I felt sure he would have liked me to make a break for it along the corridor, when he would have shot me with the greatest of pleasure. It was all very unsettling.

Some time in the middle of the day, the gaoler came with a battered aluminium saucepan with mashed potatoes and cabbage, cooked without salt and stone cold. Hungry as I was, I couldn't eat it. I asked him if I could go to the toilet, and he indicated that he was unarmed and slammed the door on me. No one else came near until the following day.

January 3 dawned, and I was very thirsty having had nothing to drink since the afternoon of the first. Mid-morning, an officer arrived wearing a long great coat with a brown velvet collar and wearing a peaked cap, high at the front and with the peak low over his eyes. He let me out to a toilet, but by then my insides had given up, I suppose; with nothing going in, it was unreasonable to expect much to come out. I asked him if I could have some water, and he shouted, "Nicht Wasser!" and started carrying on again about killing women and children. He got more and more worked up and started lashing out at me. I was able to ward off his blows, and eventually, he patted his revolver and, pointing at me, said, "Kaputt!" He slammed the door as he left.

About half an hour later, he came back with a young girl of about fifteen who spoke a little English. He asked if I were an officer and appeared to disbelieve me when I said "Yes". I probably looked a sorry sight, my battle dress soaked in engine oil and not a sight of soap or water for nearly three days. He also asked me how many times I had bombed German cities, we were after all on the edge of the heavily bombed Rühr. Remembering the shooting threat I was glad to be able to say "none". I tried to point out how many cities all over Europe had been bombed long before the German ones began to suffer, and I think but for the girl he would have turned nasty again. I was again returned to my cell.

Around the middle of the day, a Luftwaffe feldwebel came, and I was taken away in an ancient prewar Opel car. I sat in the rear, the feldwebel in front next to the driver. It wasn't a very secure arrangement, and I felt more like royalty than a prisoner.

I was first taken to the site where the plane had come down. It had gone in nose first between two houses on a corner. It was a built-up residential district, and they were lucky there was no damage to buildings and no one hurt. The earth had been thrown up around a crater and only about the rear third of the fuselage was showing from where I sat in the car. The feldwebel got out of the car, climbed the rim, and peered down into the crater. I wasn't invited to follow him. When he got back in the car, he pointed to the plane and then at me, obviously connecting me to the plane, I wasn't sure if he was asking me or telling me.

After another two or three miles, the Opel's engine spluttered and died. We coasted to a standstill, and several attempts were made to restart the engine until, quite quickly, the battery showed signs of weariness. The feldwebel signed to me to get out and help him push. I suppose I should have refused, but in about a foot of snow, with no top coat and no proper food in what seemed like living memory, my teeth were beginning to chatter, and I was glad to do something to get moving again.

Our efforts were to no avail anyway, and we pushed the car along to where a long drive ran slightly downhill between an avenue of trees to a farm house about a quarter of a mile away.

The feldwebel set off down the drive to try to get help or the use of a telephone, leaving the driver in his seat and me in the back. The driver had his rifle between his knees, but on the floor in the back was a tow rope with a big galvanised eye on one end. It was tempting and should have been easy to overpower the driver, and I considered this. I think it was the thought of travelling lightly clad in the extremely cold weather through hostile country and with the prospect of crossing, almost certainly by swimming, the Rhine and the Meuse rivers that really dissuaded me from trying.

The moment passed and eventually the feldwebel came back looking annoyed and had obviously had no luck at the farmhouse. After some discussions the driver fished out the starting handle and while the feldwebel sat at the controls, put all his considerable beef into winding up the engine. Surprise, surprise, it started. We drove a few more miles to a small town where another shop, open fronted, had been laid out with trestle tables and made into an army mess hall.

A meal was brought to us, mostly potato and cabbage, and a mug of their ersatz coffee. It was said that they made this coffee from ground acorns. From the way it tasted, I could believe it. At any rate it was hot. Although the mess was crowded with soldiers, no one took any notice of me.

After lunch the feldwebel and I walked through the town to another gaol, where I was put in a cell to spend the night. This cell was larger and cleaner than the previous one, but so cold. A fire was lit, and the single pipe along one wall of the cell got hot but made little difference. During the evening bread and cheese as well as another mug of coffee appeared through a hatch in the door. Soon after, the heating pipe slowly cooled off. I don't think I slept at all that night, I was so cold. I tried moving about doing exercises etc, but I couldn't keep that up for hours. The bed was on the floor and consisted of a board fixed on edge, bordering a mattress hard packed with straw. There were no blankets or pillow. In desperation I tried lying underneath the mattress, but I was still too cold to sleep and the dust and dirt coming out of the mattress finally drove me out again. I spent the whole night with my teeth chattering, until soon after day break when a couple of slices of bread and jam, and another mug of hot coffee suddenly appeared through the hatch.

Shortly afterwards, I was taken to another nearby cell where two Luftwaffe N.C.O.s were waiting, and then the feldwebel from the day before turned up. He gave the other two instructions, handed over rations which they put in their packs and we went out into the street. There awaited a lorry with a large covered trailer behind it. The lorry already had a pretty full load of forces personnel, and the two N.C.O.s and I climbed into the trailer, which was pretty well full mostly with displaced persons (D.P.s). D.P.s were people from countries occupied by Germany and forced into slave labour. They were in a shocking state; all looked grey and gaunt, underfed and dirty. Their coats were in tatters, one had his toes poking out of his boots which were bound round with strips of cloth. Another had no footwear at all, just rags bound round his feet.

These men appeared curious about me, and one tried to talk, I gathered they were from Italy. He peered closely at the wings on my battledress top and spelt out R.A.F. He turned to his comrades, and there was some excited chatter among them. I heard "R.A.F." repeated several times and derisory laughs directed at the Germans in the trailer. Then they started making actions with their hands, mimicking bombs falling and yelling loudly, 'Boom . . . boom . . . boom . . . boom!' at the end of each action, and all the time grinning fiendishly at the German soldiers. Remembering all too well my recent lack of popularity, I was glad when we stopped and they dropped off the back of the trailer, still yelling, "R.A.F. OK!" and giving 'V' signs.

We came to the outskirts of a city and even I , used to the damage caused by German bombs in London during their 'Blitz', was awed by the devastation. We bumped and wound our way at walking speed over and through piles and piles of brick rubble. There wasn't a building standing in a habitable state for mile after mile, and the road was buried under it all somewhere.

Eventually, we reached Essen railway station, where we alighted. There, we waited for something like two hours for a train. Nobody seemed to have any idea of when a train might be coming. It was pretty obvious that their transport system was having a hard time, and schedules and timetables had gone by the board.

I hadn't any idea where we were going, but wherever it was, it looked like being a slow journey. At times the train slowed to a crawl and often stopped, sometimes in stations, sometimes not. By now I was on first-name terms with my two guards. They were both men in their fifties, and though burly and of rough appearance were friendly and in fact quite kindly. They tried to talk, which was difficult since neither spoke a word of English, and I had about a dozen words of German. One, a Gefreiter (Lance Corporal), was called Fritz; the other was an Unteroffizier (N.C.O.) named Hans. Fritz had been a prisoner of war in the First World War and became quite nostalgic about his time spent in England.

We reached Marburg around lunchtime on 5 January, having so far taken a day and a half to cover the ninety odd miles from Essen. At Marburg we had lunch in a crowded waiting room. Hans managed to rustle up some mugs of 'coffee', and we ate bread and wurst from their packs. Afterwards we sat on a seat on the platform and Fritz and Hans went off in turn to find a wash room. Fritz loaned me his razor and soap and I had my first wash since the afternoon of 1 January. It worked wonders even if the water was cold, the soap ersatz, the razor blade blunt, and my beard five days old.

Eventually, after another long wait a train came into the station and we set off again. This train was crowded and many of the travellers appeared to be families carrying most of their belongings in a sheet tied at the four corners. After travelling about an hour the train stopped and then backed up until it was in a cutting. Fritz indicated that it was an air raid, and after a few minutes everyone crowded to the windows. Over their heads I saw several Lightnings pass over quite low. I got one or two filthy looks and I began to wonder if my two guards were there to prevent me escaping or for my protection.

After about two hours we started moving and eventually reached Frankfurt after dark. From what I could see Frankfurt seemed in an even worse state than Essen. We then caught a local train to Oberhausel, from where we walked about two miles through deep snow to my next place of residence, which turned out to be an interrogation centre. As we went, Fritz said, "You'll be OK now, with many friends", and what was left of our rations were given to me.

Inside the gates of the camp I found myself in a long single storied building constructed from wood and plaster board. I was taken into a room and Fritz and Hans shook hands and left. I was made to strip and was searched, the first time anyone had thought to do that. I was allowed to dress and allowed to keep my watch and the food I had with me. I was taken down a long central corridor with doors on either side. Outside each door there was a pair of shoes, I didn't think they'd been put out for cleaning. At intervals along the corridor there was a guard carrying a machine gun.

A door was opened, I was ushered in, and it slammed behind me. Once again, I was in solitary. My new cell was about six feet by eight, a window was in the wall opposite the door with an electric radiator beneath it. The bed was along one side and comprised an angle iron framework with a few boards across it, and a mattress filled with straw and shavings. There was a single small and very thin blanket. A light was set into the ceiling with a wire grill over it. A red button by the door operated a red arm in the corridor so that you could attract attention should you want it. The heater was operated by a large rotary switch outside the door, which went on and off with a loud *clunk* so that you could hear them being switched on or off all along the corridor.

That first night, I was very cold. The radiators were switched on and off all night at about four hour intervals. When they were on, it was bearable—barely—and you would dread the *clunk* . . . *clunk* . . . *clunk* approaching along the corridor as they went off. I would lie there hoping that they would miss mine; they never did. I came to realise that the bed was clever too, designed to prevent rather than encourage sleep. There were enough boards to support you, but with wide gaps between them. They were also on the short side so that if you did by some chance start dozing and moved, a board would fall through and as you bulged into the gap others would slide together and you'd wake up with a start and your backside on the floor. The blanket was roughly square, and not long enough in either direction to cover both shoulders and feet, so that one end or the other was always freezing. I was glad when morning came!

Eventually there was a clattering out in the corridor, doors banging and boots clumping up and down. Then my door opened and breakfast arrived, two slices of black bread, a dob of bright red jam (no butter) and a bowl of their ersatz coffee (no milk or sugar).

Around mid morning the door opened and a small, weedy, clerk came in with two guards and a thick bundle of forms over his arm. He peeled off one of these and gave it to me together with a small stump of pencil, saying, "You write please" before leaving.

The form was about foolscap size and started innocuously enough with "Name? Rank? Number? Next of kin?" but went on to "Squadron? Where based? Call sign? Type of aircraft?" and so on. We were only supposed to give answers to the first three, but I couldn't see any harm in giving next of kin, and I couldn't pass up any chance that my family might get to know that I was okay; the rest I ignored. The clerk when he returned got agitated and said, "You must write, please" I suspected that that was all the English he knew.

After that came lunch: a bowl of watery soup, made, I'm sure, from meadow mowings boiled up. There were several bits in it which I recognised as weeds.

I had noticed that at intervals numbers would be called out in German, and passed from guard to guard along the corridor, followed by doors banging and feet thumping along the bare boards of the corridor. I gathered that people were being taken out of other cells, but for what? Interrogation? Beating? Torture? Shooting? My imagination was running away with itself. Shortly after lunch, the number *neun und zwanzig* (twenty-nine) was called, and this time the footsteps stopped outside my door which was then opened. I was taken along the corridor by two armed guards, out into the open, through the snow to another similar building and ushered into an office. The guards left. Behind a desk a tall slim man was putting a blue grey tunic onto a hanger in a cupboard. After closing the cupboard door, he turned and, reaching across the desk, offered his hand, saying, "Hello, Ron, I'm George!" In almost R.A.F. blue trousers, light blue shirt, black tie, and an accent-free English, I could have been meeting my new C.O. Without thinking I took the offered hand but then realised what I was doing and dropped it as if it was red hot.

George was not in the least put out and indicated that I should sit down. Then he talked, and talked, and talked—in impeccable R.A.F. officers mess English, with all the current R.A.F. slang in all the right places. You could be forgiven for thinking you were talking to a rather garrulous colleague.

"What's Ealing Broadway looking like these days?" No answer. "I used to live just off of the Ealing Road, a nice place to live, I was very happy there." He went on to talk about London generally, and obviously knew it better than I did—and I was a Londoner! He went on to sport; football; cricket; women. Onto cars and the various merits of various marques, and all sorts of subjects, but never the war.

I realised that he was trying to get me involved in the conversation, but during training, both in the army and airforce, we were warned of this ploy. Once you start talking, it is very difficult to stop, and the subject is soon brought round to things other than sport and women.

At the end of this marathon one-sided chat, he said quite casually, "How about this silly form, it has to be completed in order to definitely identify you as the pilot of a particular crashed plane. There are probably thousands of your agents in our country who have done their filthy work and would love to get into a nice safe prisoner of war camp until the war is over. Let's just get it done so that the system is satisfied, and then we can get you out of here to a proper camp where you will be more comfortable, and among your friends." Silence. "Look, old chap, you don't think someone of your rank can tell us anything we don't know already, do you?" He produced a booklet from the drawer of his desk and said, "What would you like to know? At Volkel, we have squadrons . . .", and he rattled off squadron numbers, aircraft identification letters, radio call signs, together with C.O.'s names. I was supposed to be impressed—which I certainly was! Only one item was incorrect: he gave Spike Umbers as our C.O.; he was in fact a flight commander.

Since he only spoke of Volkel squadrons, it was obvious that he already knew the aircraft that I had been flying. I said that I was only bound to give him my name, rank, and number; the guard was called, and I was returned to my solitary home—*neun und zwanzig*—to brood on the matter. I had been in 'George's' office for over three hours. And brood I did for a further five days.

I think a sign was put on my door, for the lack of comfort increased. I cannot say that I was ill treated, but if I pushed the red button, no one came for an hour or so. The heater switches were clunked on one after another, but just as I was in a frenzy of anticipation expecting mine to go on the footsteps would retreat. Then just as I had reached the depths of despondency—*clunk*—it would go on.

I was so cold. I tried sleeping under the mattress one night but it didn't improve matters and in fact dirt and bits of shaving came out of the mattress. I must have swallowed a shaving, and could feel it stuck in my throat for weeks afterwards. Another dodge which was more successful was to drag the bed up near to the radiator, and sit on the bed rail, feet on the radiator, with my blanket over my head and the radiator. That way I hoped to confine what little heat there was in a smaller space and perhaps raise the temperature to where I could stop shivering. I suppose it might have helped, but I was still pretty miserable. Our shoes were taken away each night which was a pity for I still had my fur lined flying boots which would have at least kept one end of me warm.

Lying on the bed I found a small piece of glass mirror. In this position I could also see the days scratched off by my unknown predecessors. Six vertical lines and a stroke across for each week on the underside of the angle iron bed rail. I started my own set using a corner of the mirror. I was encouraged to see that none of these others seemed to have spent more than three weeks there.

Days went by, and I was beginning to wonder if I had been forgotten. I would listen to the numbers being shouted up and down the corridor, but I never heard mine. The trouble, too, was that *neun* sounded very much like *ein*, and sometimes, I would get off of the end of the bed, all braced for another battle with George, only to hear another door down the corridor being unlocked. I quickly got to the state where I would have welcomed anything happening, as long as something did.

Then after five days, my number was called, and I went again across to see 'George'. He didn't waste time on idle chat this time but started straight away about how silly I was not to give him the few details required on their form. He said he knew that they weren't able to keep people at Oberhausel in any sort of comfort. Then there were the excuses about the food. "Germany is short of food, because of the indiscriminate bombing by your people we cannot get food to where it is needed. Our own people also are short of food, so why should we feed you any better than them? Are you cold? I'm afraid we have to ration the power, the power station has been damaged, and fuel is short. You would be better off in a proper P.O.W. camp, among your friends and where they are better able to look after you!" He carried on a bit about our bombing: "Did you see Frankfurt? Such a beautiful city, ancient buildings, all in ruins!" I couldn't help reminding him that German bombers had attacked open cities such as London and ancient country towns like Canterbury long before we retaliated. Then realising that I was in danger of joining a discussion, I shut up again.

He got up and paced up and down behind his desk, still talking and I reached over and picked up his information booklet which was lying on the desk. He started forward as if to stop me but I suppose he thought it couldn't hurt and let me flick through it.

I tried not to dwell longer on one page than another, which was pointless really, since I was sure he already knew that I was flying a Tempest which were all based at Volkel. It was really amazing the information that had been gleaned from various sources, and I couldn't help but wonder what, or who, those sources might be. But that was that for the moment and I went back to my cell for what turned out to be a further eight days. During this time I could hear other people moving about and it added to a feeling of despondency and doubt. Was I being silly? Nothing much they didn't know already. It's surprising the way thoughts and imagination can run riot when you are kept away from your fellows.

One day, in the corridor on the way back from a long-overdue toilet visit, I met Ken Brant, whom I had been with in Florida and hadn't seen since. He said he had already been there three weeks and didn't intend to say anything however long he stayed. Before we could say much more we were brusquely parted, but the meeting short as it was did wonders for my morale.

One day, an American colonel was moved into the cell next to mine and at intervals during the day I could hear discussions going on. That evening I heard his door open, and voices of at least two others in with him and I could clearly hear him answering all their questions without hesitation. Aircraft details, base, personnel, radio call signs of his and other squadrons. At the time I was mad as hell and could hardly restrain myself from banging on the wall. Later, I wondered if it wasn't a put up job. He was only there less than a day, he was moved out shortly after the interview.

On a couple of occasions during my stay, there were lightning searches. There would be the thudding of many feet along the corridor, key turned in lock, door thudding back with a crash, and a couple of officers and a couple of N.C.O.s would crowd in.

One tipped the mattress up and went all round the cell, the other went through my pockets. There wasn't much to search after all, I think it was more for effect, it was all accompanied by a good deal of shouting and banging about. Anyway they didn't find my piece of mirror or the scratches under the bed rail, so that was a minor victory for me.

Eventually, I was again taken over to see 'George'. The tactics were changed; this time, he commiserated with me on the conditions under which we were kept. I probably looked a mess. I hadn't had a proper wash or a shave since the railway station at Marburg. Come to think of it, I hadn't had a bath or shower since leaving England some three weeks ago. My oil-soaked battle dress smelt like a back street motor repair shop, and I'm sure lack of sleep and proper food had taken it's toll. George was all sympathy and said, "Hang on, I'll see if I can get you some food!"

He came back in a few minutes with a soup plate filled with macaroni with a thick meat gravy over it. He placed it in front of me with a fork, and I must admit that I whacked into it with relish. Food never tasted so good. Of course, while I was eating, he started talking.

"We gave your fellows a good pasting New Year's morning, really caught them with their pants down! Planes shot up on the ground, and transport." I couldn't stop myself from laughing. I said "The only planes damaged where I was were two FW190s shot down by our aircraft just off of the airfield. There were no aeroplanes or transport damaged on the ground that I heard of."

He took my plate when I had scraped clean the last morsel and went out. In a few minutes he returned and I was taken along the corridor to another office, far more luxuriously appointed, and with an obviously high ranking officer sitting behind a large desk. I was asked to repeat what I had already said, and grilled about how our planes appeared to be airborne and waiting. This was not so, of course. No 3 squadron were returning from a sortie and 486 and 56 had not long taken off. They were all recalled and directed to where the action was taking place.

I returned to my cell, but later that night was taken across to the interrogation block again. This time I found myself in a well appointed room with drinks set out on a table. I was now in the company of three Germans. 'George' wasn't there, but an officer introduced himself as major somebody or other and said.

"These two gentlemen are pilots from one of our fighter squadrons."

I felt like a tramp at the Ritz! They were immaculately turned out. Highly polished black jack boots, the pilots in beautiful black leather jackets, and there was I in an ill fitting army battledress, black with evil smelling engine oil, unwashed, unshaven, and probably rivalling my jacket in foulness of smell. However I was offered cognac which I didn't refuse; it was warming and contained calories after all. A cigarette was offered which I refused.

The pilots tried to start a conversation on the relative merits of their aircraft as compared to those of the British, but I wasn't going to be drawn into that, and an uneasy silence developed. The Germans standing together on one side of the room, and I alone on the other. I think a bell push must have been pushed, for before I could get a second cognac the door opened and I was ushered out and returned to my cell.

Later that evening I was taken across the camp to another cell. Fuel shortage or not this was certainly warmer, and although we were still in solitary confinement no attempt was made to stop us from shouting to one another.

The next morning, I was interviewed by a civilian political officer. A very half hearted affair. A few questions about any political affiliations that I might have, and a long speech about all the good Hitler and the National Socialist Party had done for Germany. Later that day, I was moved into a large room with about fifty other American and British N.C.O.s and officers. That night we had to sleep where we could. There were no beds and I was lucky to commandeer a table top. Most others were on the floor, curled up where they could find space.

Early next morning, by now 20 January, we were moved out to a *Durlagluft* (transit camp) near Wetzlar. Most went by train, I was one of the lucky few who managed to get aboard a bus. On arrival we were searched again, had more pictures taken, were fingerprinted, and were issued with U.S. Army underclothes—close-knitted 'long johns' and long-sleeved vests that buttoned up to the neck, all in a delicate shade of khaki. We were also given soap, but they were short of supplies and several items were not available. Of these the one I missed most was a toothbrush. I also got a tin of pipe tobacco but no pipe to smoke it in. All this was by courtesy of the Red Cross. We then had a shower and a change. It was wonderful.

The food at this camp was quite good but in short supply and despite it being supplemented with Red Cross food we were hungrier than at Oberhausel. We were free to wander about in the camp; maybe the extra exercise made the difference.

One night while at Wetzlar, there was an air raid—quite a display from our windows and said to be on the Leitz Optical factory. There was also a daylight raid on 22 January by Thunderbolts on an ammunition train which was quite spectacular.

Now that we were together there was a lot of discussion after being in solitary, and I was able to discover that Bob Cole had passed through on his way to Barth up on the Baltic on 19 December. I was glad to hear that he was okay.

On 24 January we started on our way to Barth ourselves. About one hundred and fifty of us were marched to the station, and boarded box cars. These had a central sliding door, to the left of which wire netting had been put over a wooden frame with a door of similar construction in the centre. Small windows were open to the elements and were criss crossed with barbed wire. The floor had been covered with straw and a wooden form had been put along either side.

Thirty eight of us were herded into this cage, six guards occupied the remainder of the truck. We had been issued with a Canadian Red Cross parcel between two men and Frank Lock, a South African, and I shared one. Damp had got into many of the parcels and some of the contents spoiled. Luckily, ours was okay.

The truck was very crowded and there was no question of everyone sitting or lying down together. The forms of course were more nuisance than they were worth. It was also cold and draughty. We spent our first hour trying to block up some of the cracks with the straw.

Except for a lot of shunting, we didn't move for hours, and by next morning we found ourselves stationary in yet another marshalling yard. Then via Kassel to Halle where we were again stationary for hours. The story went around that we'd missed a fast train which we were due to be hitched onto, and they didn't know what to do with us.

After four days the rations issued to our German guards for the journey ran out, and they were only able to issue two loaves of their black bread per car each day. Luckily while in Halle they were able to get us an issue of a good oatmeal soup.

Eventually, we arrived at marshalling yards south of Berlin. We had been told to expect a five day journey and by now our Red Cross parcels were also running low. We were able to trade cigarettes for bread with rail workers through the window and Frank Lock and I were able to get a loaf for twenty. By now we had teamed up with two Americans Al Robertson and Charlie Loring. We fought for our own bit of floor space and took it in turns to stand or lie down under the bench for about four hour stretches. Frank and I shared our loaf with the other two. One of the Americans faked up a packet of dog ends to look like a full packet of cigarettes and traded it for bread. Everyone thought it a great joke, but of course trading came to an end.

On our first two nights in the marshalling yards at Berlin, there were air raids. The guards left the box car as soon as the alarm went, the sliding door was slammed shut, and we heard the padlocks go on. It was pretty scary listening to the A.A. fire getting ever nearer, and at the height of the raid the racket from guns, bombs, whistling shrapnel and on occasions the thump as a spent shell hit the ground too close for comfort. It was said they were Mosquito raids, though how anyone knew was a mystery to me.

On our third day in Berlin we moved to more marshalling yards nearer the city. We got some more rations including some soup, which was very welcome. The bread was two weeks old. Later we were to be given bread over a month old. It didn't seem to ever go stale. Al Robertson said this was due to the fact it was made of compressed saw dust. I could quite believe it.

Our fourth night in Berlin was spent in yet further rail yards in the Templehof area. That day we were given bread but nothing else and were reduced to melting snow to drink. The strain was beginning to tell on the guards, and they were pretty short when we asked for water, or to get out onto the track to relieve ourselves. This was always an embarrassing business. About a dozen of us would be let out of the car at a time to accompanying shouts of "Schiesen, schiesen!!" We got the drift. So there we were, open to the gaze of all and sundry, stood over by half a dozen guards, dropping our pants and exposing our tender parts to the icy blast blowing across some foot and a half of snow, trying to obey a call of nature which would only be heard two hours later when we were once again locked in our all too familiar box car.

During that fourth night an American named Shirley went down with a fever. In the morning we saw several trains heading north loaded with tanks and all sorts of other war materials. By now the Russians were advancing fast along the Baltic coast and that's no doubt where these trains were headed. We were informed that due to the war situation they could no longer get us to Barth and would be moving us to a nearer camp. We were transferred to a local train that afternoon and travelled about forty or fifty kilometres south of Berlin to Luckenwalde. From here we marched about three kilometres to Stalag IIIA. By now some of our number were so weak they only made camp with help from others.

Once in the camp we went through the usual de-lousing and shower routine. The shower was quite an experience. At least fifty of us at a time, shivering in an almost 'out of doors' shed under an array of piping. We were warned that water would be turned on for one minute only. Then the warm water was turned on; what bliss. Then came the realisation that seconds were ticking away and a frantic rush to soap all over and get it washed off. Most of us managed it. Luckily, the German ersatz soap produced practically no lather. Out at the other end we dried, and our fumigated clothes were handed back to us.

We were led between rows of barbed wire, through gates into a compound which had a row of probably twelve long single storied wooden huts. We were led into the second of these. To the right about half the available floor space was taken up by three double rows of three tier bunks. In the middle was a tiled stove. The bunks were made of wood with loose wooden slats (bed boards) laid across. On this was laid a straw filled mattress and we were each allocated two blankets. There weren't actually enough bed boards or blankets to go round, luckily our crowd were in early and we got our share. I was even able to claim a top bunk. There were 150 of us in the hut and an overflow of about a dozen Americans were put in the first hut which already had a contingent of Polish army officers in it. They looked very smart in their light brown uniforms and square topped caps. They had all been prisoners since the outbreak of war in 1939 and were rather subdued compared to the noisier of our American friends.

We had barely settled down when it was announced that Shirley, who had been taken ill on the train, had been diagnosed as having scarlet fever. We were immediately put into quarantine. That is, a wire was stretched across the compound between our hut and that containing the Poles and a guard put on it to ensure no one crossed over. However, we had contact with those in the other hut because we both used the same toilet facilities.

Somewhere on the camp a radio was obviously operating and within minutes a bulletin was issued via the toilets giving details of the Russian advance along the Northern Baltic coast, and we were all encouraged to hear how far they had got. Our incarceration might not be very long after all.

Soon after our arrival we were issued with a bowl of oatmeal, one fifth of a loaf of bread and some ersatz coffee. Thinking this was one meal and still being pretty hungry we ate the lot, only to learn that this was our ration for the day.

We soon learned that we were the first English-speaking prisoners to arrive at the camp. Most others were French, with a compound of Norwegians, and the few Polish in the next hut. There were also a large number of Russians somewhere on the camp. They were ill clothed for the wintry conditions, ill fed and used for all the nastiest jobs around the camp. Rumour had it that they were dying at a rate of eight a day.

The French did most of the running of the camp and some were trustees, allowed out of the camp and down to the town. They ran the kitchen and we soon found that it was necessary to bribe them with cigarettes in order to get our proper allocation of rations.

It was terribly cold in the hut. Fuel for the stove was doled out in meagre amounts, and even when the stove was lit it hardly made any difference.

At night some of the Americans slept together, partly for warmth, but also because we did not have enough bed boards or mattresses to go round. Bed boards were always in short supply and vanished in an amazing way, mostly I'm sure into the stove. Demands for more turned out to be a favourite way of aggravating the Germans. I don't think I ever had more than four, four inch wide boards, and since these were not fixed, they had to be strategically spaced so that the right parts of the anatomy sagged through. Sometimes a board would suddenly slide along, and you would wake up suddenly to find yourself in danger of falling onto the person beneath.

Our compound comprised an area with a long line of wooden huts. In front of these was a space of about twenty yards bordered by a high wire fence with a gate in it's centre. Through the gate was an exercise area which we called the football pitch, although we had neither the necessary ball or the energy for such games. This was bordered by a double barbed wire fence some ten feet high and overlooked by wooden watch towers. Inside the wire fence and about fifteen feet from it was a single wire about two feet from the ground. We were warned that anyone crossing beyond this wire was liable to be shot. The whole area with the huts and football pitch was bare earth. Very dusty when the wind blew.

The toilets were on a steep sided mound some twelve feet high with wooden steps and handrail at it's centre. On top was a wooden enclosure about six feet wide and with a canopy along each side, the centre being open to the sky. There was a board running along either side with round holes at about two foot intervals and partitions between. At the left it had been extended by another half a dozen seats on either side. Here they had dispensed with canopy and partitions. The sides of the partitions were adorned with the most amazing exhibition of erotic art. Easily recognisable Hitlers, Ribbontrops, Goebbels, and Mussolinis were depicted having the most painful atrocities, sexual and otherwise, performed upon them by over developed giants.

The toilets had to be dug out every few weeks and this was a typical job given to the Russian prisoners. When you saw a party of a dozen or so enter by the gates, pushing a large cart with an enormous iron tank on it, it paid to get upwind of the toilets—fast!

We were continuously hungry. From our arrival at Oberhausel onwards rations were insufficient to sustain life. In the early days at Luckenwalde our rations consisted of the following. A bowl of coffee in the morning, the coffee being made from roasted acorns. At midday we had a bowl of soup. This was a watery brew and had all sorts of grass and recognisable weeds in it. It was as if a meadow had been mowed and the cuttings stewed up. It's taste was a little bitter, there was no trace of salt or seasoning. At week ends we did a little better and were given a weak pea soup and sometimes a little oatmeal in it. There was always a rush to get near the front of the soup queue so that you could get on the back of the queue hoping some would be left over for seconds.

With the pea soup we got a handful of potatoes, two or maybe three if they were small. These were steamed in their skins and a fair amount of mud. We ate these complete, skins, mud, eyes, and if there were maggots they went down the same way. Two of us were detailed each day to fetch the potatoes from the kitchen in a large wooden tub, carried by means of a wooden pole slid through two holes at the top.

When the last potatoes were issued there would be a rush to the tub to scrape the sides. The first half dozen would be head and shoulders into the tub while others tried to pull and elbow them out. Aircrew were considered to be the elite among our forces, but hunger had them behaving like animals.

At tea time we had a loaf of their black bread between five with some sort of spread. Margarine, a rather vivid red jam or a meat paste. Again a bowl of coffee or sometimes tea.

Our girlfriends or wives would have been upset to have known how little we thought about them. Our sole subject of conversation was 'food': restaurants where we had had good food, menus, and recipes.

A request had been made for toilet paper and a large box had been dumped in the centre of the hut full of waste paper, most of it quite useless for the purpose it was intended, being cartridge paper, corrugated etc, but I dug out some with plain white parts and made a small notebook. A stub of pencil was passed from one to another and we avidly collected all these recipes etc. swearing we would try them all when we got home.

Jimmy Hendry, a New Zealander, used to eke out his rations, making them last as long as he possibly could. There was a small table at our side of the hut and he would sit there with a large penknife that someone had acquired slicing his fifth of a loaf carefully into as many wafer thin slices as possible. He always had a crowd around him watching, sitting on the upper bunks, their own meagre ration long gone. The process of preparing his food took a good while, but he would then ration himself to one slice every half hour until it was finally gone. The loaves had a date baked into their underside, and we found that they were usually three or four weeks old.

On the fourth of February, a large party of British and American aircrews arrived having marched from Sagan. We were still in quarantine and so had no contact with them immediately, but stories said there were two and a half thousand coming in, and there were four group captains and several wing commanders among them. One of them Group Captain Willes was senior officer and took command of our compound.

In a few days our quarantine ended and an American officer Major Smith took over command of our hut, and what organisation there was quickly went to pot.

At this time too, all the N.C.O.s were moved out of our compound. The American enlisted men were moved into huge marquees which had been erected in an area adjoining our compound. This was a bit rough because there was still a foot or so of snow on the ground, and there were several further falls soon after they moved. They lived in pretty squalid conditions, sleeping on straw on the ground. They were required to work also. Commissioned officers were not expected to work, but I think most of us would have welcomed something to do to pass the time. In fact later on we requested permission to cut wood to use in the stove, it was so cold in the hut, and when this was granted there was a rush of volunteers.

I was one of a party of about a dozen let out of the camp with guards to cut down small trees and scrub, and carry it back to our compound. We were out best part of a day and most of us would have gone again. However permission was never granted again and the wood was burnt in the stove in no time.

Now that we were able to move freely between the huts, we found some of these people had been prisoners a long time, four years some of them, and they had been able to have uniforms including greatcoats sent from home. Some possessed Swiss Rolex watches which could be ordered from neutral Switzerland, the money having been sent from home direct to Switzerland.

Some still had stores of Red Cross food which they had dragged on sledges for weeks on end.

With the empty cans from the Red Cross parcels many had made cooking pans, and little fires called 'Smoky Joes'. It was amazing what some of these people had acquired during their stay, and pliers and hammers could be borrowed quite easily. Where they were hidden goodness knows, but frequent searches of the huts by our guards never found anything. Materials to make the 'Smoky Joes' came from cans. First the top and bottom were taken out using the tiny tin opener which came with the parcels, then they were cut down the seam and flattened. If larger pieces were needed, say for a pan, the edges of two pieces would be turned back with pliers, slid together and hammered flat.

The 'Smoky Joe' consisted of a little pan to hold the fuel, with a little fan underneath to provide a draught, the fan being driven by a little hand wheel and belt made from a piece of string, or a boot lace. A few small chips of wood, or coal found by rummaging around the stove, and with the fan wound frantically, a glowing red hot fire could be produced to heat anything. The 'Smoky Joe' was a masterpiece of ingenuity, they also caused no end of trouble over the number of bed boards they consumed. I suppose their making and use used up time, and that was important. One thing we had plenty of was time.

Someone had acquired a pair of nail scissors from somewhere and we gave one another hair cuts with them. A hair cut could take anything up to half a day. Then there was a call for anyone to see a dentist. I had a tooth that had bothered me at times and about half a dozen of us were conducted to another part of the camp where a French dentist did a filling for me. I'm not sure it was the one which had been hurting, but it was a change of routine, scenery and another half day gone. I even went to a church service on a couple of occasions, held in a corner of one of the huts by an American who seemed to know the right words even though I'm sure he wasn't a chaplain or even ordained. I derived some comfort from these sessions I suppose when you are in desperate straits anything that might bring succour has to be tried.

It was then decided that the British and Empire people should stand for 'Appell' with the rest of the British on the football pitch, and this suited us well enough.

Twice a day, whistles were blown, and among much shouting of "Schnell!" or "Was ist das?" we were shepherded from the huts and compound onto the football pitch, and the gate locked. This provided endless opportunities for mucking up the system, and there were always a few chased out of the huts or the toilets after the gates had been locked, pretending they hadn't heard. We then each had our allotted block of about two hundred all formed up in fives. The trick then was for some of the centre files to move half way between those in front so that when the officer counting went along counting in fives, he ended up with a four in the last file and with much grumbling and shouting he would have to start at the beginning again. He would then come along making sure he'd got each file of five lined up and shouting, "Fünfs, fünfs!" (Fives, fives!) and a chant would start up from everyone, "Fünfs, fünfs, fünfs", which 'caused great hilarity except for the German counting.

When they had got us all counted, we were held in the football pitch while they went through the huts, counting those in sick bay etc. When this was completed a sign was given to the guards on the gates and they were unlocked. Well, as the snow melted a large puddle formed in the gateway, and as the gate opened there was a surge through it and the guards found themselves left splashing about in about three inches of muddy water. You could see the look of apprehension grow on the guards faces as they unlocked the gate. They knew what was about to happen.

Somewhere on the camp the radio was still functioning and every evening there would be a news bulletin read by someone going from hut to hut. We waited avidly for this to hear news of advances from both east and west. Though that from the east seemed to offer more hope for us. While this was going on someone was posted at the doors on either end of the hut and should a German guard approach they would call "Goon up!" In fact, if at any time a guard came through the hut this call would go up, and all the illicit tools etc would quickly vanish. One guard, unusually with a sense of humour, would open the hut door and call out "Goon up!" himself as he walked through.

Depending on the news bulletin our spirits mostly soared, but occasionally plummeted when there had been some set back.

On several occasions we saw flights of Luftwaffe planes go over. One afternoon in February I saw a flight of about 200 Me109s and Fw190s go over, the most German planes I'd seen at one time since 'Blitz' days. These were travelling in a south easterly direction and everyone seemed to think it a good sign. Later, I saw one of their jet Me262 fly westwards at great speed, and on another occasion a three engined Ju87s came over at rooftop height.

Rations varied from time to time. A loaf was normally shared between five men, but sometimes it went to seven to a loaf and towards the end of our stay as many as twelve. On one occasion the Norwegian army officers in the next compound gave up some of their Red Cross food parcels to us, and this was a very much appreciated gesture. These worked out at one parcel to five men. These were Danish parcels and next morning we cooked oatmeal on a 'Smoky Joe'.

By now we were all showing the effect of malnutrition, and one day we tried to get some exercise and went for a walk round and round the football pitch. It had been suggested that we should try to keep as fit as possible and save some food, in case of a further move or in the case of the chance of escape. I was amazed at how weak we had become. Everyone was becoming very thin and this I noticed particularly in a chap called Charlie Loring. My own arms scared me whenever I rolled up my sleeves. I had already moved the buttons on my underpants over three inches, and now they were loose again.

Eventually after endless rumours we got our very own issue of Red Cross parcels. These were American and contained things like dried milk, tinned meat, dried fruit, jam, chocolate 'D' bars and all sorts of other goodies.

I'm afraid that we were no longer used to such rich food, let's face it we were no longer used to food, and we also made pigs of ourselves. Most of us felt queasy, and during that night there was a steady stream of sufferers across to the toilets to be sick.

These parcels did not all have the same contents and soon a certain amount of bartering began. Someone who didn't like gooseberry jam would swap it for blackcurrant. Quite soon among the Americans, dealers appeared who would swop anything for anything so long as they made on the deal. It was surprising how quickly they built up a considerable stock of food.

On the beautiful sunny morning of 7 March, there was some trading going on over the fence with the Norwegians in the next compound. A guard tried to stop this, and an American as he turned away spat on the ground. The guard enraged at the insult levelled his rifle and actually pulled the trigger. Luckily there wasn't a round in the breach, and other guards rushed up before the situation could develop any further.

The yank was marched off to solitary and later we were assembled and addressed by the camp commandant. He said that any further such incident would result in someone being shot as an example. He also said that if any more bed boards were cut up for fuel we would be moved into tents. The next morning the rails were missing from the toilet steps. We waited with bated breath for the uproar, but nothing happened.

Then a wager was struck between two Americans that one of them could not consume a whole parcel in twenty four hours. It was a pretty stupid wager when food was so short, but Colonel Oakes condoned the whole thing by holding the I.O.U.s for six hundred dollars and acting as referee. The one challenged nearly made it, but he had left the salt and pepper until last and with only these left and minutes to spare, the salt made him sick and he lost both the food and the money. Anyway, it provided a full day's entertainment for the rest of us.

In early March, the boxer Max Schmelling visited the camp. This was presented as a rare privilege by the Germans, and the 'kriegies' crowded into the huts to see him, remembering him as a great prewar heavyweight champion. Most of the British refused to be impressed. Some remembered how he had double crossed his manager, and that he was a German who had fought against us in Crete.

It was 11 March, Joy's birthday. In the afternoon the Polish officers in the next hut who had formed a choir, gave a performance and the singing was beautiful. In the evening I had a quiet party for Joy up on my top bunk. Hot coffee and cheese and potato pie cooked among the ashes under our big tiled stove. Actually, when I say cooked, the potatoes were already, of course, and it was just a case of melting the cheese and getting a nice brown crust on top. As we were turning in, Al Robertson's and my will power broke down. We were still hungry, and we ate the prunes and bread which we had been saving for the next morning's breakfast.

About this time, I met Wing Commander Beamont, who I hadn't realised was in the camp. He was among those who had marched in. He told me that also among his party was Bill Hart, a New Zealander from 486 Squadron.

We arranged to meet for a brew up in each of our bunks in turn and we had several good talks about events in the Tempest Wing. This again broke the monotony.

Rumours were rife at this time about an impending move. The Russians were advancing fast along the northern areas which was why previous parties had already been marched from Poland and the Baltic. A large party of Russians had already been moved out, said to be fourteen hundred strong. The emergency food we had been advised to save had been eaten once parcels started arriving but Frank Lock and I decided that we would make some iron rations in case we were on the road during a move, had the chance to escape, or were left on our own resources for any other reason. We melted the plain chocolate 'D' bars and mixed in butter, dried milk, dried fruit, oatmeal and let them set into slabs. Bits broken off tasted delicious and I don't know how we managed to get them into our kit bags.

Then on 9 April, there was a strong rumour of a move to a camp in the south near Nürnberg. The following day the Senior British Officer was interviewed by the Camp Commandant following which the S.B.O. announced that the move was definitely on.

11 April was a day of rumour, the main gist of which said that the move was at the instigation of the Gestapo, and that we were to be held hostage until they got the terms they wanted from the Allies when Germany capitulated. No one liked the idea of the Gestapo being involved. The Wehrmacht was one thing. They behaved in a reasonably soldierlike manner, but the

Gestapo was a different matter, quite unpredictable. We all had a healthy dis-respect for them. Word went around that we were to employ every delaying tactic that we could think of. The day ended with the posting of a German movement order in each hut.

The move started bright and early next morning. Only the British ini-tially, and two of our Group Captains had left at about four o'clock the evening before. It started hut by hut from the far end of the compound, and each person and their hut was searched as they left the compound. Almost immediately delaying tactics were used. People supposed to be in one hut would be visiting American friends and would have to be looked for. Chased out of one hut they would vanish back into their own hut, supposedly emp-tied, to find something and vanish again. At the search point kit would be deliberately emptied everywhere, and the re-assembling and re-packing was the slowest imaginable. Loud cries of items missing after the search, and accusations of theft. Two senior R.A.F. officers had insisted on staying to wit-ness the evacuation and search, and when the Germans shouted at some slow and impossibly inept youth would shout back even louder and I'm sure that but for them murder might well have been committed.

Extra guards had been brought in for the move and these were all young arrogant, ex–Hitler Youth types who shouted and snarled and tried to push people where they wanted them. Our old camp guards were still around but taking it fairly easily, with a smile and a shrug when there was a particularly violent outburst from one of the newcomers.

Our hut was the last out, and by now it was late afternoon. By now the pressure had eased and the search was pretty cursory. I couldn't see that they had had a very big haul. A few penknives and the odd hammer or two. By the time we had marched down to the station it was about six in the evening. Already, news bulletins were being passed up and down the plat-form, so the radio had obviously got through. There was still a lot of shout-ing going on as the young guards tried to herd people into the cattle trucks. Many had 'Smoky Joes' going on the platform and these were going well on coal stolen from the station stock. The station master was near apoplexy and drew an automatic which he waved in the face of one offender caught black-handed at the coal pile and who stubbornly refused to understand the order to "P— off!" given in German.

We had some rations issued on the station and eventually as dusk fell, we were herded into the trucks. Forty of us to a wired off end, about one third of the truck in area. The doors were slammed and padlocks went on.

The night was hell for me. I had had a headache coming on all evening, and during the night this grew rapidly worse. In addition I felt sick and all trembly inside. To make matters worse I badly needed to make water and no one would come near to let me out. It had to be contained until one of my long suffering companions passed me an empty can which I was able to use and tip between the barbed wire out of the window.

I did get a couple of hours sleep after that in the early hours of the morning. It was a relief when day break came and a certain amount of shunting took place. The word went up and down the train that due to our delaying the departure, the engine scheduled for us had had to be used elsewhere, and we had been moved into a siding out of the way. Rumour also said that in the confusion the previous evening several of our number had walked off the end of the platform and quietly disappeared.

By now my headache had grown to monstrous proportions, I felt sick, and couldn't stop trembling. The right side of my face was swollen. As soon as we were let out I saw our doc, and with two others on the sick list was taken to see a German M.O. The upshot was that all three of us were marched back to the camp, and installed in the lazarette. Here I was put to bed and fed sulphur drugs.

The next day I was feeling much better but the swelling on my face persisted. My spirits rose when at midday the rest of the British lads marched in from the railway station. Our tactics had won the day and the move had been foiled, for the time being at least.

That night, 14 April, there was a night raid on Potsdam. This was quite spectacular with the flares, flashes, against the illumination of the fires. Everyone turned out and many stood on the banks of the toilets to get a better view. Every fresh conflagration brought cheers from the crowd, and the guards became angry and tried to chase us back into the huts. As fast as one hut was filled, another would creep back out. Bayonets were fixed to rifles and a nasty situation only abated when the distant action abated.

I had a visit from Frank Lock in the sick bay, and Al Robertson turned up with a slice of fruit cake. Where he got it, goodness knows; it probably originated down in the town somewhere and came to me via any amount of weird deals. It tasted good to me.

16 April was my birthday, and the day turned out bright and sunny. Since we were in a continental climate, the change from winter to summer had been quite sudden, and on this day it was warm enough to sit outside and bask in the sun. Frank Lock presented me with some pipe tobacco, and I was able to sit puffing quietly in the sun, real bliss after the dog ends I had been smoking. Before I had been shot down, I had been a heavy pipe smoker, getting through an average one ounce of tobacco a day. When I was shot down, I had none of the makings, of course, but at Wetzlar with all the other Red Cross issues was a ration of cigarettes, but I was able to take mine in a two ounce tin of Ogdens Best. Unfortunately, they had no pipes, but I thought I

might pick up one along the way. I kept the tin for quite a while, until in our darkest days, before Red Cross parcels were issued, when some of the boys found the lack of tobacco harder to bear than the shortage of food, I gave the tin to Al Robertson and Charlie Loring. They were sitting on a bunk sharing drag for drag on a cigarette made from other peoples dog ends, rolled in wetted newspaper, and about an eighth of an inch in diameter. They were so grateful you would have thought I had given them the crown jewels. Later of course the inevitable happened and I acquired a pipe but had no tobacco.

I found that Bill Orwin from 3 Squadron was in the N.C.O.s compound and had a shouted conversation across the wire. He had been shot down into the sea just off Den Haag (Tempest EJ540 10/9/44), and had swam to shore only to find a rather unfriendly reception committee waiting for him. It was good to see him looking well.

Seven officers who had escaped from the train were returned to the compound. There were no punishments. I think by now the German guards realised that the end was nigh and had given up. Sounds of warfare could be heard both to the east and the west and we had seen planes strafing and dive-bombing away to the south west of the camp.

On 19 April I was deemed fit enough to move back from sickbay to a hut. During the day there were American raids to the south and to the east and on the twentieth there was a raid by Marauders to the south. Everyone crowded onto the toilet steps at dusk and you could see the flashes in the sky both to the east and west. At lights out the S.B.O. came and told us that the Germans had told him that the Russians had broken through to the south, and that we were more likely to be released by the Russians than our own people. He said we must be ready to take over the camp at a moments notice. Contingency plans were already made.

The following dawn we awoke to the sound of battle to the south east. You could clearly hear not only artillery, but also small arms fire. At one o'clock the German guards were suddenly gone and we took over the camp. There was a visitation from an officer from an S.S. artillery battery installed near the camp, and he said we must stay within the camp's boundary, and if they had any trouble from us a hundred would be taken and shot.

The first thing we did was to take down white ceiling panels and lay them out in the football pitch in the form of the letters P.O.W. It didn't stop us from being strafed by German planes during the nights of 22 and 23 April. The first time it was a Ju88, and I was out of my top bunk like a flash, and under the bottom one opposite. Silly really, I was just as safe up on my own bunk, the wooden bunks wouldn't have stopped a shot but that is the effect of the noise and confusion in a strafing attack.

A group of local women gathered at the wire, terrified, with good reason, by tales of the treatment they could expect from Russian soldiers. Baring their breasts and pleading with British and American officers to move in with them in the hope that the Russians might then leave them alone. A forlorn hope as it turned out, as some who took up the offer found out.

During the morning a Russian officer and driver appeared in a jeep. Everyone crowded round and there was a lot of cheering, back slapping, and hand shaking. He didn't speak English, and no one among our number had even a smattering of Russian. However we managed to glean that he was reconnoitring ahead of the main Russian lines but that they were moving fast and wouldn't be long arriving.

Around mid day several Russian tanks and trucks arrived. The tanks parked along the road running between our compound and that of the N.C.O.s. The wire bordering the road was in the form of a double barbed wire fence about eight feet high, and holes had been made in the two fences to get out onto the road, and we all crowded out and around the tanks.

Some of the tank crews climbed down and again there was much comradely hand shaking. Although these were spearhead troops, each tank appeared to have at least one woman in its crew. These were all of the well built type, being chivalrous, and in their grey uniforms, high black boots, forage caps and greatcoats, looked far from glamorous, but to us they were a welcome sight.

Someone among them decided that they had better get on with the job and they all jumped aboard, engines were started and the leading tank rumbled forward. There was such a crowd around the tanks that there was a rush to get out of their way. This turned to panic as the leading tank swerved to the right, into the barbed wire fence, and then left to flatten the wire all along it's length.

The only way I could go was back through the fence into our compound. The trouble was that the holes were not in line, so that you had to go through the hole in the outer fence, along about three yards between the fences and then through the inner fence. I only just cleared the inner fence as the poles with the wire still attached came crashing down behind me. A pole missed me by inches, but the wire caught the back of my shoulder and tore my battledress. That evening the main Russian force arrived. An officer told us that a village had been allotted to feed us. Some people went down to the town and returned with radios and other goodies, and we could sit and listen to the news ourselves.

Now that we could move freely within the camp I had quite a few brew ups with Bill Orwin in the N.C.O.s compound. I also met Ken Brant again. Ken had been with us in Florida.

On 23 April there were funerals of eight dead Russian prisoners and the remainder were formed up into columns and marched out of camp. They were in terrible shape, but put on a brave show, and there was many a smile and cheer as they left. In the light of what we now know happened to most Russian P.O.W.s after they returned home, I wonder what became of those poor devils.

On the radio there was news of some P.O.W.s being repatriated and everyone cheered up, especially at the announcement of six weeks of leave for repatriated P.O.W.s. However, while we could move freely within the camp, there was a cordon of Mongolian soldiers around the outer wire and we could not go outside the perimeter.

During the first few days of our 'liberation' some strange things happened, and stranger tales told. Some of our ex-guards, including some of the officers, were seen being marched into the camp with shovels, looking quite ill and unkempt and were shovelling coal. Power and water supplies were intermittent, and the lines were said to be broken between the camp and town. Some water could be obtained from a pump, and other supplies from a lake just outside the camp boundaries. Rumour said that two German work parties had been sent into the woods to effect repairs with written permits and been shot by Russian patrols. A third was sent up with an armed escort and after several days supplies were restored. All the Russian troops I saw were Mongolian and probably could not read or write.

One or two people who had taken off for the American lines crept back with tales to tell. Two Americans had heard firing in a wood and hid in a ditch. After a few minutes two German soldiers and a nurse broke out of the woods and ran across open ground towards the road our hero's had been travelling on. Some Russians reached the edge of the wood not far behind the Germans and shot all three. The Americans lay still in their ditch until all was quiet again and scuttled back to camp, glad to be within the safety of barbed wire again.

Three N.C.O.s had gone down to the town and were living with some women, their children, and an old grandfather. When the Russians appeared, they didn't approve of the situation at all. Apparently, rape was okay, but you mustn't treat them like humans. The three N.C.O.s were locked in a downstairs room, the grandfather thrown into the street and shot, from the screams upstairs from the women and children it was obvious what was happening to them. Automatic fire added to the din as china, glass, pictures and anything else which might be valued was shot and smashed. The three didn't wait to find out what the Russians had in mind for them, but climbed through a window and raced back to camp.

Rations began to have priority in our thoughts again. Red Cross food had run out, and we were dependent on food brought in by the Russians. Their troops lived off the land, and from then on so did we. A village would be told to feed us for a week, and we got whatever was available. One time it came in lorry loads of flour, and we all sat round making chappattis from the flour mixed with water. Another time milk giving cows were driven in. Someone somewhere must have known enough to butcher them and cut them up. The resultant slab of meat that I got could not be made edible, not even by beating it hard with a bed board, and this was all there was, no bread or potatoes to go with it. It was a peculiar diet and I think that while I was putting on weight again we were pretty unhealthy. I found that any little scratch festered, and twice I had my arm in a sling. I also had a cut on my foot which festered and took a long time to heal.

All this while there were sporadic sounds of fighting around us. On 1 May there were sounds of a battle somewhere fairly close and the rumbling was pretty continuous all night. At two o'clock in the morning there was quite a panic when a shell landed on our football pitch. We were told that the immediate area had been cleared on 3 May.

Our C.B.O., after several attempts to find a senior Russian officer sober enough to talk sense to, managed to get permission for us to walk outside the outer perimeter of the camp. This brought some variety for it included the lake and the cemetery. Around the outer limits of the camp the Germans had cleared an area of about a kilometre in width which was grazed meadow land. I suppose anyone escaping, even if they got through the wire then had this open space to cross with no cover whatsoever and patrolled at night by guards with dogs. The N.C.O.s told the tale of three of their number, two Canadian and an Englishman, who got through the wire only to be caught by the dogs. The two Canadians were killed while the Englishman managed to get back through the wire unhurt.

We were now allowed to walk in this open area close to the perimeter wire, but not to cross it. This gave a grand sense of freedom, but brought risks also from the guards making up the cordon. In those first few days several of our people were stopped and searched, and had pens and watches taken from them. Again these troops were Mongolian and were completely undisciplined. If they saw someone watching them they would fire at anything around to impress. I saw one once firing at the insulators on the telephone lines.

The lake was quite idyllic. It nestled in amongst wooded hills and secluded among the trees were little chalets, where no doubt the camp's officers disported themselves with their ladies during off duty hours. The chalets had all been wrecked during the fighting that had taken place all around us, but it was very pleasant to walk around the lake. Some of the Norwegians were trying to catch fish and fresh water crayfish which were to be seen in the lake. I only saw one crayfish caught which wouldn't go far, but it was a pleasant way of passing the time, both for the fishermen, and the watchers and jeerers.

The cemetery was something else. There were quite a few Europeans buried there, including one British person, and these were all in individual graves each with a wooden cross bearing rank and number, occasionally a unit was also shown. The Russian section was quite different. Here there were two long rows of earth mounds, each mound about forty feet by eight, and each of which contained the bodies of two hundred Russians. The last of these pits was still open and earth thrown in to cover whatever lay in the bottom. We were appalled especially when we counted the mounds, and from memory the total came to well over two thousand bodies.

We rarely missed the news on the radio. We heard when the Americans and Russians met up our side of the Elbe and morale soared. Many of the Americans took off for their own lines; most were turned back. The Chief British Officer had let it be known that he wanted no undisciplined behaviour and that we should wait to be evacuated in an orderly manner. However when the Russians first arrived everyone thought they would be home in a few days. As time went by and still we were confined within barbed wire with a cordon of armed guards around the place, morale sunk to a low and when the Americans heard that their own people were just a few miles away it was too much to bear. Many slipped through the cordon at night and vanished, presumably to their own people, but stories came back that those caught by the Russians were being interned and would eventually be returned by boat from Odessa—a process we reckoned could take months.

Rumour was rife. One strong one said we were to be moved on foot to Wittenburg and the American lines. On 3 May the Russians started registering prisoners. Slowly, but we were glad something was happening. That afternoon, two American war correspondents arrived in a jeep. They said that no one knew the camp had been liberated and that it was thought there was still heavy fighting in the area. It wasn't until some G.I.s showed up that they knew anyone could get through. According to news reports the Russians had taken 120,000 prisoners and killed 60,000 Germans in the area within the last few days. Among the American prisoners was a war correspondent named Beatty, and he went back with the other two in the jeep promising to stir things up.

The visit and the definite news that someone had got through to the U.S. lines made our American friends even more mutinous and that night over a thousand of them took off for their own lines. The next day, 4 May, a jeep arrived with two signalmen. They gave further news that P.O.W.s were being evacuated in large numbers from Wittenburg. It was all very unsettling and the temptation to leave was almost unbearable.

Mid afternoon brought the arrival of a U.S. Colonel in an armoured car and news flashed around camp that seventy-five U.S. trucks were on their way to take us out.

Al Robertson and Charlie Loring had already gone for a walk from which they said they might come back. The Americans went wild when it was said trucks were on the way and Al and Charlie did come back having met the armoured car on their way out.

Registration continued and everyone expected to be on the trucks and away next morning. The weather had brightened and spirits were high. The evacuation had come just in time for food supplies were becoming very low and we were continually hungry.

Saturday, 5 May, started with a rumour that the Russians would not give the okay for us to move out. Spirits sank to a new low. Then there was another rumour that they had. As soon as there was any uncertainty, a large number of the lads took off, but by lunch time most had returned having been turned back by the Russian cordon around the camp.

During the afternoon ambulances arrived and started evacuating the sick bay, they brought the news that a convoy was on it's way with 'K' rations and bread. We drooled at the thought. In the event our rations for the day was a bowl of dubious soup and a little American bread. Many of the Americans were making preparations to take off, saying that they would sooner walk today than ride tomorrow. This seemed unwise especially when we heard that the American forces had withdrawn to the far side of the River Elbe. This not only meant a good deal further to walk but also a good sized river to cross before you were greeted by friends. You could be sure that all the easy crossings would be guarded. We also learnt that all the German forces in West Germany, Holland and Denmark had surrendered to Montgomery's forces.

During the night ninety Russian trucks arrived loaded with food, mostly flour and sugar. Blast it, chapattis again!

6 May started well with an issue of 'K' rations. My share was a fifteenth part of five men's rations—little but very welcome. We also got some American bread.

At about two thirty the first of the evacuation convoy arrived, twenty five trucks. We heard that American G.I.s were being loaded on sixty men to a truck, and that they were only able to take what kit they could get in their pockets. However, the Russians wouldn't let them leave, so they were all unloaded again. Then the trucks waited in the town and G.I.s were sneaked through the wire and loaded onto the trucks outside the camp. We later heard that the Russians had put a cordon round the area, a machine gun had been set up in front of the convoy and they were told they would be fired on if they attempted to leave. They did leave, but empty. This caused panic and a good deal of speculation among us all. What was going on? Why wouldn't the Russians release us?

The following morning another twelve trucks showed up. Our senior officer announced that the Russians would not release us until registration was completed, and they had orders from higher authority for our release. After consultation it was announced that remaining trucks would go back empty and await further orders. The Russians promised action within two days.

During the morning the Norwegians marched out. Rumour said that they are marching one hundred and sixty kilometres. Not all the trucks had returned empty and during the night Al Robertson and Charlie Loring had got away in one of them as had quite a few of the Americans who had been with us since Wetzlar.

Then another hundred and twenty five trucks arrived and the convoy commander said he was going to stay until he could take us out. Later, we heard that he had gone to General Farmin's headquarters to obtain permission for us to leave. On his way he passed a Russian general on his way to Luckenwalde.

At two o'clock it was announced that the war in Europe was over. It didn't have the impact it should have had, we were only interested in one thing. Getting home!

That evening many of the Americans went out through the wire, climbed aboard the trucks and spent the whole night sitting in them . Quite a few of the trucks left when they were full and presumably somehow got through. Later ones leaving however were stopped outside the west gate, and stayed there all night with the boys sitting in them.

Also that evening after it was dark bonfires were lit in both the officers and N.C.O.s compounds. 'Smoky Joes', radios, and bunks all went on. Someone even set fire to one of the wooden watch towers, a most impressive sight. Everyone seemed convinced that tomorrow was the day we would be leaving.

The following morning we woke early to the news that all of the trucks were already full. After snatching a quick brew and some food Frank Lock and I made our way out through a hole in the fence to see for ourselves what was happening. On the way out we passed some others returning, who said that the trucks were all full, and that evacuation would only be allowed in an orderly manner.

Frank and I found that there were only about thirty of the trucks left. These were apparently jam packed with 'kreigies', but someone pushed up, making room for us, and Frank and I climbed aboard. We were so packed in you couldn't have scratched your nose, but after a few minutes the trucks started up. We thought we were away, instead of which we were driven into the camp and everyone was made to get off.

Various rumours floated around. One said we were all to be evacuated in accordance with a nominal role, and the one which proved correct saying that the trucks were to be sent back empty, that they would be checked at the gates and again at the Elbe, and anyone found aboard would be interned. Later, an American Colonel Hurdy told us that a commission was still arguing over the exchange of prisoners, and that the Russians would not let us go until it was all settled. Since the war a lot has been written about the incident where British troops were ordered to force Russian P.O.W.s onto trains for return home against their will and at bayonet point, and a lot of blame placed on those who issued the order. Perhaps we were the reason behind this unpleasant incident, and it had to be done to get our own men home. Meanwhile we were still virtually prisoners, behind barbed wire, and with armed guards patrolling it. I saw Bill Orwin later that day and he was actually fired on by the guards while trying to get out to the trucks. Frank and I resigned ourselves to the fact that we weren't getting out that day.

It was brilliant weather and I sat in the sun reading, and actually did some washing. At least, with so many already gone, there was plenty of food which had been abandoned. We had a share out and were amazed at the amounts some people still had. They must have been in the rackets.

There was plenty of room too. Our hut had about thirty left in it, whereas it had once held about one hundred and fifty. I had my own bed which I used to keep my meagre collection of belongings on, and the one next to it which had been rigged with a blanket to make a hammock which was quite comfortable. During the day the few American G.I.s still living in the tents were moved into one of the huts and the tents set light to. Quite an impressive blaze and there must have quite a lot of ammunition secreted away as it was going off and bullets whistling around all the time we were on parade on the football pitch. Some seemed far too close for comfort, but no one was hurt. It was the only thing they could have done with the tents, the lads in them had been living in appalling conditions. Hundreds had been crowded into one large marquee, sleeping on piles of straw on the ground, huddled together for warmth, and running alive with lice.

The senior British officer had the British on parade in the morning while the tents were burning and thanked us for our conduct during the liberation, deplored the mass hysteria, and the piecemeal evacuation of the past few days. He said there would be no more of that and that we must wait for the Russians to get us out in their own time. He also said that there would be a return to R.A.F. discipline and among other things we would all appear clean shaven, clean, neat and tidy each morning.

Well, we had had no means of shaving and had all grown beards. Mine was a wispy blonde thing with a slight ginger tinge, the moustache long on either side of the mouth. I looked a bit like Dr Fu Man Choo. Consternation was relieved a little when we got an issue of one razor blade each. A razor circulated among us, and as the days went by and there was no replacement blade, it became a painful process, even after trying to get an edge on the blade by honing it on a glass window.

A hundred trucks moved into camp and hopes rose that they might be for us. Hopes were once again dashed the next day when the remaining Norwegians moved out in them, and then on the 11 May the French did so.

In the meantime the weather had become very sunny and we spent a lot of our time by the lake. A lot of the lads were swimming, but I still had a cut on my foot which refused to heal.

From the time the Russians overran the camp they had been herding D.P.s into the camp. These were people from the German occupied countries who had been rounded up and sent to Germany as slave labour. There were some women among them and some children.

The tale was told in the early days that a request was put to the Russians of milk for the children. The Russian officer reading the request didn't believe the small amount asked for and added a couple of noughts to the figure with the result that the few D.P.s we had in those early days were practically swimming in the stuff.

Anyway when the Norwegians and the French were gone, they moved in large numbers of these people. That same evening a large contingent of Belgiums pushing their belongings on home made carts arrived. About a third of them were women. We had by now several thousand D.P.s in the camp of almost every European nationality. A story went round that a brothel had been set up behind one of the huts, and an American 'D' bar (chocolate bar) would buy you all the delights of paradise and, we suspected, a good deal more, too. We'd seen the V.D. films!

The area around the lake was very beautiful, but not ideal for sunbathing because of it lying in a hollow and because of the surrounding trees. However, the path between the compounds and the lake ran across an open grassy area which was ideal, and most days now there would be hundreds of completely nude male bodies, all sizzling gently in the hot sun. I remember the first time some of the D.P. women joined the party. A man with a woman on each arm all completely nude sauntering down the path to the lake. The only thing raised among all those young males might have been the odd eyebrow and the only emotion curiosity. We must have been in a very low state indeed.

To make way for more D.P.s we were moved to an area just outside the wire fence surrounding the compounds. These had been the quarters of the German camp guards, and were really quite pleasant. Bungalow type truppenlager buildings standing among lawns and shrubs. Much cleaner than the huts and quieter too. Of course, we were not too pleased at first at being moved down there, only a move home would suffice! We were especially peeved when we found we had to move a double tier bunk from a block near the east gate to our new billet some way out beyond the west gate. We managed to borrow a barrow and got all our kit and bunk down in one journey, but we were dead beat at the end of it. We were without doubt, in terrible condition.

Frank and I shared a room with two others, Misty and Jimmy, and we had cupboards for our gear, a table and chairs, and to our amazement were issued with sheets for our beds. Such luxury! About this time as part of the getting back to normal we started having morning parades, and an orderly officer rota was posted up. I did my turn without event. By now my foot had healed, but I had a burn on my hand which festered, and a red mark right up under arm. I had to keep my arm in a sling. The slightest cut or graze immediately festered.

That evening we four went for a walk up into the camp. We learnt that a New Zealand lad, Ronnie King, had married a Belgian D.P. woman. They'd only met two weeks before. The Senior British Officer only learned of the affair after the ceremony and was more than a little put out. There had also been weddings between two Dutch men and German women.

Our old hut was full of Dutch people, some whole families. They seemed quite a good crowd and were looking after themselves better than most of the D.P.s who looked a pretty disreputable bunch on the whole. One of them spoke English and he insisted that we were being held back because the Russians were annoyed at the unofficial evacuation which had taken place.

Getting back to our quarters in the truppenlager through the west gate proved more difficult than we expected. Several people were gathered around inside the gate which had a sentry with rifle, lounging in a hut at the side. As we approached he came out of the hut and took up a threatening attitude, rifle extended, in the centre of the open gate. We gathered from his signs that we must go back. Several times we approached and each time the rifle was levelled and signs made for us to go back. Someone among the crowd spoke English and told us, "He won't let you through, he has been told not to let anyone through the gate, and he won't. But there's a gap in the wire just down there and nobody has told him to stop anyone from going through that".

So we made our way along the wire and sure enough not a hundred yards from the gate and well within sight of the sentry was a gap in the wire. We hurried through expecting shots to ring out any second, but nothing. We got back to our quarters breathless, and had a good laugh at the stupidity of it, but later there was an incident when a Russian started shooting at chaps going between the *Truppenlager* and the main camp.

The author's POW dog tags.

The next few days were mainly spent sun bathing, and wishing we had some food. We didn't try any more visiting.

On 19 May the siren was sounded which for us British was the general recall. Shortly afterwards the S.B.O. issued a statement saying we would be leaving the next day. A dance was organised in the kitchen which went on until two thirty in the morning. I couldn't imagine who would dance with who and didn't bother. Frank looked in but said I hadn't missed much.

CHAPTER 5

Homeward Bound

Next morning, 20 May, at nine o'clock we were all roused and told to be ready to move to the camp entrance in fifteen minutes. We hurriedly packed what we could, and moved out leaving a wonderful haul for the D.P. scavengers who were moving in as we moved out.

There at the camp gates was a line of gleaming new Dodge trucks with Russian drivers. After a couple of hours to get ourselves organised twenty five men to a truck, and several false starts, we left Luckenwalde Stalag IIIA behind us at last, just a month after our taking over the camp from the Germans.

The Russians drove quite fast, but about every ten miles there was a stop during which all the wheels were changed round. I suppose an instruction book somewhere advised this for even tyre wear, but had been badly interpreted. It's usually done every few thousand miles, not every ten.

When we reached the main autobahn near Wittenburg we found that the bridges had all been demolished. The first of these caused quite a hold up with lots of conflab. Eventually, we all got out of the trucks, which then wended their way down one embankment, between broken off tree stumps, across the road beneath and up the far embankment. We walked across. There were several more of these crossings where we stayed aboard and an exciting ride it was.

We finally reached the Elbe where a pontoon bridge had been put across. Several Russian officers were enjoying themselves in speedboats which they had commandeered from somewhere, and on the far side a beautiful sight, a line of trucks with the American star on their sides, drivers smoking or talking in groups, and awaiting our arrival.

We walked over the bridge onto the trucks and were driven to an aerodrome near Hallé which was staffed by Americans. Here we were given the de-louse treatment, showered, re-clothed, and then food.

Hot sweet tea, white bread and jam and tinned meat. That white bread was about the best thing of all. After months of heavy black German bread, it was so light and white and absolutely beautiful.

Three good meals a day certainly did wonders for morale, and as we began to reacquaint ourselves with things like pork chops we really began to believe that we were out. Kriegy chappattis, black bread, the smell of the 'aborts', 'appell' all receded into the past like some bad dream.

There was little for us to do except wait and we had had plenty of practice at that. We would tire ourselves out wandering around the airfield inspecting the various wrecked aircraft, seeing pictures in the evening, and sleeping like a babe.

People had been leaving in batches by air and on 25 May our turn came. We left at a moment's notice in U.S. Dakotas which had flown in Russian workers. We landed at Brussels Evere airport and were billeted in a nearby barracks. Here we had more showers, clean clothes, and a big meal in a real officers' mess, complete with music. We were also issued with five pounds, but by the time we had had dinner it was too late to go out on the town. Beer and spirits had several of the boys under the table already.

Next day, half way through lunch, we were rushed back to Evere. I don't know why for we waited hours before being moved again to Melsbrook. There we boarded a Lancaster III and flew to Oakley near Oxford, arriving around 6.50 pm. A cheer went up as we crossed the English coast, and it was certainly good to see old Denge roll past underneath us once more.

Trucks were waiting and these drove us to Cosford. The English countryside in late May seemed so green and lush and absolutely beautiful. At Cosford a P.O.W. reception centre had been set up. Here we were re-kitted in air force blue. There was a brief debriefing and it was with sadness that I saw Jimmy Mannion's name on a list of those they wanted news of. Obviously he had not turned up in any of the camps, and since we were pretty well the last home, hopes for him were getting very slim.

The first thing of course was to phone families and I witnessed one rather sad incident. One officer who had been 'in the bag' more than four years had a photograph with him of his wife. She was a very good looking girl, and he proudly showed the picture to all and sundry given the chance. He came away from the phone looking glum. His particular friends asked what was wrong. He hesitated and then said, "Yes, she's gone."

The Cosford people had everything very well organised, and were very sympathetic in their approach. I suppose by then they had dealt with a large number of returned prisoners and had met most of the problems. We were quietly and efficiently processed, bedded down for the night, and delivered to the rail station next morning with travel warrant home, cash and ration cards in our hands. Home of course to a rapturous welcome!

Most of my family and friends had been expecting a starved, gaunt looking Ron to turn up, instead of which I was fatter than my usual handsome self. It was, however, an unhealthy fat, put on over the last few weeks due to the weird diet supplied by the Russians, followed by gross over eating once back in the lands of plenty. In fact during those first few days I couldn't look at food without just having to eat it, and to this day I cannot bear to see food wasted.

But Stalag IIIA wasn't finished with me yet. I had only been home a couple of days when large red patches which irritated like mad came up all over my face. My mother said "I'll soon fix those!" and dabbed them with some sort of strong antiseptic. I was due to see Joy and her family, and by the time I arrived the red patches had become large angry sores. I went to Ramsgate General Hospital, and having spun my tale I got lots of attention and sympathy from a bevy of beautiful nurses. It turned out as I suspected by now, to be impetigo, aggravated no end by mother's well intended attentions. I was again painted in great splashes of purple, no longer my favourite colour. However it slowly cleared up, meanwhile I felt more conspicuous than any sore thumb possibly could.

Back home my face ached and was swollen. I went to a local dentist and he said it was an abscess under a tooth. I expect nowadays penicillin would clear the thing up in a couple of days, but I lost a perfectly good tooth. I saw it before it went in the bin, and it was perfectly clean without a mark on it. At least my swollen face went back to normal and the pain stopped.

I was notified that my kit was in store at Colnbrook some miles west of London. A family friend whose business necessitated a petrol ration volunteered to run me out to collect it. I was very grateful, especially when we got there and found that, as well as a kit bag, there was also my camp kit, including a camp bed and chair, canvas wash bowl, and bath. Without my friend and his car, it would have been a struggle getting that lot home.

My first couple of weeks at home were taken up with visiting friends. Most of my own friends were still away in the forces so it was their parents who I mostly saw. I also took the dog and went on long walks over local commons, but as time went on I was running out of things to do, people to see, and time began to drag.

August came and with it the end of the war in the Far East and V.J. night. People went mad with the cessation of all hostilities. After six years of war, peace was a dream that took getting used to. On V.J. night my mother, Pam Boyd, and I went up to London, and converged with hordes of others on Piccadilly Circus. There was singing, and fireworks being thrown about, and people climbing on the hoardings where in normal times Eros stood, and the crowds were so jam packed you couldn't have fallen over if you had fainted. Some girls and women did faint, and were passed over the heads of the jubilant crowd to where they could be attended to. The pressure at times was quite frightening, and it's surprising there weren't some casualties.

We thought we would try to get down The Mall to the palace, but this was quite impossible, and eventually we wended our way home.

Time passed and to help it on it's way I carried out one or two projects. One of these was the building of a photographic enlarger. Very Heath Robinson, but the optics were studied in a book, and it worked well.

Then, after about ten weeks, I was called for an interview at Bentley Priory in Stanmore. The interview, I think, was to discover my intentions. Would I want to stay on and make a career out of the air force? Would they want me to? So after being home twelve weeks, I received my posting to 56 Operational Training Unit at Milfield in Northumberland as an instructor.

Arriving at Milfield, which is about four miles north of Wooler and probably fifteen miles south of Berwick on Tweed, I found quite a few old friends. No one from the squadron but some I had last seen in Canada and Bournemouth. I soon found that there were nearly as many 'instructors' as there were pupils at Milfield. I think we were probably an embarrassment to the authorities now that the war was over, and they didn't know what to do with us until they could sort us out for de-mobilisation. I was asked if I minded joining station flight, and I readily agreed.

The duties of station flight were to air test planes as they came out of the hanger following more major services. Some planes, needing more work than could be handled at Milfield, were ferried away. We also ferried visitors south to York where they could catch a fairly quick train to London. This would be done in a Miles Master or a Percival Proctor II which seemed to be kept mainly for this purpose. We also took parties of A.T.C. cadets for joy rides in the Proctor at week ends.

Our quarters were a single-storied building on the airfield near the control tower. One of the duties of our ground staff was to look after visiting aircraft, including refueling and carrying out any other maintenance work needed before they took off again.

It was quite an enjoyable time really, the weather was still quite good and no-one was shooting at you, so you could really enjoy the flying. Two other pilots were assigned to Station Flight, Flight Lieutenant Joe Payton and Flying Officer Geoff Wylde. They each owned a prewar Ford Eight Saloon (these sold for £100 in 1939!), and we were able to explore the surrounding countryside in our off duty moments. Pilots were entitled to a ration of petrol, but it wasn't enough to take you touring. These old cars ran mostly on a mixture containing lighter fuel, paraffin and anything else flammable we could get our hands on, even I have to admit, a good deal of aircraft fuel. It was handy on station flight with the re-fuelling bowser parked alongside. Geoff's car was running badly and he had the engine overhauled at his father in laws garage and he said the valves came out with their heads looking like drumsticks! I myself, during this time, bought a motor bike, which gave me a good deal of mobility.

We also climbed the Cheviot on foot. It's only a walk but a steep one, and in R.A.F. shiny soled black leather shoes was quite hairy enough.

Apart from local air tests, we did a fair bit of ferrying between Milfield and a satellite airfield at Acklington. We also ferried Typhoons and Tempests for inspections and maintenance to Woolsington and another airfield near Lichfield. Collecting a plane after a major overhaul could be quite interesting. Quite frequently the fixed trim tabs would be altered and I remember once taking off from Woolsington near Newcastle and having to use both hands to prevent the plane rolling violently to port.

Taking visitors to York was an easy trip, so far as navigation was concerned. We flew south keeping the coastline in sight to our port. Beyond the Tyne we headed for the column of smoke rising up from Hartlepool. Abreast that we turned half right and headed for the column of smoke rising from Middlesborough. Keep on that heading and you met the main line railway just south of Northallerton and which could then be followed south to York, and Hucknall Aerodrome. Once I flew directly over Middlesborough and the smoke was so thick I had to fly on instruments until I came out of it. There was no clean air act, or any concern for the environment in those days. I felt quite sorry for people who had to live and work under that pall of filth.

The war might be over, but who ever is up top regulating matters wasn't through with me yet. Joe Payton and I were asked to air test two Tempests. These were parked on the grass at the end of the hanger, on the opposite side of the perimeter track, and about a hundred yards along from our building. Joe and I went out together, and started up. Joe taxied out first, and as soon as I saw he was on the perimeter track I followed.

I taxied in a wide turn on the grass, and had just got onto the perimeter track when there was a loud clanging crash, and about four bod's flew out from under the front of the wing. I sat horrified; I thought I had somehow run into a party of men on the perimeter. I imagined the prop. churning into flesh and bone and blood pouring everywhere. Meanwhile the plane had slowly tilted up on it's nose, and caught fire. For one moment I thought it was going right over on it's back, but it rocked a couple of times and settled on it's nose. As I've said previously in this epistle, I never did like the idea of getting burned, and the sight of flames galvanised me into action. Meanwhile a crowd had already come running, and were yelling at me to jump. It's a long way down from the cockpit of a Tempest on its nose, but many hands were there to break my fall. My first words were "Is anyone hurt?" and it was a relief to hear that no one was. Walking round to the front of the plane I saw that a tractor was well embedded under the remains of the propeller.

Apparently, what had happened was that a sergeant and a party from the hanger had come over to borrow our tractor. The sergeant went in to ask permission for the loan, while some of his party tried to start the tractor. Never an easy beast to start, this time it fired first turn of the handle. Unfortunately, someone had left it in reverse gear, and instead of stalling as you might expect, it went charging backwards across the grass, with about four aircraftsmen trying frantically to reach over the big nobbly rear tyres to get to the controls to stop it. Meanwhile, I was taxiing in a curve and it must have been out of sight under the nose of the Tempest the whole way.

Of course once alight the plane burned fiercely! The fire tender was only about fifty yards from it, but they used every bit of foam on the station. It still didn't go out until the whole thing was ashes, except for the tail which had broken and dropped to the ground clear of the main blaze. Rivulets of molten metal were running into the tarmac, burning with an intense white light, and a column of black smoke went up which could be seen for miles. Except for the fire fighters everyone had to keep well back because with the tanks full, there was a very real fear of the lot exploding. At least there was no ammunition on board.

As usual the tarmac of the perimeter track melted over an area about thirty feet in diameter, and flying had to be suspended until more supplies of foam were obtained.

Joe Payton and the author on the summit of the Cheviot, September/October 1945.

I was later taken aback when trying to get a replacement parachute. The store man seemed quite upset that I couldn't have stayed in the plane long enough to drag my old parachute out of the cockpit. He then wanted what was left of the old one returned, and when I said it was completely burned he said "The buckles wouldn't have burned!" I think he wanted me to sift the ashes for them.

There was a big Hoo Hah about it. There was to be a court of enquiry, and the sergeant was on open arrest pending a court martial. I was sorry for him really, he was a good scout, and he wasn't even there when the attempt to start the tractor was made, but I suppose they took the view that he was in charge of the party and responsible.

No one suggested that I was in any way to blame and all the evidence was collected from everyone involved by the station adjutant. Up until I left for demobilisation some weeks later there had been no court of enquiry and the sergeant was still on open arrest. Nor was I ever called back to attend either event. My guess is that the whole thing was quickly forgotten. It wasn't long before they were breaking these planes up and burning them anyway. The incident appeared with some of Geoff Wyldes photographs as an article in Tee Eem (Training Memoranda) as an example of how a moment of carelessness could destroy thousands of pounds worth of airforce property.

We had a new station commander arrive at Milfield, Group Captain Donaldson. Donaldson was a character. He had a very charming American wife and a black Scottie dog called Hersham We all approved of the wife, but Hersham was a pest. Always somewhere you could hear Hersham's yapping bark. He would chase after anyone on a bike yapping at their heels, and they didn't like to give him the kick he deserved in case the Groupy got to hear and was riled. The Typhoons and Tempests were started with a Coffman cartridge starter and whenever he heard the bang of one, he would race across the airfield and stand in front of the plane barking and jumping up at the propeller. It's a good thing he wasn't a better jumper. No one wanted to be the one to carry back the pieces and declare, "Sorry, boss, we've chopped up your dog!"

The station commander was allocated a light aircraft, and Donaldson had a Tiger Moth at that time. One day in a howling gale and driving rain, when all flying on the station had stopped, Donaldson decided he had somewhere to go in the Tiger Moth. Undaunted by a little bad weather he taxied out with several unfortunate aircraftsmen hanging onto either wing tip to hold it down. Turning into wind on the runway, he had them running until at a signal they let go and the Tiger Moth went almost straight up to about two hundred feet. On his return he must have telephoned ahead, and a party were waiting each side of the runway. When he came in in the teeth of the gale, his ground speed was so low the reception party were able to race alongside and practically pull him down onto the ground.

Tempest (SN110) ablaze after a collision with a moving tractor at Milfield, 8 October 1945.

One day the Station Commander called an emergency officers mess meeting. Having ensured himself that all officers were in, and everyone else out, he said, "Right, lock the door! It's come to my notice—" God we thought, what have we done? "—that mess funds stand at something over two thousand pounds [a fortune in 1945]. Now you and I will soon be gone from here, and it seems a shame to leave all that loot for the benefit of strangers! Let's spend it!"

So a series of parties was arranged which were as lavish as anything I remember before or since. The mess was draped with camouflage netting to make it look like a cave. A six piece band were dressed as pirates and U.V. lamps borrowed from the sick bay to make skulls and skeletons shine with luminous paint. Drink was free and food was tremendous. After war time rations it seemed like a dream. In Northumberland there had been very little hunting and fishing during the war and game was abundant. I remember whole salmon cooked and sliced on a silver salver, venison, pheasant, and other delicacies. We had a tremendous time. Group Captain Donaldson made the news after the war by holding the World air speed record for a while in a Gloster Meteor.

Meanwhile, demobilisation began to be talked about and we were all given a demob. number based on age, length of service and a few other things. Since I was older than most of my contemporaries, and had been in the service, army and airforce, my number was pretty low and I looked like getting out early. Meanwhile someone came to give aptitude tests and advise on careers. He said that my test hadn't thrown anything in particular up, that I would probably do well at anything I put my hand to, and why didn't I become a teacher! He probably said that to all the boys, they were short of teachers after the war.

I was asked if I would go on an air gunnery course at Catfoss near Hull. It seemed to me a bit late in the day, but when I found we would be flying Spitfires, I readily agreed. I had never had a chance to even sit in the famous 'Spit', and I relished the thought of trying one.

However, down at Catfoss, we'd had a couple of lectures but not got near an aeroplane when they somehow discovered my demob. number, and said that it wasn't worth doing the course if I was to be demobilised almost immediately. So I was taken off the course and returned to Milfield. I never did fly a Spitfire.

Again, I was asked to do a course at Westlands on helicopters. Well, nobody at that time was taking helicopters seriously, and after Catfoss there didn't seem much point, so I turned down the offer. With hindsight probably a mistake, but it's no use looking back over your shoulder at what might have been.

So we came to December 1945 when I set out from Milfield on my Matchless motor bike amid shouted farewells and good wishes from all my friends. Kitbag lashed on one rear footpeg and the mudguard, raincoat flapping round my knees, and cap jammed on my head, through the Cheviot Hills and down to Newcastle, train to London, and demob.

The next day I reported at the dispersal unit at Uxbridge. Very efficiently, in no time at all, I found myself departing a civilian, with about one hundred pounds gratuity, a light grey chalk-striped suit so tight across the shoulders I daren't breathe in hard, shoes which pinched, and a trilby hat which was only ever used as a football some years later when it fell out of a cupboard I was rummaging in.

Epilogue

Well, that's it: my war as I remember it after some sixty years. The story was written for my son and his boys in the hope they never have to face a similar time.

As I've said many times since those days, I wouldn't have missed it, but on the other hand nor would I wish to go through it again. On the plus side it did quite a bit for me of course. I had left school early at the age of fifteen without qualifying in anything. By the time I reached my initial training in the R.A.F. at Cambridge, school was around seven years behind me. Yet I competed with young men straight from university on equal terms, and often won through when they failed. It was a great boost to confidence and showed me that I could do better than I had been doing before the war. The various scrapes I got into and got out of taught me the difference between hardness and toughness; hardness is brittle and breaks when pressure is applied. Since those days, I've never felt the need to prove myself to anyone.

Prison camp gave me an abhorrence of waste, especially of food, which is to this day practically a mania which has to be kept mostly to myself in our wasteful modern society.

On the squadron there was a comradeship that I've not met anywhere else. However big the formation, the basic unit was a pair. Attack from the air would come from behind, and you each watched the other's tail. If one of a pair had trouble, and had to leave the formation and return while still over enemy territory, his partner went with him. Each of our lives depended on the vigilance of the other.

This made it all the more poignant when any of these talented, carefree, young men failed to return, as so often happened. Of those who didn't return, those I regretted most were Jack Collins and Vic Smith, who eased me through my early days on operations with the squadron. Both were experienced pilots for whom I had the greatest admiration and respect. Another was Jimmy Mannion, who vanished without trace on what should have been a routine patrol. He was with us so short a time, but he was a good friend and a talented pianist. Then there was Frank Reid, whose demise was so unnecessary. One learned not to show feelings, and the chances are that an evening

243

following such a loss would bring an even rowdier-than-usual party in some pub or other. Their faces parade past in the mind's eye. Many have names attached; many do not. Many were not with us long enough to make a lasting impression. This was the down side of it all, which no amount of pluses could ever balance out.

Stackpole Military History Series